DEAF + PLUS

A
Multicultural
Perspective

Kathee Christensen, Editor

with
Gilbert Delgado, Guest Editor

DawnSignPress

Printed in the United States of America.

Published by DawnSignPress

Library of Congress Cataloging-in-Publication Data

Deaf plus : a multicultural perspective / edited by Kathee Christensen ; guest edited by Gilbert Delgado.
    p. cm.
  Includes bibliographical references and index.
  ISBN 1-58121-017-5
    1. Deaf children--Education--United States. 2. Children of
minorities--Education--United States. 3. Multicultural education--United States. I.
Christensen, Kathee M. (Kathee Mangan) II. Delgado, Gilbert L., 1928-

HV2440 .D43 2000
371.91'2'0973--dc21

                        00-022086

10   9   8   7   6   5   4   3   2   1

Attention: Schools and Distributors

Quantity discounts for schools and bookstores are available.

For information, please contact:

DAWNSIGNPRESS
6130 Nancy Ridge Drive
San Diego, CA 92121
www.dawnsign.com
858-625-0600 V/TTY 858-625-2336 FAX
ORDER TOLL FREE 1-800-549-5350

ACKNOWLEDGMENTS

Many people have contributed directly and indirectly to the ideas that led to the publication of this book. If spaced allowed, I would thank each one individually. Let me begin by saying that every Deaf child, every Deaf parent and every Deaf graduate student with whom I have interacted over the years has taught me most of what I know and appreciate about the world we call Deaf–Plus. To be Deaf is to be multicultural.

To my friend and guest editor, Gilbert Delgado, thanks for persevering in the task of improving opportunities for Hispanic Deaf persons. You began and you continue this important work.

Thanks to Jay Innes, Steve Nover, Oscar Cohen, Joe Fischgrund, Colleen Smith and Mary Kane for hours and hours of dialogue about culture and communication. Thanks to Becky Ryan from DawnSignPress for navigating the manuscript to completion. Thanks to Kim Pogorelsky for her editorial "eagle eye."

Special thanks to my husband, Ben, who is tireless in his efforts to lead me along new cultural roads—pot-holes and all! Thanks to Kyra and Chip whose rainbow of friends made our home more interesting. And an enormous thank you to my father, Ken Mangan, who had the wisdom to raise me at the cultural hub of the Deaf community—a state residential school for the deaf.

!Gracias a todos!

Kathee Mangan Christensen
San Diego, California

Contents

Introduction

Teaching is more than the transmission of knowledge. Teaching and learning are processes founded in a multiplicity of cultural traditions. Culture is a dynamic, ever-changing phenomenon. This truth became apparent during the construction of the present text.

This text, originally, was intended to be a revised edition of an earlier text that considered multicultural issues in the field of education of children who are deaf (Christensen & Delgado, 1993). The chapter authors of the original text were invited to review their contributions to the first edition and update, revise, and resubmit chapters that would inform contemporary practice. Early on, however, it became clear that what was needed was not a simple revision. The research and practice in the field had grown to the extent that an entirely new text, founded on the earlier work but significantly different and more complex, was required. The first book was based on the premise that the life experiences of Deaf persons constitute a unique cultural journey (Lane, Hoffmeister & Bahan, 1996). The book established a framework for the consideration of multicultural issues within the broader scope of Deaf Culture (Humphries, 1993). The new work assumes that readers have a basic understanding of Deaf people as a cultural/bicultural entity. Deaf-Plus builds on this basic knowledge. It explores recent accomplishments which have expanded the bilingual and multicultural dimensions of the Deaf community at large. For example, the Council on Education of the Deaf (CED) now mandates multicultural competence for prospective teachers of children who are deaf; CED has developed bilingual education standards; in school districts such as Dade County and Los Angeles, more attention is being paid to the situation of deaf children from families that speak Spanish; the national American Council on the Teaching of Foreign Languages (ACTFL) has endorsed American Sign Language as a member of the category entitled Less Commonly Taught Languages; collaborative efforts between ACTFL and the American Sign Language Teachers Association (ASLTA) have begun. Because of all of this activity around cultural and linguistic inclusion of ASL and Deaf Culture at a broader national level, it was necessary to rethink the conceptual framework of the text and contact new authors to expand upon the earlier work. A new treatment of the original multicultural perspectives construct was required.

The present text embraces the perspective that the presence of multicultural identities in the field of education represents a positive social condition. The title, Deaf-Plus, suggests that diversity within Deaf Culture enhances and enriches the quality of the culture. The new text stretches the limits of the original work and explores the importance of cultural and multicultural influences on contemporary education of children who are deaf. Emerging in the discussion are the critical needs to restructure teacher preparation, to confront "linguicism," and to prepare strong leadership for the 21st century.

Successful education of children who are deaf evolves through dynamic relationships among communication, cognition, and cultural influences. Implicit in this text are the following assumptions:

1. Learning occurs in a variety of social and cultural settings.

2. Learning is a result of dynamic interactions and collaborations.

3. Learning is negotiated among deaf children, their families, their teachers, and others through mutually comprehensible communication.

4. Learning, for deaf children, is founded on and mediated through visual, face-to-face encounters and experiences.

5. Individual development is a result of personal assimilation of and accommodation to a variety of social and cultural experiences at school and elsewhere.

No two individuals come to a point of "knowing" in exactly the same manner. Knowing (learning) is a result of unique cultural and communicative experiences perceived and tested in the personal space of an individual. This personal space extends to what Vygotsky has termed the "zone of proximal development," or the level of potential development which is possible through creative problem-solving under the guidance of a competent other (Vygotsky, 1978, p. 86).

To effect significant, positive change in education of children who are deaf, teacher preparation practices must be examined closely. Reform in teacher preparation will not be effective unless it is consistently applied across preservice and inservice settings. Discord between research and practice cannot produce the positive outcomes needed so desperately in the profession. This text represents a collaboration among teachers, administrators, and university professors. The diverse backgrounds of the authors reflect Deaf, Asian, African-American, Hispanic, and Native American Indian heritages. Most of the authors learned languages other than English as young children and are bilingual or multilingual.

Chapters One and Two establish the framework for the text. Welch examines multicultural education from a global/social justice perspective and makes suggestions for adaptations to education of the deaf. Delgado provides an historical review of multicultural programs for deaf children in the United States and presents some challenges for current educators. Chapter Three makes a transition to the classroom where teachers, the majority of whom are monocultural, are required to develop appropriate instructional strategies to enhance literacy in deaf learners with diverse linguistic and cultural strengths and needs.

Chapters Four through Ten deal with the specifics of educational and social programming for deaf children and families from culturally diverse backgrounds. Cheng discusses the ways in which Asian and Pacific Islander cultures regard deafness. Akamatsu and Cole describe a variety of issues related to schooling and family involvement which confront deaf children from diverse immigrant or refugee backgrounds. Chapters Six, Seven, and Eight focus on the complex needs of deaf children from Spanish heritage backgrounds, including persons who identify themselves as Hispanic, Latino, or Chicano. Ramsey shares experiences with a border population. Gerner de Garcia expands on the historical and legal issues facing children from diverse linguistic backgrounds and introduces the term "linguicism" into the dialogue on education of the deaf. Struxness presents data on service delivery to Hispanic deaf students in a specific geographical setting. Then Fletcher-Carter and Paez present a framework for exploring the personal cultures of deaf and hard-of-hearing students within an educational setting.

The final two chapters look at challenges for the new millennium. Redding calls for a positive attitudinal change among educators. Christensen charges the profession to respect the shifting cultural margins and growing diversity in both deaf and hearing populations.

The authors of this text are hopeful that their contributions on the topic of multicultural issues will enhance the current educational dialogue and inspire future educational research efforts that move toward sound theoretical practice. It is our profound wish that services provided for deaf children in the 21st century will meet the complex and multifaceted cultural and linguistic needs of this growing population.

REFERENCE

Humphries, T. (1993). Deaf culture and cultures. In K. Christensen & G. Delgado, (Eds.), *Multicultural issues in deafness.* White Plains, N.Y.: Longman.

Lane, H., Hoffmeister, R. & Bahan, B. (1996). *Journey into the DEAF-WORLD.* San Diego, CA: DawnSignPress.

Vygotsky, L. (1978). *Mind in society: The development of higher psychological processes.* Cambridge, MA: Harvard University Press.

1

Building a Multicultural Curriculum: Issues and Dilemmas

Olga M. Welch

How open is the social system to individual or group advancement? How do we explain the many obvious forms of inequality we see around us, such as rich and poor neighborhoods in our communities, unequal educational outcomes, and unequal earnings? By the time we become adults, we hold well-ingrained beliefs about the social system, human nature, and the character of various sociocultural groups based on our own life experience as well as the ideology we have learned to use to interpret that experience. Usually, however, these beliefs are so taken for granted that we do not recognize them as beliefs, nor do we see the constraints they place on our interpretation of the world; rather we regard such beliefs as "truth" (Sleeter, 1996, p. 36).

This chapter presents an overview of some of the issues predominant in discussions of multiculturalism in general education and relates these issues to the education of persons who are deaf. Further, the chapter suggests strategies for teachers in deaf education to consider using in their classrooms.

During the past decade, there have been several workshops and institutes which have attempted to redress the lack of attention paid to diversity in American classrooms. Too often, however, this has caused a distillation of complex issues of multiculturalism, ethnicity, and diversity into paradigms that relegate cultural identities to boxes or fixed images to which teachers are provided "special" responses. This approach to multicultural education preoccupies these same teachers with supplying "accurate" and "authentic" representations of particular cultures in the hope that such corrective strategies will automatically promote tolerant attitudes in students. These revised versions of cultures are then taught as either a seamless parade of stable and singular customs and traditions or in the form of individual or particular heroes whose accomplishments, while exemplary, serve to buttress the idea of America as a society where success is distributed fairly, based on individual merit alone (Britzman et al., 1993). Thus, for some educators, it becomes the means through which to instruct "majority" students about the "problems" encountered by their "minority" counterparts and a way of instructing "at-risk" students that "through hard work, patience, delayed gratification, etc., (they) can carve out their rightful place in American society" (Omi & Winant, 1986, as cited in Sleeter, 1996, p. 14). This has turned several classrooms into arenas where words like "racism," "classism," and "sexism" become provocative means of eliciting emotionally charged discussions, resulting in one group or the other "owning" the problem or reinforcing a dynamic where groups of participants become polarized, unable on the one side to get beyond the suggestion that they are partially guilty of perpetuating an unjust system or unable, on the other, to relinquish the self-satisfaction at finally getting "the oppressor" to admit guilt (Hodges & Welch, in press).

Proponents of multiculturalism in deafness have tended to avoid discussions of racism, sexism, or classism, preferring instead to turn the study of these forms of discrimination into examinations of Deaf Culture. Still others have focused on the preparation of teachers for bilingual/bicultural programs that, in some cases, give only peripheral attention to issues of race, class, gender, and sexual orientation. Still others have used multiculturalism as a demarcation point, separating those who are "authentically Deaf" from those who are "hearing in the mind."

This lack of agreement on goals and outcomes of multiculturalism for Deaf students impedes the development of implementation strategies, since the meanings and representations affect how knowledge of social difference changes and disturbs the identities of the knower and begs the question of how knowledge of identities and cultures is produced, encountered, and dismissed in classrooms both self same and diverse (Britzman et al., 1993, p. 189). Indeed, a more accurate beginning for would-be practitioners of multiculturalism in deafness might be to recognize the "ambivalence (existing) in the meaning and the detours of representing identities that are always already overburdened with meanings one may not choose, but nonetheless, must confront and transform" (Marks, 1984, p. 110, as cited in Britzman et al., 1993). Further, how multicultural education for Deaf students is framed depends on the political perspective from which it is understood. Thus, oppression and inequality within these interlocking representations cannot be understood simply through a curriculum aimed at promoting cultural sensitivity within existing school content and contexts.

Olneck (1990) suggested that in order to have any meaning, multicultural education must achieve three goals: (1) it must enhance the communal or collective lives of groups that constitute society, (2) it must be serious in recognizing the claims of disenfranchised groups as legitimate, and (3) it has to support the validity of group membership as a basis for participation in society (p. 148).

Multicultural education for learners who are Deaf is no exception. Although experienced individually, oppression of the Deaf cannot be understood in individual terms alone because people are privileged or oppressed on the basis of social group status (Adams *et al.*, 1997). "One of the privileges of dominant group status is the luxury of simply seeing oneself as an individual" (p. 9). Thus, a hearing male is rarely defined by either his hearing or his maleness. If he does his job well, he is accorded the positive recognition that his individual work merits. On the other hand, if he does poorly, he alone receives the blame. However, as Adams *et al.* (1997) remind us, the situation is quite different for persons whose individual identities are inextricably linked in the public consciousness with that of a subgroup. "Those in subordinated groups can never fully escape being defined by their social group memberships" (p. 9).

Thus, an African American, Deaf female, for example, may wish to be viewed as an individual but may instead find her accomplishments scrutinized through the dominant society's assumptions about her racial/ethnic group, deafness, and gender. If she excels, then she may be seen as atypical or exceptional on several levels, while her failure may be viewed as representative of the multiple groups to which she belongs.

Although not all members of a particular group will define themselves identically, the above examples illustrate how group identity, influenced by societal assumptions, history, and the tension that exists between individual and group identities can affect the particular experiences of targeted groups within an unequal society (Adams *et al.*, 1997, p. 10).

While attention to the importance of Deaf Culture (its history, values, and commitments) is critical in preparing teachers who will work with Deaf students, uniform definitions which exclude or seek to downplay issues of race, ethnicity, gender, class, and sexual orientation provide these same teachers with only a partial understanding of that culture. Further, this approach encourages teachers to treat Deaf Culture as peripheral to the "real business" of educating Deaf students for the 21st century, that is, as a "politically correct" gesture rather than as a central component of their curriculum planning. To become more than another "diversity initiative," teachers of Deaf students who wish to implement multicultural education, like their public school counterparts, must begin to understand how educational institutions work to limit some groups even as they empower others. This means understanding the myth of an unbiased school "meritocracy," which perpetuates a view of achievement that blames the individual for failure while ignoring or underplaying the pervasive barriers that exist. Nor does such an analysis ignore individual capability or responsibility but rather it seeks to examine how privilege and subordination operate within schools and, in the process, affect student achievement even in the face of the most conscientious teacher's efforts.

I did not accidentally select these issues related to multicultural education. Rather, I chose them because of my position as a teacher with over twenty-five years of teaching experience in day and residential schools for the Deaf and as a teacher–educator in a teacher preparation program in deafness at a major research university. Moreover, for the past eleven years, I have been conducting research on the relationship between identity construction and academic achievement for educationally disadvantaged adolescents (hearing/Deaf /White and Black American). This research, along with my experiences as a classroom teacher, has convinced me of the importance of implementing a multicultural curriculum that is neither reductionist nor superficial. In seeking to develop such a curriculum, however, I have come to understand the particular issues and dilemmas that multiculturalism raises for both teachers and students. Some of these concern definitions, while others center on goals and outcomes. For example, how does a teacher, confronted with the task of providing Deaf students with the appropriate knowledge and skills needed to achieve academically, define and give attention to multicultural education in the classroom? Further, given the constraints of school policies, the individual differences between and among Deaf learners, and the necessity to attend to "regular" curricula objectives, how can teachers be expected to give more than superficial consideration to diversity issues? These questions and others have led me to study the literature on multicultural education in order to discover its applicability for teachers of the Deaf. Because I prepare future teachers, I wanted to explore the benefits of multicultural education for ALL Deaf students. In this chapter, I offer some of what I have learned. Specifically, the chapter presents a review, though not exhaustive, of the literature on multiculturalism and the unique issues and dilemmas facing educators who want to implement multiculturalism in their classrooms and a summary of particular areas for teachers of the Deaf to consider. In general, the chapter uses the work of earlier influential researchers to present a model that can be used when developing multicultural curricula for Deaf learners.

What Is Multicultural Education?

Sleeter (1996) suggested that a fundamental question within which multicultural education situates itself is: How can educators act in a way that actually furthers social justice? She asserted also that "as a field, multicultural education has tended to be action-oriented in that much of its literature is prescriptive. Multicultural education attempts to frame and advocate what educators can do" (p. 45). Thus, although theorists in multicultural education are aware of the systemic nature of oppression (especially racism), much of the literature maintains a naive, traditional stance that offers suggestions for schools and practice that address schools specifically, but do not consider their context in larger systems of power (Sleeter, 1996). Indeed, Lila Bartolome suggested that the preparation of teachers is hampered by its "myopic focus on methodology," a focus that conceals real questions of power within schools, questions that reveal the unequal access met by subordinated students that hinders their academic success. "In fact, schools often reproduce the existing asymmetrical power relations among cultural groups" (Bartolome, as cited in Sleeter, 1996, p. 45).

Thus, the meaning of multicultural education and how one should implement it continues to shift in direction, causing that meaning to be declared unclear as attempts have been made to put it into effect. Banks (1995a) and other researchers and educators (McCarthy & Apple, 1988; Grant & Sleeter, 1986; McLaren, 1994; Olneck, 1990) who examine multicultural education refer to the goal of providing educational equity for all students, regardless of race, class, gender, ableness, and lifestyle. While the importance of realizing this goal has been underscored by the numerous conservative, liberal, and radical formulations of multicultural education (Sleeter & Grant, 1988, as cited in Sleeter, 1995) and the explosion of research in the field, it has been complicated and at times impeded by the divisiveness fueled by various conservative and radical critiques (Sleeter, 1995). The conservative critics, Sleeter explains, wary of the radical nature of the literature on multicultural education, take a largely assimilationist, universalist stance which places more emphasis on establishing a common curriculum while diverting attention from politically charged issues. The critics from the radical left, in contrast, decry the all too conservative nature of multicultural education and accuse it of "embracing individuality within an economic system while neglecting to address more vigorously systems of oppression which are not limited to schools but mirror deep, troubling aspects of the larger society" (p. 89).

The disputed nature and function of multicultural education notwithstanding, proponents have presumed that the consequent reforms it is expected to bring about will be accepted and affirmed within existing school structures by teachers who will translate their awareness of cultural diversity and its issues into effective instructional revisions. Again and again, teachers have been sensitized, had their consciousness raised, and even been admonished about "politically correct" behavior, yet seldom have they been encouraged to look inward to scrutinize their personal ideology and identity construction.

Nor have they been given the opportunity to examine how these factors and the narrow limits imposed by the educational contexts in which they work relate to and affect what happens in their classrooms (Hodges & Welch, in press).

In the face of this reality, it is not surprising that teachers believe in the neutrality of curriculum strategies and the classrooms in which they are practiced. Nor is it surprising that they are more likely to produce multicultural curricula that adhere to White, conservative renditions of the United States. Since this rendition is the "taken for granted" reality of most content in the disciplines, the meaning of "diversity" is filtered through that lens. Such an understanding of the aim of multiculturalism results in a curriculum that is integrated, but in a subsuming sense; that is, representations of diverse groups are blended into grand narratives that still favor the positions and perspectives of those who control power and wealth (Sleeter & Grant, 1991). Left unexplored is the nature of these perspectives, how they came to be produced, their historical groundings, and who benefits from their acceptance as "fact."

Instead, through a focus on cultural sensitivity and tolerance, educators become preoccupied with what to add to the curriculum, which literary selections, which historical figures, which artistic representations, and so on, while leaving unaddressed such questions as, "Who decides?" "What is the nature of the curriculum into which these 'additions' are made?" and "Whose stories are being told?" (Sleeter, 1996, p. 92).

In classrooms for the Deaf, this form of subsuming multiculturalism may take the form of "inserting" Deaf History or heroes into the "taken for granted" content of academic courses without equal attention to the nature of the content itself or how deafness and Deaf people are represented within it.

According to Sleeter (1996), these grand narratives contain the following dominating Eurocentric and patriarchal themes:

> The United States is the land of wealth and opportunity; it is open to all who try; anyone can get what he works for.

American history flowed from Europe to the East Coast of North America; from there it flowed westward.

American culture is of European origin; Europe is the main source of worthwhile cultural achievements.

National ideals consist (as they should) of individual advancement, private accumulation, rule by majority as well as by market demand, loyalty to the United States government, and freedom of speech.

Some social problems existed in the past, but they have been solved.

Most problems that society faces have technical solutions, for which science and math offer the best keys.

Americans share consensus about most things; differences are individual and can be talked about (usually in one story).

Other places in the world may have poverty and problems, but the United States does not; we tend to solve other nations' problems.

America is basically white, middle class, (able bodied), and heterosexual; white wealthy men are the world's best thinkers and problem-solvers and usually act in the best interests of everyone (p. 93).

While some may debate them, these themes support a view of America that "presumes to account for and tie together the 'substories' into a seamless 'universal' story in which all are included. Since they are largely unstated, also, these themes structure the grand narrative of curricula fashioned within this world view" (p. 92). Thus, in their haste to create classrooms in which the unique cultural identities of the students are recognized and the tolerance and celebration of diversity encouraged, teachers may lose sight of the hybrid nature of all cultures in favor of a unified, homogeneous concept of cultural identity that is passed on in their instruction and grounded in the above worldview (Hodges & Welch, in press). In many cases, such an outlook offers what Said (1993) described as an uncritical and un-thinking form of education. Said calls for an approach to multicul-turalism that rejects the static concept of identity and uses curriculum as the site for reflecting on and discussing that which separates as well as that which integrates the political and social interests of various groups. Such an approach incorporates the goals of a multicultural curriculum suggested by Banks (1995a).

WHAT ARE THE GOALS OF A MULTICULTURAL CURRICULUM?

If teachers are to assist students in questioning the "taken for granted" knowledge offered in school curricula in order to understand and fash-ion an inclusive dialogue on diversity, they must confront an issue cited by Paul Robeson, Jr. (1993). In his questions "Which culture?" "Whose diversity?" Robeson contends that the controversy over mul-ticulturalism represents less a struggle over the politics of race and gen-der and more a manifestation of an ideological conflict over the values of American culture and the nature of United States civilization. In-deed, it is a debate over whether the melting pot culture (with its grounding in White, Anglo-Saxon, Protestant values) which has been the foundation of the American way of life should be replaced by a mosaic culture incorporating the values of the diverse groups that make up America's population (p. 1).

> The issue of *which* culture we should have is linked to the issue of *whose* diversity we are talking about: the diversity of those who peer out at the world from the confines of the monocultural melt-ing pot, or the diversity of those who move comfortably through the spreading multicultural mosaic. These questions relate to the support of melting pot culture which defines diversity as the recog-nition of different individual cultural styles, or the challenge of a mosaic culture that accepts the value of group cultures within American society." (Robeson, Jr., 1993, p. 17)

Robeson further asserts that the debate over melting pot and mosaic culture raise another fundamental question: which individualism will be supported, the uniform radical individualism of assimilation (i.e. the melting pot), or the diverse individualism associated with group identification; the individualism of those merged into a melting pot culture, or the individualism of those whose self-image stems from their mosaic ancestral culture? The conflict between these two different notions of individualism contributes to the ideological debate currently raging in *America* and the social fragmentation which has accompanied it. (p. 17)

These issues, as well as discussions of monoculturalism, biculturalism, and ethnic identity (Spring, 1995; Cross, 1991), are central to the model of a multicultural curriculum suggested by Banks (1995a). In proposing his model of multicultural education, Banks offers as a major goal the transformation of the content of curriculum, pedagogy, and the ways students learn. He envisions this transformative interaction of teaching and learning occurring within a curriculum organized around powerful ideas, highly interactive strategies, active student involvement, and activities that require students to join in personal, social, and civic action to make their classrooms, schools, and communities more democratic and just. Within this transformation, teachers and students together participate in a multicultural curriculum with the goal of developing decision making and social action skills as well as cocreated forms of knowledge.

For Banks, this knowledge construction involves several complex factors, including what actually occurs within a given context as well as the interpretations that people make of their experiences and their positions within particular social, economic, and political systems and structures of society (Banks, 1993, p. 5). He maintains that in the Western tradition, knowledge construction within each academic discipline has been viewed as evolving without the influence of the researcher's personal or cultural characteristics (Greer, 1969; Kaplan, 1964, as cited in Banks, 1993). However, the research of postmodernists (Cherryholmes, 1988; Foucault, 1962; Habermas, 1971;

Rorty, 1969; Young, 1971, as cited in Banks, 1993) has challenged this ideal of objective knowledge formulation, stressing instead the influence of personal, cultural, and social factors on the construction of knowledge in a discipline. Banks' idea of knowledge growing out of these traditions includes the ideas, values, and interpretations that individuals bring to the social contexts in which they operate. Thus, the importance of positionality (e.g., gender, race, class, age, ableism, and other aspects of identity) in the construction of knowledge challenges the Western notion of a neutral and objective process. He offers a "knowledge typology" for use by teachers and curriculum specialists to identify the perspectives and content needed to make the curriculum multicultural. The typology includes the following five types of knowledge. (a) *Personal cultural knowledge,* e.g., the concepts, explanations, and interpretations that students derive from personal experiences in their homes, families, and community cultures. From this knowledge, students extract assumptions, perspectives, and insights to develop screens through which to view and interpret the knowledge and experiences that they encounter in school and in other institutions within the larger society. (b) *Popular knowledge,* e.g., the facts, interpretations, and beliefs that are institutionalized within television, movies, videos, records, and other forms of mass media. The tenets of popular culture, conveyed subtly rather than overtly, include some of the patriarchal and Eurocentric themes explored earlier in this chapter. (c) *Mainstream academic knowledge,* e.g., the concepts, paradigms, theories, and explanations that constitute traditional and established knowledge in the behavioral and social sciences. Representing the Lockean belief in a set of objective truths, which are verifiable through rigorous and objective research methods, these are uninfluenced by human values and interests although they are universal both in nature and in application. (d) *Transformative academic knowledge,* e.g., a counter to the view of knowledge as objective, which expands the historical and literary canon and is based on different philosophical assumptions about the nature of knowledge, about the influence of human interests and values on knowledge construction, and about the purpose of knowledge. It proposes that the most important purpose for knowledge construction must be to help people improve society. (e) *School knowledge,* e.g., the facts, concepts, and generalizations presented in textbooks, teachers' guides, and the other forms of media designed for school use. School knowledge also involves how teachers interpret and mediate that knowledge.

For Banks, these knowledge forms represent conceptual tools for thinking about and planning multicultural curricula. He suggests their usefulness as overlapping and interrelated categories for formulating shared teacher and student investigations of the nature of the "taken for granted" knowledge that exists in society. This investigation occurs within a classroom context that represents a forum for multiple voices and perspectives. The voices of the teacher, of the textbook, of mainstream and transformative authors, and of the students constitute important components of classroom discourse. Thus, in presenting different types of knowledge, teachers assist students in understanding the social context within which knowledge construction occurs while enabling the students to develop the skills required to become knowledge builders themselves. Moreover, while participating in the critical analysis of the knowledge they master, students learn how to produce their own interpretations of the past, present, and future (Banks, 1993).

To further facilitate the process, Banks offers the following additional goals of a multicultural curriculum:

1. **A multicultural curriculum should result in reflection and social activism.** Banks (1995b) views multiculturalism as a vehicle through which students develop the ability to reflect on issues related to ethnicity and through that process to take personal, social, and civic actions to help solve national and international racial and ethnic problems. In the case of Deaf students, opportunities to engage in activities that foster reflection or activism seldom occur in the classroom. Adams *et al.* (1997) describe an ableism curriculum that includes a chronology of disability his-

tory in the United States and reflective questions that require students to discuss their own experiences of discrimination as well as the "unearned privileges" they enjoy, despite their deafness, because they belong to a dominant ethnic, gender, or socioeconomic group.

Deaf students might be given many opportunities to learn about their multiple identities, including their ethnicity. This means interviewing their family members, tracing their own genealogies, understanding how historical events (e.g., the Westward Movement or The Alamo) might be viewed by ALL of the participants in them, examining how the "master texts" discussed earlier have evolved and how these "truths" affect knowledge construction.

Further, Deaf students can be encouraged to use their knowledge of their multiple histories to develop their own agendas for social activism at both the individual and the group level. For example, students can investigate whether because of race, class, and/or gender Deaf individuals receive differential treatment when they apply for loans to begin small businesses. Through this process of reflection and social activism, they begin to understand their own roles and their ability to offer solutions to national and international issues of discrimination.

2. **A multicultural curriculum should assist students in understanding the role of their own and other ethnic perspectives on contemporary history.** For Banks, this requires students to view historical and contemporary events from diverse ethnic perspectives. To accomplish this, students must clarify their ethnic identities and function effectively within their own cultural identities, a process which permits them to relate more positively to people who belong to different racial and ethnic groups. Teachers may involve Deaf students in activities that require them to explore their own ethnic identities. Helms (1990) offers a discussion of White and Black identity development which

teachers can use to understand the stages of identity development for both groups. The work of other researchers in identity development also confirms the applicability of Helms' (1990) structure to other racial and ethnic groups.

For Deaf students, particularly, such explorations can be invaluable since they deconstruct the popular fundamental definition of Deaf Culture and expose ALL Deaf students to the variety of ethnic and racial cultures that have been excluded from that definition. Further, such a deconstruction can lead teachers and students into additional explorations of the history of Deaf people that includes the perspectives of those "left out" of traditional discussions of both Deaf History and American History. It can also create a space for examinations of contemporary issues of discrimination within and external to the Deaf Community and how they impact access for ALL Deaf individuals. However, Banks cautions, such self-awareness must never become a vehicle for promoting ethnocentrism but rather a process through which students can begin to examine their own perspectives and standpoints.

3. **A multicultural curriculum must help individuals develop cross-cultural competency.** With social justice as a central tenet, transformative education must assist students in developing the ability to function within a range of cultures. This means that students learn to operate within a pluralistic society, accepting their own ethnic and cultural identities while becoming equally comfortable interacting *within* other cultures and interacting positively *with* individuals from different ethnic and cultural groups.

Deaf students also need to develop cross-cultural competency. Like most Americans, much of what they learn about others occurs within homes or communities which are largely segregated along racial, ethnic, and social-class lines (Feagin & Sikes, 1994; Hacker, 1992). As a result, in addition to few opportunities to interact with other Deaf youth or adults, these students also experience limited opportunities to learn firsthand about the cultures of people from different racial, ethnic, religious, and social-class groups.

Deaf students, like their hearing counterparts, internalize viewpoints and misconceptions about those who are different from themselves. Although teachers of the Deaf have given explicit attention to the misconceptions of hearing people held by some of their students, few have tackled the misconceptions about persons from different racial or ethnic groups that constantly confront these same students.

4. **A multicultural curriculum must help individuals avoid cultural encapsulation by providing them with cultural and ethnic alternatives.** Multicultural education must assist students in becoming more knowledgeable about their own cultures even as they gain greater self-understanding by viewing themselves from multiple cultural perspectives. For Deaf students, cultural encapsulation can occur when they define themselves or are defined as "authentically deaf" only if they embrace exclusively the values of Deaf Culture. Instead, a multicultural curriculum invites students to investigate and identify their own cultural selves and opportunities, to learn about how those selves are viewed from multiple perspectives (e.g., What does it mean to be a Deaf/Italian/White/oral/female? How do these multiple "selves" offer both complementary and contradictory roles and issues? How are these multiple "selves" viewed by others? How do these views influence how this individual operates?). With these kinds of discussions, there is no one view of deafness or Deaf Culture. Rather Deaf Culture becomes an idea that evolves and expands to include multiple perspectives.

5. **A multicultural curriculum should help individuals gain a greater understanding of what it means to be human.** Using these expanded perceptions, students learn to accept the viabil-

ity of diverse ethnic cultures, not as subordinate to a dominant culture, but rather as functional and valid. In this way, they come to understand that any culture can be evaluated only within a particular cultural context. Providing Deaf students with a wider lens through which to gain knowledge of the world is critical. Too often, school curricula limit rather than expand their access to and understanding of non-Western history and cultural traditions. While some teachers use February to introduce Black History and March to "pay attention" to Women's History, such "additive" approaches may unintentionally trivialize these studies, reinforcing student perceptions of these groups as marginal contributors to the larger history of America. Further, by failing to make these studies "a part of" rather than "apart from" human history discussions, teachers make it more difficult for Deaf students to understand their relationship to the wider issues of access and equality which directly impact their own social, educational, and economic opportunities.

6. **A multicultural curriculum should help individuals to master essential reading, writing, and computational skills.** The multicultural curriculum should be interdisciplinary so that students master important skills in the content areas. As such, it operates within the existing curriculum content.

   Banks (1995a) suggested that an effective multicultural curriculum also must be broadly conceptualized, comparative, decision making, social-action focused, and viewed as a process of curriculum transformation (p. 51). Within such a curriculum, oppressed peoples are not depicted only or even primarily as victims. Rather, they are described as people who helped to shape their own destiny, who built institutions to foster their own advancement, and who played a major role in attaining their civil rights. This requires teaching concepts like prejudice, discrimination, and racism in concert with such concepts as protest, empowerment, interracial cooperation, and ethnic institutions (civil and political) in order to portray a full and accurate view of the experiences of disenfranchised groups in the United States (Banks, 1995a).

In the case of Deaf History, for example, it means demonstrating how from the beginning Deaf people were actively involved in securing equitable education, access to economic parity, and social/political power. The role of hearing people in that history and the examples provided by other disenfranchised groups (e.g., the Civil Rights Movement; the Women's Movement) that influenced the Deaf struggle for equality must also be acknowledged and explored. In addition, those issues (e.g., sexism, racism, classism, and homophobia) that operate within American society in general, and which also exist within the Deaf Community, must be recognized and discussed.

How Should a Multicultural Curriculum Be Designed?

In designing a curriculum that moves students and teachers away from superficial examinations of diversity, educators must develop a classroom climate where, within a shared dialogue about differences, attention is paid to the multiple cultural identities that constitute each individual and which nurtures the diversified awareness that is the foundation for that dialogue (Sleeter & McLaren, 1995). Developing this kind of climate involves going beyond the concerns of curriculum reform and toward restructuring the discourse by "defining a new conversational terrain" (Perry & Fraser, 1993, p. 18), with the teacher as the key negotiator, aware of the social and cultural constructions and frames of reference embodied in his/her identity as well as the identities of the students. Perry and Fraser (1993) explain:

> Negotiated meanings are always critically informed by the racial, class, and gender identities of the faculty and student participants and by the power relationships represented in the classroom and the larger educational institution. (p. 20)

By moving beyond the curriculum to consider these important contextual factors, educators become involved in practicing critical teaching. Teachers adopt theoretical constructs and an ‚ideological stance in teaching approaches that engage the students in critical examinations of themselves and their surroundings and which encourage them to challenge the power relations which permeate their lives (Sleeter & McLaren, 1995).

Assumptions

Establishing a relationship between multicultural education and critical teaching requires teachers to be guided by certain instructional assumptions. In their book, *Teaching for Diversity and Social Justice: A Sourcebook,* Adams, Bell, and Griffin (1997) outline five such useful assumptions that guide their work with students. These can be illustrative for teachers of the Deaf who want to implement the kind of multicultural curriculum suggested by Banks (1995a):

1. **It is not useful to argue about a hierarchy of oppressions.**
   In dialogues about oppression, elevating one form of oppression over another is neither useful nor desirable. To be sure, understanding similarities and differences between different forms of oppression as well as the interlocking nature of oppressions (e.g., how discrimination operates at multiple levels against an individual who is Deaf and female or male and homosexual) is critical. This assumption is predicated on the authors' belief that the eradication of one form of oppression, while others continue, will still affect all members of society.

2. **All forms of oppression are interconnected.**
   The authors contend that each participant in a classroom (both teachers and students) is "a collage of social identities" (p. 65). Thus, although at different moments in the course teachers may focus on one form of oppression (e.g., ableism), they and their students must not forget that their perspective on ableism reflects

their own race, class, religious beliefs, sexual orientation, and gender positions and also how they experience ableism in the course. In addition to having students explore the intersections of their different social group memberships, the authors encourage them to explore the similarities in the dynamics of different forms of oppression (p. 66).

3. **Confronting oppression will benefit everyone.**
   An important aspect of a multicultural curriculum that engages teachers and students in critical examinations of oppression is an understanding of how that oppression adversely affects all members of society. Too often, for example, eradicating barriers to the full participation of Deaf individuals into society is viewed as beneficial only to them. Adams, Bell, and Griffin suggest that the eradication of the oppression of Deaf individuals benefits non-Deaf individuals as well, since when any segment of the population is unfairly limited, potential talents and achievements are lost to all members of society.

   Moreover, those who are the targets of oppression must live with feeling guilt, shame, or helplessness, never being sure that their individual accomplishments are earned and not the result of their membership in a particular social group. "Confronting oppression can free members of all social groups to take action toward social justice. The goal is equitable redistribution of social power and resources among all social groups at all levels not the reversal of the current power inequity through alternating the groups in power positions" (p. 66).

4. **Fixing blame helps no one, taking responsibility helps everyone.**
   Class discussions aimed at furthering understanding of oppression can be derailed when one group is made to feel guilt or responsibility for the actions of its ancestors or contemporaries toward another group. This activity, which the authors label "fixing blame," does little to advance the discussion and can lead to

a sense of helplessness on the part of participants. Instead, students are encouraged to understand their positions within a historical social context which they must understand but for which they are not responsible. Emphasis is placed on students making use of that knowledge in their everyday lives to confront injustice (p. 66). The practice of blaming the disenfranchisement of Deaf individuals exclusively on the intolerance of hearing people is one example of this practice of affixing blame.

5. **Confronting social injustice is painful AND joyful.**
   Many students find confronting their own prejudices against another group a painful experience. The accompanying discomfort and uncertainty that result are difficult and troubling. As the authors explain, "facing the contradictions between what students have been taught to believe about social justice and the realities of the experiences of different social groups is complex. Like their hearing counterparts, deaf students learn that some of what they were taught is inaccurate likewise, some information that they need was not taught at all" (p. 66). Yet, these very contradictions push them and their teachers into a reflective analysis of the "taken for granted" required to experience what the authors term the "joy of understanding social oppression and taking action against it" (p. 66). Engaging in this kind of critical reflection can have a positive and profound effect on students' personal and professional relationships.

Implementing a multicultural curricula that represents these and other assumptions means that teachers do more than tinker with existing canons or definitions of knowledge. As Banks (1995b) maintains, "an important goal of teaching about racial, cultural and ethnic diversity should be to empower students with the knowledge, skills, and attitudes they need to participate in civic action that will help transform (the) world and enhance the possibility for human survival" (p. 30). For teachers, this requires a conceptual shift from "banking" notions of education, in which knowledge becomes a commodity held exclusively BY them for deposit INTO students. Instead, the role of the teacher becomes that of coach, strategist, iconoclast, and negotiator (Freire, 1970). This means that in classrooms in which multicultural education is practiced there is an attempt to create or expand the space and time for discussions of race, class, gender, ableism, and sexuality with attention to what it is that makes these social markers significant (Britzman *et al.*, 1993, p. 197). Thus, to engage in multicultural education that moves beyond the celebratory to a process of critically grounded dialogue requires teachers and students to locate themselves both personally and ideologically. From these positions they can explore the historical, political, economic events, and social issues that have led them to these positions. As Banks suggested, these locations influence the knowledge which together they construct and reconstruct. Establishing a classroom in which these dialogues can occur, however, poses pedagogical dilemmas that must be confronted.

Dilemmas

Educators who are interested in designing a transformative multicultural curriculum confront several pedagogical dilemmas. Having abandoned the practice of celebratory or additive multiculturalism, these individuals accept the implicit focus on social justice involved in teaching that places issues of racism, sexism, classism, ableism, and sexual orientation at the center of discussions of diversity. Such a focus is not without controversy. In deciding "what to teach," teachers also must change "how they teach" (Culley & Portuges, 1985, as cited in Adams *et al.*, 1997, p. 43). This means permitting themselves and students to take risks and make mistakes in an atmosphere that is fair, safe, and respectful.

In implementing this kind of social justice curriculum in their own classrooms, Adams *et al.*, (1997) identified five pedagogical dilemmas that can be useful to other educators. These are summarized here:

1. **Balancing the emotional and cognitive components of the learning process.** Dialogue cannot occur in a classroom where students feel constrained by issues of personal safety (e.g., the freedom to express ideas without being castigated within a classroom where teachers are in control of the discussion and will intervene, if necessary, to prevent personal attacks, even as they assist students in subjecting blatantly false beliefs to mature and thoughtful criticism (Rothenberg, 1985, as cited in Adams *et al.*, 1997, p. 37). It also cannot occur in an environment without clearly stated and understood norms about interaction, voice, and authority, as well as guidelines for group behavior. To create such a space, teachers must understand not only how knowledge is constructed but also how cognitive development affects the readiness of students for creating meaning "from the classroom experiences, interactions and ideas" (p. 30).

2. **Acknowledging and supporting the personal (the individual student's experience) while illuminating the systemic (the interactions among social groups).** This kind of pedagogy is culturally relevant because it "maintains equitable and reciprocal teacher–student relations within which student expertise is highlighted, teachers encourage their entire classes rather than singling out individual learners, and students are partly responsible for each others' academic success" (Ladson-Billings, 1996). Participants in such a class learn to take multiple perspectives on their own prior knowledge and beliefs, on each others' viewpoints, and on the course content. Students learn to ask questions such as "Whose version is this?" "Who is disadvantaged or advantaged by this version?" "Whose voices (perspectives) are omitted?" "Who is listened to?" "Why?" (McIntosh, 1992; Hooks, 1994).

3. **Attending to social relations within the classroom.** This involves teaching that assists students in identifying the behaviors

that emerge within group discussions and understanding how groups operate while improving their own abilities to communicate effectively and respectfully in those groups. This means not assigning blame or making judgmental assertions (p. 42).

4. **Utilizing reflection and experience as tools for student-centered learning.** This requires recognizing that both teachers and students bring to the classroom their own biases and perspectives which in turn become the "lens" through which they filter curriculum content, the accompanying discussions, and classroom experiences. Thus, it is this "standpoint" which forms the starting place for both dialogue and problem posing, not a set of "prepackaged" teacher assumptions which remain intact and disassociated from the worldviews and experiences of the students themselves.

5. **Valuing awareness, personal growth, and change as outcomes of the learning process.** Developing a multicultural curriculum that focuses on social justice without also centering on personal growth, awareness, and change within the learner is to engage in irresponsible teaching. Tatum (1992) writes that "raising awareness without also raising awareness of the possibilities for change is a prescription for despair. I consider it unethical to do one without the other" (pp. 20–21, as cited in Adams *et al.*, 1997). Indeed, teachers who do not assist students in making the connection between awareness and their own personal perspectives on issues of diversity and social justice perpetuate a kind of "tourist" multiculturalism that permits students to disassociate from or assume themselves incapable of challenging discrimination or oppression.

Teachers who develop transformative approaches to multicultural education deliberately help students to make the connections between their own awareness and direct action. They do so by "(assisting) students to recognize various spheres of influence in their daily lives; analyze the relative risk factors in challenging discrimination or oppression in intimate relations, family networks, and institutional settings; and identify personal or small group actions for change" (Adams *et al.*, p. 38).

WHERE DO WE GO FROM HERE? MULTICULTURAL EDUCATION IN CLASSROOMS FOR THE DEAF

In the chapters that follow, authors will explore various strategies for working with culturally different learners who are Deaf. Although the authors will concentrate on particular issues of race, class, and gender, each will do so within a multicultural framework that seriously considers educational interventions intended to ensure culturally relevant pedagogy for ALL of these learners.

In this chapter I have reviewed some of the dilemmas and issues that could inform the development of curricula that go beyond inviting students to engage in cursory examinations of the "contributions" of individuals from diverse backgrounds or to celebrations of diversity in dress, customs, and traditions. Instead, such dynamic curricula would involve Deaf learners and their teachers in an interrogation of their own cultural frames of reference and the relationship of these to how both interact with school content and each other. Moreover, these approaches to curriculum would make explicit the similarities and differences between and among these cultural frames of reference. That is, there is no attempt to suggest that in studying Deaf Culture, one has "taken care" of issues related to sexism, racism, classism, or sexual orientation. Nor are related discriminatory practices relegated to the "back burner" because they are viewed as drawing attention away from those equity issues considered critical for all Deaf individuals. Instead, this kind of multicultural curriculum recognizes the interlocking nature of multiple forms of oppression affecting both Deaf and hearing individuals, discourages the kind of hierarchical approaches that privilege the discrimination of one group at the expense of another, and works to achieve social justice.

Educators of Deaf students need to consider a form of multicultural education that is not an isolated addition to the curriculum nor a vehicle for promoting a monocultural, uniform Deaf Culture. Multicultural curricula can and must provide educational opportunities to build the kind of critical dialogue about diversity that includes and benefits Deaf students from all ethnic and cultural backgrounds.

REFERENCES

Adams, M., Bell, L.A., & Griffin, P. (Eds.). (1997). *Teaching for diversity and social justice: A sourcebook.* New York: Routledge.

Banks, J. A. (Ed.). (1995a). *Multicultural education: Transforming knowledge and action.* New York: Teachers College Press.

Banks, J. A. (1995b). Multicultural education: Historical development, dimensions, and practice. In J. A. Banks & C. A. M. Banks (Eds.), *Handbook of research on multicultural education* (pp. 3–24). New York: Macmillan.

Banks, J. A. (1993). Multicultural education: Characteristics and goals. In J. A. Banks & C. A. M. Banks (Eds.), *Multicultural education: Issues and perspectives* (2nd ed., pp. 3–47). Boston: Allyn & Bacon.

Britzman, D. P., Santiago-Válles, K., Jimenez-Munoz, G., & Lamash, L. M. (1993). Slips that show and tell: Fashioning multiculture as a problem of representation. In C. McCarthy & W. Crichlow (Eds.), *Race identity and representation in education* (pp. 188–200). New York: Routledge.

Cross, W. E., Jr. (1991). *Shades of black: Diversity in African-American identity.* Philadelphia: Temple University Press.

Feagin, J. R., & Sikes, M. P. (1994). *Living with racism: The Black middle-class experience.* Boston: Beacon.

Freire, P. (1970). *Pedagogy of the oppressed* (M. B. Ramos, Trans.). New York: Continuum.

Grant, C. A., Sleeter, C. E., & Anderson, J. E. (1986). The literature on multicultural education. II. Review and analysis. *Educational Studies*, **12**, 47–71.

Hacker, A. (1992). *Two nations.* New York: Scribners.

Helms, J. E. (Ed.). (1990). *Black and White racial identity: Theory, research, and practice.* Westport, CT: Greenwood.

Hodges, C. R., & Welch, O. M. (in press). *Making the familiar strange: Inside a learning community on multicultural education.* Baltimore: University Press.

hooks, b. (1994). *Teaching to transgress: Education as the practice of freedom.* New York: Routledge.

McCarthy, C., & Apple, M. (1988). Race, class and gender in American educational research: Toward a non-synchronous parallelist position. In L. Weis (Ed.), *Class, race, and gender in American education* (pp. 9–39). Albany: SUNY Press.

McIntosh, P. (1992). White privilege and male privilege: A personal account of coming to see correspondences through work in women's studies. In M.L. Anderson & P.H. Collins (Eds.), *Race, class, and gender* (pp. 70–81). Belmont, CA: Wadsworth.

McLaren, P. (1994). Multiculturalism and the postmodern critique: Toward a pedagogy of resistance and transformation. In H. A. Giroux & P. McLaren (Eds.), *In between borders: Pedagogy and the politics of cultural studies* (pp. 192–222). New York: Routledge.

Nieto, S. (1992). *Affirming diversity: The sociopolitical context of multicultural education.* New York: Longman.

Olneck, M. (1990). The recurring dream: Symbolism and ideology in intercultural and multicultural education. *American Journal of Education,* **98**(2), 147–174.

Perry, T., & Fraser, J. W. (Eds.). (1993). *Freedom's plow.* New York: Routledge.

Robeson, P., Jr. (1993). *Paul Robeson, Jr. speaks to America.* New Brunswick, NJ: Rutgers University.

Said, E. W. (1993). *Culture and imperialism.* New York: Knopf.

Sleeter C. E. (1996). *Multicultural education as social activism.* Albany: SUNY Press.

Sleeter, C. E. (1995). An analysis of critiques of multicultural education. In J. A. Banks & C.A.M. Banks (Eds.), *Handbook of research on multicultural education* (pp. 81–96). New York: Macmillan.

Sleeter, C. E., & Grant, C. A. (1991). Race, class, gender, and disability in current textbooks. In M. W. Apple & L. K. Christian-Smith (Eds.), *The politics of the textbook* (pp. 78–110). New York: Routledge.

Sleeter, C. E., & McLaren, P. (Eds.) (1995). *Multicultural education, critical pedagogy and the politics of difference.* Albany: SUNY Press.

Spring, J. (1995). *The intersection of cultures: Multicultural education in the United States.* New York: McGraw-Hill.

Chapter

2

How Are We Doing?

Gilbert L. Delgado

P.L. 100-297 signed by President Reagan April 28, 1988. The Bilingual Education Act of 1988 defines "limited English proficiency 'and' native language" [soc. 7003]. The BEA reauthorization in 1992 offers the opportunity to include deaf individuals in these definitions.

Frank Bowe

This (chapter) discusses issues and trends related to the education of Non-English Speaking (NES) deaf children. It addresses the importance of recognizing the very special needs of this population and applying successful teaching/learning strategies developed in bilingual education. Included, also, is a brief history of special education legislation highlighting developments in education of Deaf children, conclusions and recommendations.

An article appearing in the *Journal of Law and Education,* "Anatomy of a Debate: Intersectionality and Equality for Deaf Children from

Non-English Speaking Homes" (1995), by Alexandra Natapoff, very succinctly describes the status of Deaf and Hard-of-Hearing children from a variety of perspectives. The debate stems from a preceding article in the same journal (1994) by Laura Parsons and Theresa Jordan, "When Educational Reform Results in Educational Discrimination: A Case in Point."

The latter article argues that because of New York State's bilingual education requirement, which also applies to Deaf children from non-English speaking (NES) families, placement or educational services for these children can be discriminatory. That is, these Deaf or hard-of-hearing children may not be able to access a special education program designed for this disability. They recommend that Deaf children from NES homes should not be entitled to bilingual education but rather should have an "individualized diagnostic program designed and directed by educational professionals"(Parsons & Jordan, 1994).

Natapoff's countering position is based on the need to attend to the intersection or interface of Deaf and bilingual identities. That is, educators in this arena have either summarily dismissed or paid scant attention to the bilingual identity or the unique and diverse needs of NES Deaf children. This "difference" is always subordinate to deafness. Deaf children from NES homes are, for the most part, enrolled in day school programs, as opposed to residential (Cohen *et al.*, 1990). Hence, other than during the regular school schedule (five days a week, for 180 days), they are in a monolingual or quasi-bilingual environment. Yet, their pervasive educational needs related to the loss of hearing and home factors such as a different language and culture are seldom considered.

During the mid-1980s and into the 1990s some attention was given to NES Deaf children. The growing population of Hispanic and Asian-Americans in our schools almost mandated that we have another look at our educational programs. Also during this period, there was growing interest in "bilingual special education." Many professionals from these branches of education had high hopes that research, educational practices and the massive amount of literature developed on bilingual education for limited English proficiency (LEP) children could be interfaced with Deaf education, especially since Deaf children are also LEP. However, what evolved was a passing interest from the bilingual education ranks. Presentations and articles from educators of the Deaf were more "esoteric" than substantive in nature. No sustained efforts occurred.

EMERGENCE OF BILINGUAL/BICULTURAL EDUCATION FOR NES DEAF CHILDREN

Progress toward meeting the needs of culturally and linguistically diverse learners who are Deaf has been minimal in recent years. Part of the inertia may stem from the focused interest in the bilingual/bicultural educational philosophy whose limited scope does not address diversity. The bilingual aspect of this movement, for the most part, includes American Sign Language (ASL) and English. The "bicultural" part is Deaf Culture and hearing culture. Deaf Culture is generally about the white Deaf population. Thus, languages such as Spanish, Chinese, Laotian, and Hmong and the distinct cultures they enfold are given little regard.

Strong (1995) did a review of bilingual/bicultural programs for Deaf children in the United States. He surveyed nine of the more established programs around the country. Two of the programs are endeavoring to apply principles of English as a Second Language (ESL) to their curriculum.

Strong (1995) concluded that most bilingual/bicultural programs are in transition. Most are approaching the move to bilingual/bicultural education cautiously and looking over their shoulders to identify what works. This educational alternative needs to convince skeptics. Several programs, including the Indiana School for the Deaf, are now including outside researchers.

Related to this topic, the writer was involved in a review of the Indiana School for the Deaf. This school was one of the first that

publicly expressed its intention to adopt the bilingual/bicultural philosophy. The school has a curriculum coordinator and an ongoing curriculum team. The coordinator is trained in ESL and conducts
in-service training for the faculty and staff. This is a good start. However, much, much more is needed. The "marriage" of bilingual (ESL)
educators and Deaf educators is not consummated. Real and applied
educational interchange and ongoing dialogue between bilingual educators and educators of Deaf children must occur at a steady pace.

The bilingual/bicultural movement, as it is practiced today, has in
some ways derailed the multicultural efforts of the past decade or so.
NES Deaf children have particular needs which are often perceived to
be subsumed and satisfied with bilingual/bicultural educational programming. This, in fact, is not true. NES children and their families
require extensive support services above and beyond the traditional
bilingual/bicultural program elements. For example, both English and
ASL communication may break down because of a different home
language. Although the bilingual/bicultural ASL–English approach is
credible, it may not be adequate for some groups of Deaf children
from non-English speaking families.

DEMOGRAPHICS AND TRENDS

Projections from the U.S. Census Bureau (1996) indicate that

> By 2050, 53% of the population will be White; 25% Hispanic ori-
> gin; 15% Black; 1% American Indian, Eskimo and Aleut; and 9
> percent Asian and Pacific Islander. The Hispanic-origin population
> would increase to 25% and the non-Hispanic White population
> would decline to 53%.

Data from the Center for Assessment and Demographic Studies at
Gallaudet University (Allen, 1996) indicate that nearly the same demographic patterns are occurring in schools and programs for the

Deaf. A very *small* percentage of schools have designed curriculum and provided special programs to address this burgeoning group.

An entire book can be written about the country's move away from cultures and languages other than English. One Nation–One Language, English as the "official" language, affirmative action repeals and other movements constitute the ingredients of a long and upsetting debate. In some ways these developments reflect how our three branches of government have addressed the needs of an ever-changing society.

Pertinent Federal Educational Legislation

The Soviet Union's leap ahead in space and the success of Sputnik triggered President John F. Kennedy and the Congress to pass the National Defense Education Act (NDEA). President Kennedy had also come to see the conditions in the United States as wrought by poverty and lack of education. President Lyndon B. Johnson's War on Poverty and the Great Society passed unprecedented legislation providing federal assistance to a myriad of disenfranchised citizens of this country. Beginning with the disadvantaged, a natural development was that the next deserving group would be people with disabilities.

This section will not discuss federal legislation or initiatives related to the disadvantaged and regular education *per se*. However, there are many areas wherein these public laws intertwine, overlap, or are viewed as being in conflict, e.g., the Natapoff/Parsons, Jordan debate previously discussed.

The objective here will be to trace federal education legislation, primarily related to people with disabilities, from 1958 to the present time. Some overlaps and conflicts will be highlighted.

Federal legislation and funding related to the disabled started very slowly. Under the National Defense Education Act of 1958 monies were first provided for teacher preparation. Also in 1958, the Captioned Films for the Deaf Act (P.L. 85-905) authorized the acquisition of captioning entertainment films for distribution to Deaf persons.

The amendments of 1962 (P.L. 87–815) authorized training, research, and production of many types of educational materials. Teachers of Deaf children were some of the first in special education to develop a media-related curriculum in a series of workshops at Ball State University. Too, development, production, and evaluation of media and corresponding technology was made available in summer workshops at the universities of Massachusetts, Nebraska, Tennessee, and New Mexico State. The universities were part of a network of Regional Media Centers for the Deaf (RMCD). Advanced degree programs in educational technology were established at Syracuse University and the University of Massachusetts. The Captioned Films legislation was very effective in providing materials, equipment, training, and research for practitioners in the field of deafness. Its effectiveness could be attributed to its focus on deafness. As the law was further amended, the programs became more dispersed and were primarily demonstration programs.

The teacher professional development (Deaf) and Captioned Films programs received approximately $9 million in appropriations in 1971. The fiscal year 1991 appropriation for special education was approximately $2.5 billion.[1] This does not include other funds for disabled students from the Education, Consolidation and Improvement Act ($5.5 billion), Carl Perkins Act ($849 million), Impact Aid to Federally Affected Areas ($741 million), and National Library Services for the Blind ($40 million).

Part B of the Individuals with Disabilities Act (IDEA) is the section that provides for Basic State Grants: States are granted federal funds on a statutory formula which is based on the state's "child count," which is multiplied by 40% of the average per pupil expenditure across the nation. About 70% of the total special education allocation goes to Part B ($1.8554 billion). State Education Agencies (SEAs) are required to "pass through" 75% of their funds to the Local Education Agencies (LEAs). Appropriations for fiscal year 2000 are close to $5.5 billion.

---

[1] Fiscal Year 1991 figures.

IDEA also includes other programs such as:

Preschool State Grants	$292.8 m[2]
Early Intervention Grants	$117.1 m
Regional Resource Centers	$ 6.6 m
Services for Deaf Blind	$ 12.8 m
Innovation Programs for Children with Severe Disabilities	$ 7.9 m
Early Childhood Education	$ 24.2 m
Postsecondary Education	$ 8.5 m
Secondary Education and Transitional Services	$ 14.6 m
Special Education Personnel Development	$ 69.5 m
Clearinghouses	$ 1.5 m
Research and Demonstration Projects	$ 20.2 m
Instruction Media and Captioned Films	$ 16.4 m
Technology Education Media and Materials	$ 5.6 m

What is puzzling about the legislative history is that:

1. the language does not mention NES disabled children, albeit priority is sometimes given to grant proposals, and programs often earmark a percentage of grant funds for this population;

2. it appears that NES disabled children can be relegated to Title VII (Bilingual Education Act), wherein they do not seem to "fit" either.

---

[2] Fiscal Year 1991 figures.

BILINGUAL EDUCATION ACT AND IDEA

Fernandez (1992) makes a strong case for the legality, if you will, of students with disabilities being eligible for support from the Bilingual Education Act, Title VII. Fernandez' rationale is based on Section 504 of the Vocational Rehabilitation Act of 1973, IDEA, and Title VI of the Civil Rights Act. IDEA and 504 require an appropriate education for students with disabilities. The Civil Rights Act guarantees LEP students a meaningful education. Using a broad stroke, one could readily maintain that *all* disabled students are also LEP. More specifically, however, it is obvious that Deaf and Hard-of-Hearing students quite naturally fall into this category. Mastery of the English language is an "Everest challenge" for the Deaf person. Again, within this framework, consider the plight of the Deaf student who comes from an NES family. Their chances of English mastery become even more remote.

A relatively small number of projects or programs for Deaf students have been supported by Title VII dollars. In general, such projects are not designed for Deaf and Hard-of-Hearing students exclusively but rather aimed at an LEP population in which some Deaf students are included. Also, provision of speech therapy, a related service, has been justified.

BILINGUAL SPECIAL EDUCATION

The basic problems with creating an *effective* union with bilingual education and Deaf education are threefold: (i) communication, (ii) logistics, and (iii) collaboration.

Strategies for teaching ESL have involved numerous protocols with varying degrees of success. The main thrust of ESL and perhaps bilingual education is either maintenance or transition. The debate continues. Should the nondominant language be maintained and enhanced or should it serve as a bridge, a vehicle, to English and then be discouraged? Add to this debate, the pervasive question of identity and intersectionality argued by Natapoff (1995) and still another debate surfaces. The language (English) problems of Deaf children are much different from those of NES hearing children. The latter have an internalized language base which is a true "leg up." Young Deaf children seldom have a solid language base in any language, (exceptions are Deaf children of Deaf parents). Still, educators need to look at these differences and devise methods of applying ESL principles to Deaf learners—this is a problem of *communication*.

Often bilingual education programs are not located close to Deaf education programs. Often the two do not exist together in any given school district—this is a problem of *logistics*.

Federal education laws compound the problem. As we have seen, Deaf children can be eligible for educational enhancement through Chapter 1, IDEA, or Title VII. The locus for looking at better educational programs of NES Deaf children is the SEA/LEA. How do we bring together the expertise and funding to address this very unique problem—this is a problem of *collaboration*.

TOWARD EQUALITY

In the field of education of the Deaf, one of the most significant documents in this century is the Report by the Commission on Education of the Deaf, "Toward Equality: Education of the Deaf" (1988). This report has served as the basis for numerous and important changes in federal educational and other legislation as it relates to Deaf persons. Dr. Frank Bowe, who chaired the Commission, completed a follow-up review of the COED report in order to track the 52 recommendations from the COED (Bowe, 1993).

During the Commission's series of forums and hearings around the country, testimony was given by numerous recognized educators concerned with the education of NES and other diverse groups of Deaf children. The final report failed to address this population, tending to merely include them with recommendations for lower achieving and multichallenged Deaf students. Bowe's update (1993) did not indicate any change in legislation or programs for culturally and linguistically diverse groups.

Delgado (1984) found that NES and other diverse groups of Deaf children were considered lower achievers. Too, whereas 24% of the overall school-age Deaf population was reported as multihandicapped, 50% of the NES group was categorized as multihandicapped.

Collectively, certain conclusions are derived and some recommendations are made:

CONCLUSIONS

◆ Though there are still some educators of the Deaf who continue to try to support NES educational efforts, these children continue to "fall between the cracks."

◆ Focus and attention to NES and other Deaf students has been diverted by the interest in bilingual/bicultural (Deaf–hearing) education around the country.

◆ "Bi/bi" is often considered *the* solution to the problems of *all* Deaf children.

◆ Cultural and linguistic diversity is not truly recognized or esteemed.

◆ Federal legislation provides little assistance to this population because it is fragmented and vague.

RECOMMENDATIONS

◆ Educators and advocates must renew their efforts to support innovative educational programming for NES Deaf children.

◆ Efforts must be made to educate members of Congress and other legislators about the growing needs of this population that are *not* being well-served.

◆ State and local education agencies, schools, and programs for Deaf children must work on ways to mingle federal dollars and embark on long-term educational changes.

◆ Bilingual educators and Deaf educators need to meet at the national, state, and local levels to develop educational goals and specific laws that coalesce the best practices of both fields.

REFERENCES

Allen, T. (1996). Personal Communication, April, 1996. Washington, DC: Center for Assessment and Demographics Studies, Gallaudet University.

Bowe, F. (1993). Getting there: Update on recommendations by the Commission on Education of the Deaf. *American Annals of the Deaf,* **138**, 304–308.

Bowe, F. (1991). Approaching Equality: Education of the Deaf. Silver Spring, MD: T.J. Publishers, Inc.

Delgado, G. (1984). *The Hispanic Deaf: Issues and Challenges for Bilingual Special Education.* Washington, DC: Gallaudet University Press.

Federal Budget for fiscal year 2000. (1994). Washington DC: U.S. Government Printing Office.

Fernandez, A. (1992). Legal support for bilingual education and language—Appropriate related services for limited English proficient students with disabilities. *Bilingual Research Journal,* **16**(3–4), 117–140.

Gerner de García, B. (1995). Communications and language use in Spanish-speaking families with Deaf children. In C. Lucas (Ed.), *Socio-linguistics in Deaf communities.* Washington, DC: Gallaudet University Press.

Natapoff, A. (1995). Anatomy of a debate: Intersectionality and Equality for Deaf children from non-English speaking homes. *Journal of Law and Education,* 24(2), 371–378.

Parsons, L. and Jordan, T. (1994). When Educational Reform Results in Educational Discrimination: A Case in Point. *Journal of Law and Education.*

Strong, M. (1995). A review of bilingual/bicultural programs for Deaf children in North America. *American Annals of the Deaf,* 140(2), 84–94.

U.S. Bureau of the Census (1996). *Population projections of the United States by age, sex, race & Hispanic origin: 1995 to 2050.* Washington, DC: U.S. Government Printing Office.

U.S. Department of Education (1992). *Summary of existing legislation affecting people with disabilities.* Washington DC: U.S. Government Printing Office.

3

Emerging Literacy in Bilingual/Multicultural Education of Children Who Are Deaf:

A COMMUNICATION-BASED PERSPECTIVE

Kathee M. Christensen

A knowledge of different literatures is the best way to free one's self from the tyranny of any of them.

Jose Marti, 1882

How is it that a child creates meaning from the abstract alphabetic squiggles on a printed page? This question has intrigued educators for decades. Doubts about "Johnny's" ability to read were voiced in the 1960s (Flesch, 1955; Holt, 1964) and debated in the 1970s (Chall, 1967; Smith, 1971). Research in the 1980s scrutinized phonics and considered whole language as an alternative to "decoding print." Reading was conceptualized as a "psycholinguistic guessing game" (Goodman, 1976). Gardner (1983) introduced multiple intelligence theory which suggested the interdependence of at least seven areas of intellect that work toward the overall development of a literate individual. Gardner and others have added to the list of intelligences, suggesting that natural and emotional intelligences and, potentially, an existential domain may exist (Gardner, 1998). As we enter the 21st century, the controversial issue of Johnny's reading status has not been resolved. Educators are, however, beginning to frame the discussion of emergent literacy within a cognitive and cultural context.

In the 21st century, it will be critical for a child to become literate from a cultural, as well as a cognitive, perspective. In order for this to occur, teachers will need the ability to read, interpret, and present literature from a cultural perspective. What has been regarded as "the community" is growing rapidly into a diverse, multilingual, multicultural environment. Literacy is a tool that assists students in locating and understanding their place amid this cultural diversity. Deaf children, in particular, need access to literacy from the perspective of a visually defined Deaf Culture. This chapter will examine ways that teachers can enhance the development of communicative competence in deaf learners from diverse backgrounds.

A literate person has been defined as "one who has acquired the knowledge and skills to engage in activities for effective functioning in the community," and it is further suggested that four to five years of formal schooling will achieve this goal (Downing & Leong, 1982). One may be considered literate by achieving only surface ability in the overall, "deep structure" task of reading, which includes "making discriminative responses with regard for any and all types of stimulus situations" (Spencer, 1970). The branch of literacy, growing from the sturdy trunk of reading behavior in general, has sprouted at least three separate research twigs. One has to do with adult literacy in Third World nations where literacy programs are viewed as vehicles that carry oppressed people toward political independence (Freire, 1970). The second area concerns itself with early intervention programs that propose to facilitate the acquisition of literacy skills in very young children from various economic backgrounds (Durkin, 1966, 1974–1975). A third and recent field of research investigates the notion of literacy in a visual–spatial language, primarily American Sign Language (Fok *et al.*, 1991; Mather, 1989; Ramsey, 1997).

Parallel to the expanded interest in various types of literacy programs are the separate but related research areas of language acquisition and cognitive development. The decade of the 1980s is rich in research which looks at these areas within the broad scope of education. Paradigms have been developed in order to investigate, manipulate, and explain various theories about the development of reading, writing and thinking in populations of children who are deaf (Keane *et al.*, 1992; Kelly, 1990; Martin, 1991).

Catherine Snow, at Harvard University, has directed research efforts toward understanding the development of oral communication and reading ability in young hearing children (1978, 1982, 1983). It is her view that the most important components of parent–child interaction which support language acquisition in young children are also present and facilitative in the early acquisition of reading and writing abilities. Snow contended that middle-class families prepare preschoolers to understand and produce decontextualized spoken and written language through semantic contingency, scaffolding, accountability procedures, and the use of routines. This model, certainly, can be adapted to the multicultural environment of preschoolers who are deaf. Parents of deaf children, however, can participate in preliteracy activities similar to those listed by Snow only if consistent, visually accessible salient communication is present among all family members. Parents representing all ethnicities must learn to communicate visually with a child who is deaf.

SEMANTIC CONTINGENCY

Learning to read English text and learning to communicate effectively with a variety of individuals are complex tasks which involve time, effort, motivation, and consistent comprehensible input from the environment. Development varies from individual to individual. It has been found that a major facilitator of language acquisition is semantic contingency in adult speech to young hearing children (Cross, 1978).

Adult utterances are considered to be semantically contingent if they continue topics introduced by the child in an immediately preceding utterance. Adults may expand the child's utterance grammatically: Child— "Me drink."—Adult— "Yes, you are drinking your milk." Adults may add new information to the topic: Child— "New shoes." Adult— "These are your new, black patent leather shoes." They may also ask for clarification: Child— "Go now." Adult— "Do you want to go to the park now?" They may also answer questions posed by the child: Child— "Daddy come?" Adult— "Yes, Daddy will go to the park with us." All of these forms of semantic contingency serve as useful models for the linguistically developing child. A deaf child will benefit from the visually salient semantic contingency of adults who use signed language, naturally, in daily routines at home and elsewhere.

The notion of semantic contingency can be applied to literacy behaviors when adults interact with children in signed or spoken language in the following ways:

1. answering questions about words (signed or spoken),
2. reading to the child, telling stories,
3. answering questions and carrying on conversation about illustrations in books,
4. assisting with writing tasks when asked by the child to do so.

Having a wealth of interesting reading and writing materials easily available at home will stimulate some of these activities. Elsewhere in this book, readers will note that in one research study, Spanish-speaking families were found to be reluctant to use pen and pencil communication with their deaf children. In addition, reading with their deaf children was a rare activity at home. Clearly, this is an area which could be addressed by educators so that Spanish-speaking parents could become empowered to engage in literacy activities with their deaf children.

SCAFFOLDING

Scaffolding (Bruner, 1978) is a term that refers to the process of reducing the difficulty of a task so that a child may find success in an initial phase of an operation. For example, memorization of the alphabet is a common short-term memory task that many parents present to a young child in the form of a game or song. These games and songs can be found in a multitude of cultural variations. In this context, the alphabet letters have little to do with literacy, per se, and more to do with enjoyable communication between parent and child. With some minor adaptations, however, alphabet play could be used by parents to develop and expand their child's preliteracy awareness. In one case, a parent might limit the number of choices of alphabet letters to those letters with which the child has some prior experience. A parent might say, "Your name starts with 'C'. Can you show me 'C' on this page? Yes! That word, cookie, starts with a C—just like your name, Cindy!" Fingerspelling can be used in this way with young deaf children. A parent may offer such scaffolding assistance, or clues, in both language and literacy activities. Letters and numbers can be introduced, incidentally, at home and at school through appropriate books and videotapes. In the Trilingual Education series, for example, children are exposed to the English manual alphabet, and additional letters found in Spanish, through trailers at the end of each videotaped lesson (Christensen, 1986).

Effective preschool teachers use the scaffolding technique in setting up multicultural learning environments in the classroom. Puzzles depicting a variety of cultural settings might be presented on trays with some of the pieces placed right side up in order to facilitate the child's completion of the task. Scaffolding makes the environment less frustrating and more appealing to young learners. It allows the learner to take "safe risks," achieve small successes, and grow confident in the ability to learn new things independently. Children who feel at ease with a task may have more motivation to discuss some of the culturally related aspects (e.g., "Tell me about the picture.").

In second language acquisition theory, Krashen's Input Hypothesis (1983) could be considered a kind of scaffolding which supports growth in communication. Krashen suggested that the adult "pitch" linguistic input at a level just above the current functioning of the learner in order to create an achievable challenge. This comprehensible input (I+1) will provide a salient language model and facilitate gradual acquisition of the target language in an affirming social context. Piaget called this the creation of disequilibrium which resulted in active assimilation, accommodation, and learning (Ginsberg & Opper, 1988).

It is often difficult for a hearing teacher, no matter how fluent in American Sign Language, to put her/himself into the situation of a very young deaf child who is engaged in the task of creating meaning from visual stimuli. The following scenario illustrates this dilemma. A young teacher with excellent ASL skills was interacting with a profoundly deaf 2-year-old child. The teacher had just completed a book-sharing activity with the 2-year-old and was attempting to gain his assistance in putting away the pile of books which had accumulated on the table. With large, clear ASL, she signed:

YOU   CLEAN-UP   TABLE.

The 2-year-old looked at her signs, looked at the table, and thought about the situation for a few seconds. Then he marched deliberately over to the table, with his right hand and forearm swept all of the books off the table to the floor and smiled proudly at his teacher, obviously assuming that he had fulfilled her request appropriately. Deconstruction of the visually perceived command to a child not yet aware of the nuances of the language would support his conclusion. He did what he saw. He went to the place indicated and followed the sweep of the arm across the table. He perceived the message literally. Teachers must be able to analyze signed communication from the perspective of the young ASL learner and set up a communication situation so that the intent of the message, as signed, is salient to the learner. For example, the teacher might have signed:

LOOK   MANY-MANY   BOOKS

MUST   (demonstrate picking up one book and putting it on the shelf)

YOU   HELP   (work together as books are put away)

LOOK   TABLE   CLEAN!

YOU   ME   CLEAN-UP   TABLE!

The point is that the young child needed more information about what was expected of him. In this simple routine, the scaffolding provided by the teacher will allow him to interpret the signed message accurately and participate in similar interactions successfully in the future.

ROUTINES

Parents typically use highly predictable routines as they interact linguistically with young children (Snow *et al.* 1982). They also use book reading routines which can contribute simultaneously to language and literacy (Ninio, 1980). Book handling skills, discovery of print, and language behavior that leads to development of a story scheme, e.g.,

"What do you think will happen next," ultimately make a contribution to reading comprehension (Snow and Goldfield, 1982).

It is suggested (Snow, 1983) that the memorized routines of childhood rhymes and stories used with hearing children have a direct relationship to later performance with interpreting familiar textual passages. Signed versions of nursery rhymes or ASL poems can be used with deaf children to achieve a similar familiarity with visual–spatial text. The work of Mather (1989) has investigated ways in which deaf adults use pictures, objects, illustrations, and signed language to connect meaning and linguistic symbols. These techniques are helpful in early book-sharing and later reading activities.

LITERACY IN THE HOME

Learning to read and learning to communicate are supported by similar interactions with primary caretakers. Why, then, do almost all children learn to communicate and many children have difficulty in learning to read? One answer to this question relates reading success with the degree of literacy in the home. Homes in which books are valued and reading is a common activity can provide children with an understanding and appreciation of the purpose and use of books. All parents communicate in some manner, but not all parents read avidly. In addition to literacy materials, children may be influenced by literate forms of discourse in the home. TTY conversations relate print to conversation. Storytelling and reading to the child, as well as general quality of discourse, may provide important models for children in acquiring literate behavior. The Texas School for the Deaf has developed CD-ROMs in ASL and signed English which can provide a wealth of interactive visual experience for families who have access to computers. Conversation in the home my serve as a means of building "shared histories" between parent and child. When questions are asked about past events, the child can be helped to acquire the ability to recount and build internal representations of time past and things not present. Photograph albums become a visual support for building shared family histories. All of these literate interactions may better prepare some children to succeed in reading and writing. "Different sets of preschool experiences contribute to literacy skill and to skill in decontextualized language use" (Snow, 1983). Parents of deaf children, of course, must be fluent in a visual–spatial communication mode and understand the importance of visual supplements (e.g., gestures, pictures, etc.) in order to facilitate acquisition of decontextualized language.

LANGUAGE ACQUISITION

The term bilingual education when applied to hearing children typically assumes that the two languages are being used alternately. Children who can *hear* two spoken languages, one at home and a different one in the community at large, are exposed to complete models of both languages, each spoken in the appropriate environment. With exposure to these complete models, the child is able to intuit rules of pragmatics and language shifts. Four common goals of bilingual education for hearing children are speaking, listening, reading, and writing fluency in two spoken languages. Currently, a heavy cultural component has been added to most bilingual education programs, so that students learn more about the cultural environments in which the languages are used (ACTFL, 1996). Furthermore, recent research in bilingual education indicated that two spoken languages can be acquired from birth on, in a parallel manner, without interference if the appropriate environment for use of each language is clearly defined (McLaughlin, 1984; Tabors, 1997). Dicker (1996) has described this process as developmental bilingual education (DBE). DBE is a pluralistic model in which the native language is developed along with the target language or second language. Both languages are given equal status.

Bilingual/multicultural education for deaf children differs significantly from that of hearing children and their families. The main reason for this difference is that the majority of deaf children, more than 90%, in fact, are born to families who know little about deafness and even less about visual spatial communication. American Sign Language may be the most natural language for a deaf child and at the same time represent a foreign language for the child's family. It is well known that first language fluency for hearing infants begins and grows naturally at home with family members who are fluent speakers and role models. Bilingual education for a profoundly deaf child *must* begin with access to visually comprehensible communication at home.

That means that an intense ASL immersion program must be provided for family members so that (natural) visual communication can be used consistently at home, as soon as possible. Parents, presumably, have an intact first language, L1. In the United States, typically the L1 is spoken English, although the use of Spanish is growing rapidly, particularly in the western states. According to the research of Krashen, Cummins, Terrell, and others, persons with native fluency in one language can use that first language, L1, as a base for acquisition of a second language, L2, when motivated to do so. Parents, then, if provided with the means of acquiring the rudiments of ASL, can begin to use ASL at home. If a DBE approach is used, both English and ASL will be regarded as having equal status. ASL may be the L2 for the family and, at the same time, be the deaf child's L1. Ideally the deaf child will acquire the natural, visual language foundation at home in order to transition to an academic environment where complete ASL and English models are provided by teams of bilingual/multicultural deaf and hearing teachers. In a bilingual classroom of this kind, ASL could be used for discussion, explanation, and story-telling, with English used for reading and writing. In this environment, competence in both ASL and English is a goal for the deaf child and the family. It may be that, for a time, the family will be just one or two steps ahead of their deaf child in signed language competence and that eventually the deaf child may surpass his/her parents in ASL fluency. However, communication is an ongoing process. An approach which includes a means for early, visually based linguistic negotiation among family members is a positive step toward eventual bilingual ASL/English competence for deaf students. It has been found that parents for whom English is not the L1 can use ASL as a communication "bridge" between two spoken languages, English and Spanish (Christensen, 1985).

In Context, Out of Context

Adult literacy has been defined as "the ultimate decontextualized skill" (Snow, 1983). Bialystok (1991, p. 128) refers to reading as "a decontextualized use of language, that is, the language is presented outside of the empirical context to which it refers." In order to accept these definitions as accurate, one assumes that a reader has achieved an advanced level of literacy in combination with Piagetian Stage IV cognitive development. It is this cognitive level which deals with ultimate abstractions, both linguistic and nonlinguistic. An adequate level of intelligible, expressive language must be present in order to fully evaluate the facility with which an individual can deal with decontextualized images and information. Reaching this level of language fluency is a major academic challenge for students who are deaf, given the current lack of consistent, comprehensible linguistic input in the daily environment of these learners.

There are some obvious similarities in the acquisition of communication and literacy acquisition. If careful attention is paid to the behaviors exhibited, one area may be used to reinforce and supplement the other. Just as children naturally acquire, use, and play with nonverbal and verbal (e.g., signed or spoken) expression, they may be encouraged to behave in the same manner with "readingwriting" expression. Creativity in fingerspelling, for example, might parallel early, natural "word play" and enhance the development of cognitive experimentation.

Decontextualization is dependent upon significant exposure and practice within contextualized settings. Initial literacy behavior is dependent upon context (Mishler, 1979) and the gradual process of context-stripping, or abstraction, is a result of development in the related areas of receptive communication, expressive communication, and cognition. Development of any one area is interrelated closely with the overall experience of the individual, first in context and later beyond the limits of context. The acquisition of literacy, then, is an integral part of the total development of the child as he or she progresses through the academic (primarily English) and social (ASL and English) requirements of a "literate" culture. A view of reading ability, from a developmental perspective, will not be limited to the ability to decode symbols in print. The overall ability to deal with the immediate environment linguistically and cognitively is fundamental to the acquisition of literacy. English and ASL are important components in assessing a learner's strengths and potentials as he/she attempts to map form onto meaning in whichever language is appropriate for the immediate cultural environment.

CONTROVERSY AND CHANGE

In the general arena of bilingual/multicultural education, one controversial issue is that of language choice and access. In 1997, the Oakland California School Board voted to accept Ebonics as a natural dialect of many of their African American students. It was suggested that all teachers respect, and to the degree possible, understand the home language(s) of the students in their classes. The premise was that if teachers accepted the communication of the child as valid, this natural dialect might provide a bridge to the achievement of standard English. In fact, the Ebonics program was based, in part, of the research of John R. Rickford, a linguistics professor at Stanford University. Dr. Rickford cited studies which suggested that a "bridge system" can help students move from a particular dialect to a standard language. One study, in particular, described a 4-month program with 500 African American students around the United States. These students used Black dialect, a transitional reader, and then a standard English text. The subjects gained 6.2-month progress in 4 months, as compared to a control group of remedial reading students who gained 1.6 months in 4 months; in other words, it could be assumed that the control group fell behind as a result of the remedial reading program. According to Rickford, "People seem to be endorsing existing methods, but existing methods are not working" (Washington Post, January 13, 1997).

The move toward acceptance of Ebonics in the schools was an attempt to ameliorate dismal statistics compiled by the Oakland Board of Education which revealed that 64% of students who repeat the same grade are African American. Black students have an average of 1.8 GPA on a 4-point system, and of the Black males enrolled in Oakland schools, 29% do not attend on a regular basis. Clearly, the existing methods were not working. There was a need to rethink the existing policies in the schools. The Linguistic Society of America endorsed the position of the Oakland School Board, calling the plan "linguistically and pedagogically sound," further stating the Black English or Ebonics is "systematic and rule-governed like all natural speech varieties." The American Speech–Language–Hearing Society (ASHA) also published a statement in support of Ebonics as a natural, social dialect with its own lexicon, syntax, phonology, and semantics.

What happened next? First of all, there was a strong reaction from some Hispanic educators who were concerned that the Oakland plan would drain funds from existing programs for bilingual students. Resource allocation rather than support of human needs became the priority for some groups. Members of the African American community were not 100% in support of the Ebonics decision, either. Many, including Walter Williams, an economics professor at George Mason University, feared that acceptance of Ebonics would dilute education for African American students and further limit their proficiency in English and prevent acquisition of English literacy. Critics of Ebonics contended that a good education in standard English is a ticket out of the slums. Acceptance of Ebonics, they felt, builds a ghetto wall around Black students. These assertions may have a familiar ring to educators of the deaf. Many of the arguments for and against Ebonics replicate the ASL/English controversy which continues to exist in our field (see Fig. 3.1).

And so it goes, despite the words of Ralph Ellison (1947) and other writers who point to common sense in the midst of chaos. In his book, *Invisible Man,* Ellison wrote:

If you can show me how I can cling to that which is real to me,
While teaching me a way into the larger society,
Then I will not only drop my defenses and my hostility,
But I will sing your praises and I will help to make the desert bear fruit.

Figure 3.1

Critics of Ebonics	Critics of ASL
1. Afro-Centric	1. Deaf Power
2. Students Won't Learn English	2. Ditto
3. Students Won't be Competitive in the Job Market	3. Ditto
4. Students Won't Assimilate into the Majority Culture	4. Ditto
5. Students Will Fail Academically	5. Ditto

Cultural and linguistic data to the contrary, there are schools and programs that cling to practices that fail to promote educational excellence rather than explore ways of achieving academic and vocational success for all students who are deaf.

If the majority of deaf children were able to read and write at a level commensurate with their cognitive potential, educators could elect to spend time in philosophical discussions about the ways in which we might agree to disagree, professionally. At this time, however, theoretical rhetoric is a luxury we cannot afford. One does not spend time deciding which hose to use when the house is on fire. All options are tested in order to determine which ones will accomplish the goal most effectively. The fact is that deaf students of all ethnic backgrounds continue to be undereducated and underemployed. Raising the communication standards for professionals who teach deaf children is a step in the right direction. Efforts to restructure education, schools, and teaching will help us to rethink our priorities. Educational opportunities for enhanced communication among deaf, hard-of-hearing, and hearing individuals can lead to collaborative efforts which benefit all groups and individuals.

Professional collaboration and ongoing dialogue are critical elements leading to the success of our profession—success in educating all children who are deaf. Multicultural collaboration can assist professionals with differing philosophies to accomplish together much more than could be accomplished alone. Our goals for the near future must include: 1. The development of collaborative partnerships across disciplines, 2. Ongoing dialogue among culturally diverse communities, and 3. Enhanced opportunities for professional dialogue regarding differing philosophical and pedagogical perspectives. To paraphrase the core practices of the Foxfire Approach to school reform, as individual teachers and professionals, we must take time to reflect, to collaborate, to guide, to make connections and to evaluate ourselves (Jervis, 1996). If we do these things, honestly and regularly, we can expect to see progress in our students and in our profession in the new millennium.

REFERENCES

American Council on the Teaching of Foreign Languages (ACTFL) (1996). *Standards for foreign language learning: Preparing for the 21st century.* Lawrence, KS: Allen.

Andrews, J., & Bruner, J. (1978). Learning how to do things with words. In J. Bruner and R. A. Garton (Eds.), *Human growth and development.* Oxford: Oxford University Press.

Bialystok, E. (Ed.). (1991). *Language processing in bilingual children.* New York: Cambridge University Press.

Bruner, J. (1978). The role of dialogue in language acquisition. In A. Sinclair, R.J. Jarvella, & W.J.M. Levelt (Eds.), *The child's conception of language: Springer series in language and communication* (pp. 242–256). New York: Springer-Verlag.

Chall, J. (1967). *Learning to read: The great debate.* New York: McGraw-Hill.

Christensen, K. (1985). Conceptual sign language as a bridge between English and Spanish. *American Annals of the Deaf,* **130,** 244–249.

Christensen, K. (1986). Sign language acquisition by Spanish-speaking parents of deaf children. *American Annals of the Deaf,* **131,** 285–287.

Cross, T. (1978). Mother's speech and its association with rate of linguistic development in young children. In N. Waterson and C. Snow (Eds.), *The development of communication.* London: Wiley.

Dicker, S. (1996). *Languages in America: A pluralist view.* Clevedon, UK: Multilingual Matters.

Downing, J., & Leong, C. (1982). *Psychology of reading.* New York: Macmillan.

Durkin, D. (1966). *Children who read early: Two longitudinal studies.* New York: Teachers College Press, Columbia University.

Durkin, D. (1974–1975). A six year study of children who learned to read in school at the age of four. *Reading Research Quarterly,* **10,** 9–61.

Ellison, R. (1947). *Invisible man.* New York: Vintage Books.

Flesch, R. (1955). *Why Johnny can't read—And what you can do about it.* New York: Harper.

Fok, A., VanHoek, K., Klima, E., & Bellugi, U. (1991). The interplay between visuospatial script and visuospatial language. In D. Martin (Ed.), *Advances in cognition, education, and deafness,* 127–145. Washington DC: Gallaudet University Press.

Freire, P. (1970). Cultural action for freedom. *Harvard Educational Review Monograph Series 1.* Cambridge, MA: Harvard University Press.

Gardner, H. (1998). *Where to draw the line: The perils of new paradigms.* Invited address, Annual meeting of the American Educational Research Association, San Diego, CA.

Gardner, H. (1983). *Frames of mind.* New York: Basic Books.

Ginsberg, H., & Opper, S. (1988). *Piaget's theory of intellectual development* (3rd ed.). Englewood Cliffs, NJ: Prentice Hall.

Goodman, K. (1976). Reading: A psycholinguistic guessing game. In H. Singer & R. B. Ruddell (Eds.), *Theoretical models and processes of reading,* 2nd ed., (pp. 497–508). Newark, DE: International Reading Association.

Holt, J. (1964). *How children fail.* New York: Pitmen.

Jervis, K. (1996). *Eyes on the Child.* New York: Columbia University, Teachers College Press.

Keane, K., Tannenbaum, A., & Krapf, G. (1992). Cognitive competence: Reality and potential in the deaf. In H. C. Haywood & D. Tzuriel (Eds.), *Interactive assessment* (pp. 300–316). New York: Springer-Verlag.

Kelly, L. (1990). Cognitive theory guiding research in literacy and deafness. In D. Moores & L. Meadow-Orlans (Eds.), *Educational and developmental aspects of deafness.* Washhington DC: Gallaudet University Press.

Krashen, S., & Terrell, T. (1983). *The natural approach: Language acquisition in the classroom.* New York: Pergamon.

Martin, D. (1991). *Advances in cognition, education and deafness.* Washington, DC: Gallaudet.

Mather, S. (1989). Visually oriented teaching strategies with deaf preschool children. In C. Lucas (ed.), *The sociolinguistics of the deaf community* (pp.165–190). San Diego: Academic Press.

McLaughlin, B. (1984). *Second language acquisition in childhood:* (Vol.1) *Preschool children* (2nd ed.). Hillsdale, NJ: Erlbaum.

Mishler, E. (1979). Meaning in context: Is there any other kind? *Harvard Educational Review,* **49,** 1–19.

Ninio, A. (1980). Picture book reading in mother–infant dyads belonging to two subgroups in Israel. *Child Development,* **51,** 587–590.

Ramsey, C. (1997). *Deaf children in public schools: Placement, context, and consequences.* Washington, DC: Gallaudet University Press.

Schirmer, B. (1994). *Language and literacy development in children who are deaf.* New York: Merrill.

Smith, F. (1971). *Understanding reading.* New York: Holt, Rinehart, & Winston.

Snow, C. (1983). Literacy and language: Relationships during the preschool years. *Harvard Education Review,* **53,** 165–189.

Snow, C. (1978). The conversational context of language acquisition. In R. Campbell & P. Smith (Eds.), *Recent advances in the psychology of language* (Vol. 2). New York: Plenum.

Snow, C., deBlauw, A., & Dubber, C. (1982). Routines in parent–child interaction. In L. Feagans & D. Farran (Eds.), *The language of children reared in poverty.* New York: Academic Press.

Snow, C., & Goldfield, B. (1982). Building stories. In D. Tannen (Ed.), *Analyzing discourse: Text and talk.* Washington, DC: Georgetown University Press.

Spencer, P. (1970). *Reading reading.* Claremont, CA: Graduate School.

Tabors, P. (1997). *One child, two languages: A guide for preschool educators of children learning English as a second language.* Baltimore: Paul H. Brookes.

4

An Asian/Pacific Perspective

Li-Rong Lilly Cheng

Look, it cannot be seen—it is beyond form.
Listen, it cannot be heard—it is beyond sound.
Grasp, it cannot be held—it is intangible.
These three are indefinable.
Therefore they are joined in one.

Lao Tsu

In this chapter, the history, languages, and cultures, including cultural values, religious beliefs, and immigration backgrounds of the Asian/Pacific populations in the United States will be discussed. Their attitudes, references, assumptions, child-rearing practices, cultural orientations toward education, and feelings about disability will be examined to yield guidelines for cross-cultural communication. Some cross-cultural implications for the deaf will also be reviewed.

Asian/Pacific people have been immigrating to the United States for over two centuries. The first records of the arrival of the Chinese date from 1785. Large numbers of Japanese farmers came between 1891 and 1907. The Chinese and Japanese were the first groups to emigrate to Hawaii, followed by Filipinos and Koreans. Filipinos and Koreans began to immigrate in large numbers to the United States mainland in the 1950s. Prior to 1975, there were very few Southeast Asians in the United States. More recently, an influx of Asian/Pacific immigrants and refugees has occurred. Since 1975, over a million refugees from Southeast Asia have settled in the United States. In recent decades, more refugees from Eastern Europe, the Middle East, Africa, and the former Soviet Union have come to the United States. Table 4.1 provides recent data on the refugee populations. Many refugees went through secondary migration and relocation. Most of them have settled in California, New York, and Texas (see Table 4.2),

Table 4.1

Ten Largest Refugee Source Countries, 1994[a]

Former USSR	43,140
Vietnam	36,998
Former Yugoslavia	7,418
Laos	6,211
Iraq	4,930
Somalia	3,508
Haiti	3,466
Cuba	2,687
Sudan	1,289
Iran	859

Note: From Report to the Congress: FY 1994 Refugee Resettlement Program. U.S. Department of Health and Human Services, 1994. Washington, DC.

[a] Not included in this table are 13,255 Cuban and Haitian nationals admitted under the Cuban/Haitian Entrant Program.

Table 4.2

Refugee Resettlement: Top Ten States, 1994[a]

California	27,379
New York	20,892
Texas	5,874
Washington	5,547
Illinois	4,431
Florida	4,125
Pennsylvania	3,554
Massachusetts	3,312
Georgia	3,312
Michigan	2,817

Note: From Report to the Congress: FY 1994 Refugee Resettlement Program. U.S. Department of Health and Human Services, 1994. Washington, DC.

where the weather is similar to their home countries or where there is a large refugee population (Te, 1995).

Many Pacific Islander groups from Samoa and Guam also immigrated to Hawaii and the U.S. mainland (Cheng, 1995). The countries included in Asia are listed in Table 4.3, and those in the Pacific Islands are listed in Table 4.4.

There has been significant growth in the Asian/Pacific Islander population in the United States, from less than 1% in 1970 to an expected 4% in the year 2000, a projected growth of 400% in 30 years (Gardner *et al.,* 1985; Rueda, 1993). In recent years, immigrants have come from Pacific Rim countries. For example, approximately 40% of immigrants to the United States in 1990 were from Pacific Asian countries. The number of Limited English Proficient (LEP) students in California public schools in the spring of 1996 was 1,323,787, an increase of about 5% over that in the spring of 1995. Besides Spanish, the top languages were Vietnamese, Hmong, Cantonese, Pilipino, and Khmer (Context, 1999).

Table 4.3

Asian Countries

Afghanistan	Israel	Pakistan
Armenia	Japan	Qatar
Azerbaijan	Jordan	Saudi Arabia
Bahrain	Kazakhstan	Singapore
Bangladesh	Korea, North	Sri Lanka (Ceylon)
Bhutan	Korea, South	Syria
Brunei	Kuwait	Taiwan
Burma	Kyrgyzstan	Tajikistan
Cambodia (Kampuchea)	Laos	Thailand
China	Lebanon	Turkey
Cyprus	Macao	Turkmenistan
Hong Kong	Malaysia	United Arab Emirates
India	Maldives	Uzbekistan
Indonesia	Mongolia	Vietnam
Iran	Nepal	Yemen
Iraq	Oman	

Note: From "Asia" (1994). In *Collier's Encyclopedia*, pp. 18–19.

Table 4.4

Pacific Islands

American Samoa	Marshall Islands	Papua New Guinea
Cook Islands	Micronesia	Solomon Islands
Easter Island	Nauru	Tonga
Fiji	New Caledonia	Tuvalu
French Polynesia	Northern Mariana	Vanuatu
Guam	Islands	Wallis and Futuna
Kiribati	Palau	Western Samoa

Note: From "Pacific Islands" (1995). In *The New Encyclopedia Britannica*, p. 232.

The Asian American school-age population has increased more than sixfold from 212,900 in 1960 to almost 1.3 million by 1990. In 1990, 40% of Asian Pacific American children were first generation, 44% were second generation, and 15% were third generation. By the year 2020, Asian American children in U.S. schools will total about 4.4 million. According to the U.S. Census 1990 (cited in Jiobu, 1996), the largest number of immigrants to the United States is found among the Chinese.

Despite the number of years that Asian groups have lived in the United States, it was not until the recent influx of immigrants and refugees that the special needs of Asian/Pacific populations have surfaced. Prior to the recent influx, the major Asian American groups were Chinese, Japanese, Koreans, and Filipinos, many of them second or third generation (nisei or sansei as the Japanese call them) who had English language proficiency and varying degrees of acculturation. The recent influx, however, represents a diverse group from Southeast Asia (Vietnam, Laos, and Cambodia), Hong Kong, China, India, Pakistan, Malaysia, Indonesia, and other Pacific rim and Pacific Basin areas. They are greater in number and face many more challenges in adjustment. For example, the Asian population in Monterey Park, California, has shifted from a mere 2.9% in 1960 to 56% in 1990 (Fong, 1994).

Professionals in the field of education and in related fields have to provide appropriate services for these populations, yet many are unprepared to deal with the cultural, social, and linguistic diversity the Asian/Pacific populations present (Sue & Padilla, 1986). According to Stewart *et al.* (1989), a large percentage of Pacific Island children in the U.S. school system failed hearing screenings. Yonovitz (1995) indicated that 90% of the inhabitants of Bathhurst Island (an island of Australia) have moderate to severe hearing loss. A number of researchers have found that children with reported extensive otitis media with effusion (OME) had poorer scores on articulation tests and delayed phonological development (Paden, 1994; Silva *et al.*, 1982, cited in Paden, 1994).

In order to better serve Asian/Pacific Island populations, it is necessary to understand something about their backgrounds, languages, cultures, and beliefs.

BACKGROUND INFORMATION: ASIAN/PACIFIC POPULATIONS

Numerous variables must be considered when working with individuals from Asian/Pacific populations: languages, religions, childrearing practices, beliefs and values, kinship system, customs, lifestyle, practices in medicine, reasons for leaving the homeland, educational levels, personal experiences, and others. Despite their many similarities, individuals from Asian/Pacific countries cannot be lumped together as one homogeneous group in terms of common views and expectations regarding lifestyles, perceptions of illnesses, methods of healing, childrearing practices, religious beliefs, or family and community support systems. Thus, while broad similarities and differences between Asian and Western belief systems and practices may be discussed, one must always keep in mind the many similarities and differences among the Asian/Pacific populations themselves. For example, many Asians and Pacific Islanders are Catholic, yet many of them also hold a strong folk belief system. Professionals need to be cognizant about such similarities but also need to be aware of the folk/cultural differences that exist.

Asian/Pacific Americans have come from the following areas:

East Asia: China, Taiwan, Hong Kong, Japan, Korea;

Southeast Asia: the Philippines, Vietnam, Cambodia, Laos, Malaysia, Singapore, Indonesia, Thailand;

the Indian Subcontinent or South Asia: India, Pakistan, Bangladesh, Nepal, Sri Lanka;

the Pacific Islands: Hawaii, Guam, American Samoa, Tonga, Fiji, other Micronesian Islands.

Australia and New Zealand are also among the Pacific nations.

LANGUAGES

There are hundreds of distinct languages and countless dialects spoken in Pacific Asia. They can be classified into five major language families.

Malayo-Polynesian: Tagalog, Illocano
Sino-Tibetan: Thai, Yao, Mandarin, Cantonese
Austro-Asiatic: Vietnamese, Khmer, Hmong
Papuan: Papua New Guinean
Altaic: Japanese, Korean.

Additionally, "the countries of the Indian subcontinent present a staggering linguistic diversity. There are at least four major language families in the region: Indo-European (Indic), Dravidian, Austro-Asiatic, and Tibeto-Burman. Each major family has many subfamilies. All families and subfamilies contain numerous languages. Each language has hundreds of dialects" (Shekar & Hegde, 1995, pp. 131–132).

Over 1200 indigenous languages are spoken among the 5 million inhabitants of the Pacific Islands; these include Chamorro, Marshallese, Trukese, Carolinian, Papua New Guinean, Korean, Japanese, Ponepean, Samoan, Fijian, Tahitian, and Hawaiian. The Hawaiian language is spoken mainly on the tiny island of Niihau, and not too many locals speak it or speak it well. The five *lingua francas* used by the Pacific Islanders are French, English, Pidgin, Spanish, and Bahasa Indonesian. Additionally, people from the Middle East are sometimes classified as Asians; they speak Arabic, Farsi and other languages. Arabic is the native language of more than 160 million people and the official language of 20 countries.

There are many dialects of Arabic (Wilson, 1996). According to Almaney and Alwan (1982), the Arabic dialects fall into five geographical categories:

◆ North African (Western Arabic)
◆ Egyptian/Sudanese

- Syrian or Levantine
- Arabian peninsular
- Iraqi.

Asian languages differ from one another a great deal, from being tonal, monosyllabic, and logographic (a property of some writing systems) to being intonational, polysyllabic, alphabetic, and agglutinational. Languages such as Mandarin, Lao, and Vietnamese rely on tonal differences for meaning. For example, there are four tones in Mandarin, the first tone is high-level, the second is rising, the third is fall-rising, and the fourth is falling. The same syllable, *"ba,"* means "eight" in the first tone, "to pull" in the second, "handle" the third, and "father" in the fourth. People learning the language must gain a mastery of the tones both receptively and expressively in order to communicate effectively (Cheng, 1991). This presents a real challenge for deaf persons.

Chinese is logographic, that is, words are represented graphically by logographs. Logographs are also called ideographs and they (a single logograph and /or a combination of logograph) represent a meaningful unit. These ideographs are not based on a system of alphabet and many of the ideographs are expressed in the Chinese sign language by their shapes. For example, the character Wong is expressed with three fingers on the one hand and the one finger from the other hand behind them symbolizing the character Wong. Japanese writing uses a combination of *Kanji* (Chinese characters), *Katakana* (generally used for names and foreign words), and *Hiragana* (cursive used to write Japanese when Chinese characters are not available) (Cheng, 1991). The Khmer and Lao writing systems are based on the Indian languages of Sanskrit and Pali. The Hmong, as well as the Vietnamese, use alphabetical systems.

The main Asian/Pacific languages spoken in the United States are Mandarin, Cantonese, Taiwanese, Tagalog, Visayan, Illocano, Lao, Khmer, Hmong, Vietnamese, Urdu, Hindi, Chamorro, and Samoan. It is important for educators to have some background concerning these languages so that they will be able to understand why certain linguistic constructs are present or absent in students' linguistic repertoires.

RELIGIOUS/PHILOSOPHICAL BELIEFS

The major religious/philosophical beliefs of the Asian/Pacific populations are Hinduism, Buddhism, Confucianism, Taoism, Shintoism, Animism, Christianity/Catholicism, and Islam. Religions in the Middle East include Islam, Judaism, and Christianity.

Hinduism is the main religion in India. Buddhism, which preaches kindness, reincarnation, and nonviolence, began as an offshoot of Hinduism around the 5th century. Confucianism exerts a strong influence in China, Japan, Korea, and Vietnam. Confucius defined social order and the rules that dictate relationships between family members, subordinates, and others. Taoism is derived from the doctrines of Lao Tzu. The basic principle of Taoism is that one must not interfere with nature but must follow its course. Those who practice Taoism display a sense of fatalism about events surrounding them because the religion promotes passivity and inaction. A Taoist accepts what comes to him and does not resist the force of nature. A poem that expresses some of these thoughts follows:

Tao is (likened to) an empty bowl,
Whose function is inexhaustible;
Bottomless,
It seems to be the "ancestor" of the Ten Thousand Things.
It blunts all sharpness,
Unties all tangles,
Softens all lights,
And becomes one with all dust.
Deep and hidden,
It seems as if it were ever-present.
I do not know whose child it is,
It looks as if it were prior to the Lord. (Fu & Wawrytko, 1988)

The principal religion of Japan is Shintoism, with emphasis upon worship of nature, ancestors, and ancient heroes and reverence for the spirits of natural forces and emperors. Ancestral worship is a prevailing theme in Asian beliefs, and it is practiced in China, Japan, Korea, and Vietnam (Cheng, 1989). Animism is another common religion in Southeast Asia. It holds that there are spirits in everything, including one's body, and that demons and spirits exist. The head is where the chief spirit resides; touching it brings bad luck. *Baci,* a common ritual in Animism, is usually performed when a person is ill or going away on a trip. This ceremony represents the religious/folk belief system of a major part of Southeast Asia; such practices are often regarded as a means of healing and getting rid of the evil spirits. Individuals may seek advice from a priest or a shaman when their family members are stricken with birth defects or illnesses. Ashes from burned incense may be used for medicinal purposes.

The Pacific Islanders have also been influenced by Christianity/Catholicism, which is practiced with a mixture of folk beliefs, such as taotaomona/spirits (Chamorro), menehune/spirits (Hawaiian), and suruhana/healer (Chamorro) (Ashby, 1983). They often seek medical advice from faith healers or "witch doctors" and may prefer herbal medicine. A small portion of Asians are Muslims, and they live in widely scattered areas, from the Malaysian Islands to the Philippines. About half of the people in Samoa belong to the Congregational Christian Church or other Protestant churches. Other residents of Samoa are Roman Catholics (Cheng *et al.,* 1995). Religion is an integral part of any culture; it impacts views of life, child-rearing practices, human relations, and disabilities. Wilson (1996) provided helpful information about the Islam culture where the religion has a great impact on daily life. The Muslims are forbidden to drink wine or liquor and they do not eat pork. Children are raised with gender-specific rules in the family. Educators would benefit from learning about how the family system is organized, how disability is viewed in those cultures and specifically how deafness is viewed.

HOME OF ORIGIN

Some of the Asian newcomers are immigrants, while others are refugees. Although immigrants planned to come to the United States, they differ in their education and degree of exposure to the English language and American culture. By law, immigrants must have a sponsor, either a close relative or an employer. They file for an immigrant visa and then must wait for a period of time (ranging from six months to five years) before beginning visa interviews and screening procedures. In recent years, immigration rules and regulations have been modified, making it more difficult to sponsor relatives to come to the United States. Additionally, with the shrinking dollars, sponsors of immigrants have to take more responsibility in financial support so as not to drain state and federal resources.

On the other hand, refugees left their countries to escape persecution; many risked their lives and left their families behind. Sometimes, they had only a few days, even a few hours, to prepare for their escape (Te, 1995). When fleeing their native countries, the refugees from Southeast Asia did not know which country, if any, would give them asylum. The conditions in refugee camps were often difficult. Medical attention was limited, and children with ear infections often went unattended. Many refugees and immigrants speak no English and had never before traveled outside their homeland (Chhim, 1989; Lewis *et al.*, 1989; Luangpraseut, 1989; Te, 1987; Walker, 1985).

American Born

Many Asian school-age children were born in the United States or in refugee camps; others are nisei (second generation), sansei (third generation), and yonsei (fourth generation) Americans. They were born and educated in the United States and may not speak the language of their parents or grandparents. (For more information about the history of Asian Americans, see Akamatsu) (1993), Cheng (1995), Takaki (1989), and Trueba *et al.* (1993). The generation gap, which affects all families to some extent, may be a particular problem in families in which immigrant parents are raising children in the United States based on their personal experiences and expectations. Here are a few examples of the difficulties encountered by Asian immigrant parents:

◆ Discourse rules in the mainstream American culture differ from discourse rules in Asian cultures.

◆ The definition of a well-rounded person in the United States is unfamiliar in Pacific Asia. In Pacific/Asian terms, a well-educated person has expertise in one area. In mainstream America, a well-rounded person should have some knowledge of many areas, including sports, music, sciences, literature, politics, art, and language.

◆ Adolescents do not want to look, act, or be treated differently from their peers especially in dress, telephone habits, hairstyles, and curfews. Asian parents may impose rules that are very different from their mainstream counterparts.

◆ Messages that youth get from schools, peers, and media play an important role in shaping their thoughts and molding their behavior, which their parents find unacceptable. (Cheng, 1996b).

Researchers in Asian studies have discussed the differences within the Asian/Pacific group. There is a great diversity in social class among the families of refugees and immigrants. About 95% of the Vietnamese and Chinese–Vietnamese came from urban backgrounds, whereas 50% of Cambodians came from rural backgrounds. Among Southeast Asian refugees, Vietnamese parents are reported to be the most educated, having an average of nine years of schooling. The Hmong have an average of one year of schooling (Ima & Rumbaut, 1989). Fathers generally have higher educations than mothers in all groups. A lack of family tradition in education may lead to school dropout and academic underachievement (Ima & Keogh, 1995).

There are major differences between early immigrants and recent immigrants. The early immigrants came to the United States in the late 19th century to work in the mines, for the railroads, and on the farms (Akamatsu, 1993; Asian Women United of California, 1989; Cheng & Chang, 1995; Chin, 1967). They experienced unfair treatment, including the Asian Exclusion Act and the internment of the Japanese during World War II. Later immigrants came after World War II to further their education, and many found employment in major industrial and academic institutions. Recent immigrants came to the United States to seek better job opportunities and to further their studies. Some came to escape Communism. Many people waited for years before a visa was granted due to quota restrictions. A large number of immigrants have come from China and Hong Kong. Many recent Asian immigrants are from Malaysia, China, India, Hong Kong, Taiwan, Korea, and Japan. The application procedure and the health requirements exclude many individuals with disabilities. Immigrants' personal life histories have a significant impact on how they feel about themselves and how they view life, and this directly influences how they view education. It behooves educators to be sensitive to their needs and views.

Refugees

Most refugees never dreamed of leaving their homes. For them, the journey to the United States was filled with trauma, anxiety, separation, fear, hunger, and unrest (Te, 1987). Refugees from Southeast Asia came in three waves. Those who came in the first wave, primarily Vietnamese, came after the fall of Saigon in 1975; many belonged to the bureaucracy and armed forces of the defeated government of South Vietnam. They were more educated and had higher than average social resources and professional and managerial skills. The second wave, or the "boat people," started in 1978. This group included a wide variety of ethnic groups as well as those from various socioeconomic backgrounds, mainly farmers and fishermen. Those from the third wave, who came after 1982, were even more diverse in terms of ethnicity, background, experience, and social class. Between 1975 and 1990 over a million Southeast Asian refugees, about half of them under 18 years, were admitted to the United States (Chuong & Van, 1994).

There is great diversity among the Southeast Asian population. They bring with them a diverse mixture of customs, education, beliefs, and values (Rumbaut & Ima, 1988). The Vietnamese, Chinese, and Hmong have similar cultural traits including sharing of patrilineal–extended family systems. Patrilineal–extended families were built on the Confucian cultural model that emphasizes family relationships, duties and discipline, filial piety, obedience, parental authority, and respect for the elderly. The Lao and Khmer people have common cultural roots, elements of which are borrowed from Indian culture, religion, and languages. The Indian languages, Sanskrit and Pali, have influenced the Lao and Khmer languages. Theravada Buddhism is a shared religion.

Pacific Islanders

Pacific Islanders from Samoa, Tonga, and Guam have immigrated to Hawaii and the U.S. mainland in large numbers. The Chamorro people of Guam hold U.S. passports and can travel freely to the United States. Western Samoa is under the rule of the British government, while American Samoa is a U.S. territory. In recent years, more than 60,000 Samoans left their homeland, leaving approximately 30,000 Samoans on the island.

The Filipinos are grouped as either Asians or Pacific Islanders. The Philippines is an archipelago of more than 7200 islands from which there has been a steady flow of immigrants since the end of World War II. In their homeland they speak a total of 87 mutually unintelligible languages, but most Filipino immigrants speak English. Many Filipino Americans either were born in the Philippines or have parents who were born there. After the Second World War, a large number of Filipinos came to the United States. Internal unrest, corruption, and economic hardship drove more to the United States to pursue a better life. They are among the fastest growing Asian/Pacific Islander communities, and it is estimated that by the year 2000 there will be close to 2 million Filipinos in the United States (Kitano & Daniels, 1988). For more information see Cheng *et al.* (1995).

ACCULTURATION

Different degrees of acculturation are present in the immigrant and refugee populations. Some immigrants, either as groups or as individuals, totally reject the new culture into which they have come. Some adapt to the new culture, integrating some of its aspects while still retaining part of their own culture. Others become assimilated into the culture, giving up their former cultural identity (Berry, 1986).

Some people are highly assimilated and still retain high ethnic identity (Cell B), whereas others give up or reject their ethnic identity to achieve assimilation (Cell A). On the other hand, some preserve their ethnic identity but with low assimilation (Cell D), while some get lost in a low cultural identity and low assimilation situation (Cell C). Berry's model described the situation of European Americans, who can assimilate completely into the majority, whereas Asians never feel completely assimilated because of their appearance.

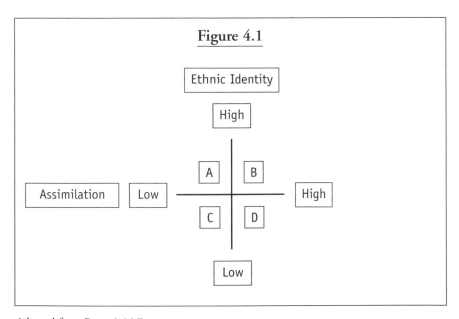

Figure 4.1

Adapted from Berry (1986)

The process of forming an identity is extremely complex. It is more complex for persons of color in the United States because of the mixed messages they receive from their environment. The children of first generation immigrants reported receiving contradicting messages from home and from their environment, causing them to be confused, lost, marginalized, or ambivalent. Asian individuals are variably acculturated into the American mainstream; some adapt successfully and move up in U.S. society, while others adapt more slowly and do not integrate into society depending on the environment. In Western societies where independence is highly valued, autonomy is a key value in childrearing. In contrast, most Asian societies value obedience, respect for elders, and family cohesion and harmony. This will result in children feeling torn and experiencing the crisis of having to deal with two separate worlds. The notion of the developmental niche is useful in studying children growing up in multilingual/multicultural settings.

Spindler and Spindler (1990) also researched acculturation and proposed the following adaptive strategies:

- *Reaffirmation* of the home culture and rejection of the mainstream culture.

- *Synthesis* of aspects of the home culture and the mainstream culture; this may be seen in religious beliefs and practices.

- *Withdrawal* by rejecting both cultures, and not committing to any cultural values.

- *Biculturalism,* or full involvement with the two cultures. This requires effective linguistic and cultural code switching.

- *Constructive Marginality* involves moderate participation in both cultures while keeping a conscious distance from both cultural systems.

- *Compensatory Adaptation* is characterized by thorough adoption of mainstream culture and rejection, or at least avoidance, of the home culture.

During any personal contact with an Asian/Pacific individual, educators should always be reminded of the cultural values associated with the individual's family background. Variables such as eye contact, physical contact, and praise and reinforcement are viewed differently by Western cultures and by Asian/Pacific cultures. Asian cultures, in general, do not encourage physical contact; eye contact is used minimally; open praise is reserved for special occasions.

The United Nations Educational, Scientific, and Cultural Organization defined culture as a dynamic value system of learned attitudes, with assumptions, conventions, beliefs, and rules that permit members of a group to relate to each other and the world. Some of the many cultural constituents, as identified by Kohls (1979), are general beliefs, religious beliefs, myths, values, and knowledge. Cultural beliefs, such as attitudes toward illness and disability, shape societal thinking. Aspects of culture, such as language, are fluid because they need not persist generation after generation. On the other hand, static aspects of culture such as kinship systems, attitudes, and beliefs do tend to persist generation after generation. Asians who are second and third generation still hold many of the same beliefs and values. The following section describes some of the cultural beliefs that are prevalent in Asian/Pacific cultures.

CULTURAL BELIEFS ABOUT DISABILITIES IN GENERAL

The following is a synopsis of some of the primary cultural beliefs, kinship systems, and childrearing practices in many parts of Pacific Asia.

What is considered a disability? Conditions that are caused by congenital or acquired injuries, such as blindness, deafness, cleft palate, and paralysis, are considered disabilities (Meyerson, 1983).

From whom does one seek medical advice? People may seek help from a medical doctor trained in Western medicine, indigenous methods of healing, and/or a folk medicine man or woman, faith healer, or shaman.

How is medicine used? People may choose a combination of Western and folk medicine, which at times has disastrous results. For example, they may alter the suggested frequency and amount of the prescribed medication. There have been reports of overdoses because the patient thought that recovery would occur sooner if more medication were taken. Some do not use measurements such as one teaspoon or two drops properly or do not take their doses at the prescribed intervals.

What are the methods of healing? These include surgery, medication, physical therapy, acupuncture, massage (Chinese, Korean, Japanese), cao gio (coin rubbing), herbal medicine, bat gio (pinching), giac (placing a very hot cup on the exposed area), xong (steam inhalation), balm application, baci (a ritualistic healing practice among Vietnamese), or ingestion of hot or cold foods (Chamorro, Hawaiian, Hmong).

What religious or philosophical beliefs affect treatment? As mentioned above, the Asian/Pacific populations have a variety of religious and philosophical beliefs. For a more complete description of these beliefs see Cheng (1989, 1991, 1995, 1996). Some Asian/Pacific people believe that a disability or deformity is karma (fate), and therefore nothing can be done about it; those with a fatalistic attitude will not seek intervention.

What are the causes of disabilities? These arise from a variety of spiritual and/or cultural beliefs, such as imbalance of inner forces, bad wind or spoiled food; gods, demons, or spirits; and hot or cold forces. Most people view a disabling condition as the result of wrongdoing of the individual's ancestors (e.g., talking about others behind their backs). Belief in reincarnation may lead individuals to accept physical deformities or disabilities as the result of the wrongdoing of one's ancestors.

How are disabled individuals treated? Some cultures view a disability as a gift from God; the disabled individual belongs to everybody and is protected and sheltered (Chamorro culture). Other cultures view a deformity as a curse and the individual may be ostracized from society (Philippines and China).

What are the attitudes toward disabilities? These vary from culture to culture. Some define deaf people as mute (considering them incompetent in learning oral language). Some view deafness as a curse. A child's disability is viewed by some as a personal embarrassment to the parents (Epstein, 1989). Attitudes are formed and influenced by religions and philosophies, including Buddhism, Confucianism, Catholicism, and Islam. For example, the mother of a child born with a disability may view this as a family disgrace and associate disability with shame and guilt (Wilson, 1996).

What steps should be taken in seeking a cure? Again, these vary from culture to culture and individual to individual. For those who have been acculturated, seeking medical advice from a physician is a common practice. Those who have recently arrived in the United States may first seek advice from family members and take folk medicine and then see a medicine man or a clan head who may communicate with the deceased ancestors for advice as they did in their home country. Next, medical advice may be sought from a physician from the same language and ethnic group, and finally, as a last resort, consultation with persons who are not members of the same ethnic/linguistic group may be attempted.

How is illness perceived? A person with mental disorders may be viewed as healthy since there is no physical evidence of disability. On the other hand, a person with a physical difference may be regarded as sick even though he or she is otherwise in good health.

What are the childrearing practices? The Asian/Pacific cultures may view children as helpless, dependent, and lacking intentionality. A good baby is one that is not fussy but quiet. Views on dressing, toilet training, feeding, and self-help skills may vary a great deal among the different cultures. Methods of discipline also vary widely (Sue, 1986). Wilson (1996) described the difference in parental attitudes between Arab parents and American parents, and one aspect is that Arab children are generally dependent on their parents for a longer period of time than are most American children.

Individuals may have mixed feelings regarding disability and the treatment of disabled individuals. For example, the cultural value of being benevolent may be overridden by the superstition that deformity brings bad luck, resulting in the abandonment of disfigured newborns. The Asian views on education, authority figures, discipline, self-direction, parent–school interaction, parent–child interaction, parental responsibilities, and filial piety of the children make it difficult for educators of the deaf to comprehend the interrelatedness of those principles and how they relate to the ultimate success of the deaf population.

TREATMENT OF THE DEAF IN ASIAN COUNTRIES

As described earlier, Asian American people have been influenced mainly by Chinese and Indian philosophies, religions, and cultures. Confucian beliefs are taught in China, Japan, Korea, and Vietnam. Other Asian countries have been influenced by the Indian religions of Buddhism and Hinduism. At the same time, indigenous belief systems are also important.

The Chinese, Japanese, Korean, and Vietnamese people have a deep-rooted humanistic philosophy which began with the teachings of Confucius. Confucius was born about 550 B.C., during a time of harsh rule; only those in the aristocracy were allowed to be educated. Since he was born into a family of lower aristocracy, Confucius himself had to struggle to gain his education.

Confucius was the first person who taught all people without regard to their position or social status. He believed that everyone had the capacity to become a virtuous individual through learning and education. To him, people were the most important component in society. They were to aspire to become virtuous and to follow "the Way." A series of steps was necessary on the journey along the Way. There were progressive degrees of achievement, each dependent on successful completion of the previous step. The attainment of the whole series constituted the knowledge for personal self-motivation.

The traits to be developed were humanity, benevolence, kindness, compassion, charity, courtesy, diligence, respect and deference to the elderly, filial piety, and responsibilities in relationships. Confucius stated that to attain these traits one must be true to one's self and free from self-delusion and practice reciprocity (loyalty to others and an appreciation of the feelings of others). Through his writings and teachings Confucius laid the foundation for the educational philosophy of the Chinese, Korean, Japanese, and Vietnamese people.

Confucius' concerns for the disadvantaged were seen in his teachings. His principles of self-cultivation, fondness for education, and vigor for learning remained a driving force in the education of disabled individuals. It was many years, however, before these teachings were applied directly to the educational needs of deaf students. The official document of Li Chi, originating from China and dating back to approximately 200 B.C., outlined society's responsibility for the care and education of the disabled. Specifically, society was deemed responsible for giving assistance to and meeting the special needs of widows, widowers, orphans, the deaf, the blind, the physically disabled, and all sick individuals. Such individuals had been protected and cared for by family members because they were ostracized from society.

In China, the earliest records of treatment of the disabled were in 1870 when Pastor William Moore established the first school for the blind in Peking (Beijing). In 1887, the first school for the deaf in China was founded in Shangtung province by Madame Annette

Thompson Mills, an American trained at the Clarke School. Later more schools were established and supported by churches and received no government funding. By 1916 there were only 12 schools for the deaf in China. In the People's Republic of China, between 1949 and 1985, the number of schools for blind, deaf, and retarded students increased from 40 to 375, as enrollment expanded from 2322 to 41,706. From 1985 to 1988, the number of schools increased to 504, serving 52,800 students (Epstein, 1989). The total number of deaf children in China exceeds 550,000. China has made progress, but currently educates less than 10% of deaf children. Also, China lacks preschools for the deaf—in fact, some deaf Chinese students do not begin school until age 9 and leave to begin working at age 16. After the Cultural Revolution, the Chinese government established an Association for the Disabled led by the son of Deng Xiao Ping, Deng Pu Fong, who became disabled during the Cultural Revolution due to an injury of the spinal cord. Other associations such as the Association for the Deaf and Blind began to publish journals and present information on the deaf and blind populations. The *Journal of Deaf People in China* not only covers stories about the deaf but also gives lessons in Chinese sign language in every issue.

In Taiwan, the first school for exceptional children opened in 1890 as a school for the blind and later included deaf children. It was a privately owned school, and later other private schools were opened to serve the deaf population. The government of the Republic of China (Taiwan) opened its first school for the deaf and blind in 1927, and during the next 10 years a few more such schools opened. The government began putting emphasis on educational opportunities for the deaf and blind, and the population's awareness of the importance of education for the disabled increased.

In 1987 there were four schools for the deaf with a total enrollment of 1965 students. Other hearing impaired students attended special classes in regular schools. In Taiwan today, most deaf individuals receive vocational training and work in sheltered workshops. A report (Lin & Ho, 1986) indicated that male students have more severe losses than female students. Another report (Chen, 1983) indicated that 76% of the special education population in Taiwan are hearing impaired/deaf. According to the 1995 Republic of China Yearbook, 99.89% of school-age children in Taiwan attend school. In 1995, there were 16 special schools including 4 schools for the deaf and 159 special classes for the hearing-impaired (Education Statistics of Republic of China, 1995). The same report indicated that 0.06% of the elementary and junior high school population had hearing impairment. The data are quite different from the data in the United States, where 0.6–0.7% of the school-age population have a reported hearing impairment. Lin (1993) reported that there was an extreme shortage of speech and hearing professionals in Taiwan.

Reports referred to societal attitudes as well as current rehabilitation efforts in Asian countries. Gokhale (1982) explained that legislation for the disabled, as well as public assistance and social security, are newly emerging concepts in most Asian countries. In the past, a child with an impairment was often denied the chance for education and intellectual stimulation. Sidel and Sidel (1982) reported that as recently as the 1940s, the blind in China were described as "isolated in a tangle of superstition, fear and contempt" (p. 121). People with disabilities were considered to be "sick" in China and were therefore "eliminated" before or soon after birth (Gudalefsky, 1989). Blindness was often considered a punishment for the parents' or ancestors' sins, and blind children were frequently abandoned or sold into slavery (Sidel & Sidel, 1982). According to traditional Shinto beliefs in Japan, illness was a state that was considered polluting, calling for temporary separation, and even ostracism, from the group (Lock, 1980). Such beliefs are prevalent in other parts of Asia, including India, the Philippines, and Malaysia.

Sidel and Sidel (1982) described the Shanghai Children's Welfare Institute, which provided care for approximately 500 patients ranging in age from newborn to 16 years. Many of the children had been abandoned by their families, probably due to the parents' superstitious ideas about physically disabled and retarded children. They were often viewed as monsters, ghosts, or foreign spirits that came to the parents as punishment for a sin. These views were particularly widespread in the rural areas, and even today such beliefs exist. A study on birth defects (Cheng, 1989) revealed that many of the Chinese people still believe that birth defects are caused by parents' wrongdoing or by pregnant women looking at rabbits or using scissors.

In Japan, disabled students are mandated to attend school under the School Education Law. Mentally and physically disabled children are placed in special schools or classrooms depending upon the type and degree of the disability. Standardized degrees of mental and physical deficiencies are used as guidelines. The Municipal Committee for Instruction, composed of doctors, school teachers, professors, and welfare facility staff, judges the degree of deficiency. Placement in special schools, special classes in normal schools, or regular classes in normal schools is recommended, depending upon the degree of deficiency. The special schools serve 11,308 children in 110 national, public, and private schools for the deaf, ranging from kindergarten through upper secondary grades. At the level of compulsory education there are 100 schools serving 5588 deaf students and 467 special classes serving 2005 hard of hearing students.

The tendency in rehabilitation efforts made so far has been to isolate the deaf in terms of special institutions and special places to work (Gokhale, 1982). It is estimated that more than 6 million children in China are in need of special education; only 6% of them are receiving services (Epstein, 1989).

In 1986, a law for special education was passed in the Republic of China (Taiwan), mandating that the disabled be served educationally. In 1976, 31% of those with hearing losses were being served by public schools, 52% by special schools and residential schools, and the rest were reported as not attending school (Kuo *et al.,* 1976). Recent publications report the latest trend to be toward integrating deaf children into the regular classroom and utilizing other methods of teaching, such as aural–oral communication. Teachers are working with the deaf in all fields in which they can achieve. One indication of this is a report stating that the conservation abilities (as described by Piaget) of hearing-impaired students had a significant relationship to their age and intelligence. A positive linear growth in conservation abilities was noted as they advanced in age (Chang, 1988). Also early home training in developing listening skills and speech has led to hearing-impaired children having better developed fine and gross motor skills, higher scores in receptive and expressive language skills, better self-help skills, situation comprehension, and personal–social skills (Hwang, 1988). Parents of disabled children are also being served through genetic counseling and information about the disability and the availability of treatment.

EDUCATIONAL IMPLICATIONS

When working with Asian/Pacific populations, the following factors must be considered:

Personal life history: immigration/migration/refugee history, including the reasons for coming to the United States, e.g., war, trauma, abuse, separation;

Lifestyle prior to immigration: many immigrants and refugees lived an agrarian lifestyle in which farming was their main focus; others from the Pacific Islands may have depended upon fishing and growing livestock for their living (Walker, 1985);

Prior education: length and consistency of schooling, amount and type of exposure to English, repeated moves or transfers, lack of schooling;

Home environment: social class, resources (educational level, employment, and income levels of parents), home language, caretakers, members of the family (especially the mother's socioeconomic and emotional characteristics), extended family, roles and expectations, activities, forms of discipline;

Prior medical information: screening, examinations, surgery, medication, birth history, illnesses, lack of medical care;

Personal status, such as detached youth, unaccompanied minor, orphan, or adopted.

Family and community support systems: childcare providers, medical assistance personnel, providers of advice during crises, medical advice, mental health counseling, family counseling;

Cultural beliefs: especially folk beliefs about medicine, birth defects, disabilities, and the causes and treatment of disabilities;

School information: past and current school performance, strengths, weaknesses, quality of school life, and classroom behavior; and

The referral: who made it and why? Who has seen the child?

Professionals face significant difficulty when they come in contact with Asian/Pacific populations. Interpreters may be difficult to locate, and resources are not readily available. Interpreters need to be trained in terminology, testing techniques, ethical issues, parent communication, and cross-cultural communication (Cheng, 1996a).

When working with such a culturally and linguistically diverse population, the following information and skills may be necessary.

Knowledge of different languages;

Knowledge of various learning styles and cultural orientations toward teaching and learning;

Knowledge of diverse values, biases, and beliefs;

Knowledge of different kinship systems;

Knowledge of different communication styles (Matsuda, 1989);

Knowledge of folk and religious beliefs;

Knowledge of recent history (refugees, camp, war, migration, death in the family);

Knowledge of family and support systems.

Professionals who do not share a language with their students/ clients must work with interpreters. A number of publications have focused on the need for professionals to team up with paraprofessionals (Hamayan & Damico, 1991; Mattes & Omark, 1991; Langdon & Saenz, 1996). Furthermore, the following critical information must be gathered through home visits with a teacher and interpreter team:

Number of years in the United States;

Language(s) of the parents (hearing or deaf);

Prior education (disruption, lack of schooling, repeated moves and transfers);

Home environment (unsupervised minors, detached youth, unaccompanied minors, single parent, parent working two or multiple jobs, multiple guardians);

Educational background;

Language(s) used at home;

Child care arrangement at home (who takes care of the children).

CONCLUSION

Professionals need to be innovative in their application of intervention strategies, since Asian/Pacific multicultural students who are deaf provide a special challenge. These individuals come from such diverse cultural, linguistic, and religious backgrounds that critical background information is essential for professionals to develop a culturally relevant and sensitive approach when working with this population.

Educators must increase their sensitivity and awareness of cultural differences in Asian/Pacific learning and communication styles in order to make the adjustments necessary to meet the needs of Asian/Pacific deaf populations. Cross-cultural communicative competence is necessary for successful interaction (Cheng, 1996a). Finally, we need to have the children educate us about their world. Only when we understand them can we empower them through the education we offer. In addition to this, we need to engage parents in the educational process, thus maximizing the natural support system.

Coelho (1995) emphasized the following points when working with diverse students. These points are applicable to teaching and communication with Asian/Pacific populations:

◆ Share cultural knowledge;

◆ Make connections with students' existing knowledge;

◆ Include the perspectives, experiences, achievements, contributions, and aspirations of Asian and Pacific Islander groups in the curriculum;

◆ Include teachers who can serve as role models and cultural interpreters on staff;

◆ Incorporate students' culture into the curriculum and into the life of school;

◆ Provide learning activities that appeal to a variety of learning styles;

◆ Create opportunities for equal-status interaction;

◆ Help all students to diversify their repertoire of learning strategies.

More research needs to be done in order to understand the needs of the population and to further our knowledge about the aspects of the culture that deaf persons from a multicultural world are facing today.

REFERENCES

Akamatsu, T. (1993). Teaching deaf Asian and Pacific Island American children. In K.M. Christensen, & G.L. Delgado (Eds.), G. L. *Multicultural issues in deafness* (pp. 127–142). London: Longman.

Almaney, A. J., & Alwan, A. J. (1982). *Communicating with the Arabs.* Prospect Heights, IL: Waveland.

Ashby, G. (1983). *Micronesian customs and beliefs.* Eugene, OR: Rainy Day.

"Asia" (1994). In *Collier's Encyclopedia* (Vol. 3, pp. 14–55). New York: Collier.

Asian Women United of California (Ed.) (1989). *Making waves: An anthology of writings by and about Asian American women.* Boston: Beacon.

Berry, J. W. (1986). The acculturation process and refugee behavior. In C.L. Williams & J. Westermeyer (Eds.), *Refugee mental health in resettlement countries* (pp. 25–37). Washington DC: Hemisphere.

Chang, B. (1988). A study on conservation abilities of hearing impaired students in primary school level. *Bulletin of Special Education, 4,* 113–130. [Taiwan Normal University, Taiwan, Republic of China]

Chen, Y. H. (1983). *Welfare policies for the handicapped in the Republic of China.* Executive Yuan Research and Development Commission. Taipei, Taiwan.

Cheng, L. (Ed.). (1995). *Integrating language and learning for inclusion.* San Diego, CA: Singular.

Cheng, L. (1996a). Beyond bilingualism: A quest for communicative competence. *Topics in Language Disorders,*16(4), 9–21.

Cheng, L. (1996b). Struggle to be heard: A call for redefinition of achievement. In *Chinese American Educational Research & Development Association Fourth Annual Conference Proceedings: Balancing academic achievement and social growth.* Rockville, MD: Chinese American Educational Research and Development Association.

Cheng, L. (1989). Service delivery to Asian/Pacific LEP children: A cross-cultural framework. *Topics in Language Disorders,* **9**(3), 1–14.

Cheng, L. (1991). *Assessing Asian language performance: Guidelines for evaluating limited-English-proficient students* (2nd ed.). Oceanside, CA: Academic Communication Associates.

Cheng, L., & Chang, J-M. (1995). Asian/Pacific Islander students in need of effective services. In L. Cheng (Ed.), *Integrating language and learning for inclusion* (pp. 3–30). San Diego, CA: Singular.

Cheng, L., Nakasato, J., & Wallace G. J. (1995). The Pacific Islander population and the challenges they face. In L. Cheng (Ed.), *Integrating language and learning for inclusion* (pp. 63–105). San Diego, CA: Singular.

Chhim, S. H. (1989). *Introduction to Cambodian culture.* San Diego, CA: Multifunctional Service Center, San Diego State University.

Chin, T. (Ed.) (1967). *A history of the Chinese in California.* San Francisco: Chinese History Society of America.

Chuong, C. H., & Van, L. (1994). *The Amerasians from Vietnam: A California study.* Sacramento: Southeast Asia Community Resource Center.

Coelho, E. (1995, February). *Cultural and linguistic challenges: Teaching and learning in a multilingual context.* Paper presented at the meeting Teaching from the Heart: Illinois Conference for Teachers of Linguistically and Culturally Diverse Students, Illinois.

Context (1999) p. 20 (138). Folsom Cordova Unified School District, Rancho Cordova, CA.

Education Statistics of Republic of China (1995). Taipei, Taiwan, ROC: Ministry of Education, Republic of China.

Epstein, I. (1989). *Special education issues in mainland China.* International Conference on Education in Mainland China, Taipei, Taiwan.

Fong, T. P. (1994). *The first suburban Chinatown: The remaking of Monterey Park, California.* Philadelphia: Temple University Press.

Fu. C. W., & Wawrytko, S. A. (1988). *Lao Tzu: Tao Te Ching.* Unpublished manuscript.

Gardner, R. W., Robey, B., & Smith, P. C. (1985). Asian American: Growth, change, and diversity. *Population Bulletin,* **40,** 1–44.

Gokhale, S. D. (1982). Rehabilitation of disabled workers in Asia and Oceania. *Indian Journal of Social Work,* **43,** 27–28.

Gudalefsky, A. (1989). The China scene. *TASH Newsletter,* Vol. 15, No. 10.

Hamayan, E.V., & Damico, J.S. (1991). *Limiting bias in the assessment of bilingual students.* Austin, TX: PRO-ED.

Hwang, T. (1988). A study on the guidance program for the speech development of hearing impaired infants. *Bulletin of Special Education,* **4,** 97–112. [Taiwan Normal University: Taipei, Taiwan, Republic of China]

Ima, K., & Keogh, P-E. (1995). "The crying father" and "My father doesn't love me": Selected observations and reflections on Southeast Asians and special education. In L. L. Cheng (Ed.), *Integrating language and learning for inclusion: An Asian-Pacific focus.* San Diego: Singular.

Ima, K., & Rumbaut, R. G. (1989). Southeast Asian refugees in American schools: A comparison of fluent-English-proficient and limited-English-proficient students. *Topics in Language Disorders,* **9**(3), 54–75.

Jiobu, R. M. (1996). Recent Asian Pacific immigrants: The Asian Pacific background. In B. O. Hing & R. Lee (Eds.), *The state of Asian Pacific America: Reframing the immigration debate* (pp. 59–126). Los Angeles, CA: Leadership Education for Asian Pacifics (LEAP), Inc.

Kitano, H. H. L., & Daniels, R. (1988). *Asian Americans: Emerging minorities.* Englewood Cliffs, NJ: Prentice-Hall.

Kohls, L. R. (1979). *Survival kit for overseas living.* Chicago: Intercultural Network/SYSTRAN Publications.

Kuo, W., Chen, Y., & Liang, C. N. (1976). *National prevalence study on exceptional children in the Republic of China.* National Taiwan Normal University, Special Education Center. Taipei, Taiwan.

Langdon, H. W., & Saenz, T. I. (1996). *Language assessment and intervention with multicultural students: A guide for speech–language–hearing professionals.* Oceanside, CA: Academic Communication Associates.

Lewis, J., Vang, L., & Cheng, L. L. (1989). Identifying the language learning difficulties of Hmong students: Implications of context and culture. *Topics in Language Disorders, 9*(3), 21–37.

Lin, B. G. (1993). *The needs for professional speech pathologists and audiologists in school education system.* Taipei, Taiwan, ROC: Ministry of Education, Republic of China.

Lin, P. B., & Ho, M. H. (1986). Research on audiological evaluation of the hearing impaired, cerebral palsied and mentally retarded in the Republic of China. In *The modernization of special education.* National Taiwan Normal University.

Lock, M. M. (1980). *East Asian medicine in urban Japan.* Berkeley: University of California Press.

Luangpraseut, K. (1989). *Laos culturally speaking.* San Diego, CA: Multifunctional Service Center, San Diego State University.

Matsuda, M. (1989). Working with Asian parents: Some communication strategies. *Topics in Language Disorders, 9*(3), 45–53.

Mattes, L., & Omark, D. (1991). *Speech and language assessment for the bilingual handicapped* (2nd ed.). San Diego, CA: College Hill.

Meyerson, M. D. (1983). Genetic counseling for families of Chicano children with birth defects. In D.R. Omark & J.G. Erickson (Eds.), *The bilingual exceptional child.* San Diego, CA: College Hill.

"Pacific Islands" (1995). In *The New Encyclopedia Britannica* (15th ed., Vol. 25, pp. 231–301). Chicago: Encyclopedia Britannica.

Paden, E. P. (1994). Otitis media and disordered phonologies: Some concerns and cautions. *Topics in Language Disorders, 14*(2), 72–83.

Republic of China Yearbook (1995). Taipei, Taiwan, ROC: The Government Information Office.

Rueda, R. S. (1993, July). *Meeting the needs of diverse students.* Presentation at the Multicultural Education Summer Institute, San Diego State University, CA.

Rumbaut, R. G., & Ima, K. (1988). *The adaptation of Southeast Asian refugee youth: A comparative study.* Washington, DC: U.S. Department of Health and Human Services, Office of Refugee Resettlement.

Shekar, C., & Hegde, M. N. (1995). India: Its people, culture, and languages. In L. Cheng (Ed.), *Integrating language and learning for inclusion.* San Diego, CA: Singular.

Sidel, R., & Sidel, V. W. (1982). *The health of China.* Boston: Beacon.

Spindler, G., & Spindler, L. (1990). *The American cultural dialogue and its transmission.* London: Falmer.

Stewart, J. L., Anae, A. P., & Gipe, P. N. (1989). Pacific Islander children: Prevalence of hearing loss and middle ear disease. *Topics in Language Disorders, 9*(3), 76–83.

Sue, D. (1986). *Counseling the culturally different: Theory and practice.* New York: Wiley.

Sue, S., & Padilla, A. (1986). Ethnic minority issues in the United States: Challenges for the educational system. In *Beyond language.* Los Angeles, CA: California State University.

Takaki, R. (1989). *Strangers from a different shore.* Boston: Little, Brown.

Te, H. D. (1987). *Introduction to Vietnamese culture.* San Diego, CA: Multifunctional Center, San Diego State University.

Te, H. D. (1995). Understanding Southeast Asian students. In L. Cheng, L. (Ed.). *Integrating language and learning for inclusion* (pp. 107–124). San Diego, CA: Singular.

Trueba, H., Cheng, L., & Ima, K. (1993). *Myth or reality: Adaptive strategies of Asian newcomers in California.* Washington, DC: Falmer.

U.S. Department of Health and Human Services (1994). *Report to the Congress: FY 1994 Refugee Resettlement Program.* Washington, DC.

Walker, C. L. (1985). Learning English: The Southeast Asian refugee experience. *Topics in Language Disorders,* 5(3), 53–65.

Wilson, M.E. (1996). Arabic speakers: Language and culture, here and abroad. *Topics in Language Disorders,* 16(4), 65–80.

Yonovitz, A. (1995). *Bathurst Island: A case study.* Presentation at ASHA Annual Conference, Orlando, FL.

5

Immigrant and Refugee Children Who Are Deaf: Crisis Equals Danger Plus Opportunity[1]

C. Tane Akamatsu and Ester Cole

start all over.
start all over.
we need to make new symbols,

make new signs,
make a new language,
with these we'll redefine the world
and start all over.

Tracy Chapman, "New Beginning"

---

[1] In Chinese characters, the word "crisis" combines the characters from the words "danger" and "opportunity."

In this chapter, we address issues concerning deaf children who are of immigrant or refugee background. We begin by presenting information pertinent to the general refugee and immigrant population, focusing on migration, adaptation and acculturation. Next, we examine issues of schooling and language and cognitive development, focusing on late-first and second language development and literacy acquisition. We also examine the role of the family in helping the school better understand their deaf child. We discuss assessment of these children in service of developing programs to meet their many educational and mental health needs. The chapter concludes with implications for school programs for deaf children, and recommendations for professional development.

Ten-year old Vasanthi arrived in Canada three years ago with her family. Although other members of her family were born in Sri Lanka, Vasanthi was born in Norway. After Vasanthi's birth, her family moved to Germany, where she lived at a residential oral school. The school forbade the use of sign; she learned no German Sign Language, no spoken German, and no Tamil. By the time she arrived in Canada, she was without any first language.

Vasanthi's history raises several issues, including:

1. the number of countries involved in her flight,

2. the education system(s) in those countries, particularly with regard to refugee claimants,

3. educational opportunities for deaf children,

4. family separation, including the deaf child's separation from his/her own family,

5. the family's ability to cope with deafness,

6. the languages that family members speak or are exposed to during the migration period,

7. the deaf child's access to any language, and

8. the implications of delayed access to language learning.

Some of these issues are common to all deaf children, and others are common particularly to immigrant and refugee deaf children. In this chapter we address these issues, specifically those concerning deaf children who are of immigrant or refugee background.

Similar to Vasanthi, many newcomer students lack not only English, but any form of language (spoken or signed), and/or appropriate study skills for North American schools. Their families may lack basic information about deafness, the importance of language and communication, the partnership role that families and schools can play, special education opportunities, and information about their and their children's rights and responsibilities as members of a new society (Turner, 1996). Yet deaf children, like any others their age, must come to feel socially and academically competent if they are to become productive members of society (Benard, 1993).

We begin by presenting information pertinent to the general refugee and immigrant population, focusing on migration, adaptation, and acculturation. Next, we examine issues of schooling and language and cognitive development. The chapter concludes with implications for school programs for deaf children and recommendations for professional development. Although the discussion is meant to focus on the general refugee and immigrant population, we illustrate these concepts using vignettes from South Asian and East African refugee children.

MIGRATION, ADAPTATION, AND ACCULTURATION: IMPLICATIONS FOR DEAF CHILDREN AND THEIR FAMILIES

Although both immigrant and refugee children undergo similar adaptation and acculturation stresses, immigrant children have the advantage of a planned migration. Emigration and immigration are planned moves, where families must make specific preparations for the move and where they usually have time to make these plans. Such research and preparations may include information about the new country, learning the new language, investigating educational opportunities for the children, and perhaps visiting the new country prior to actually making the move. Thus, the new country is specifically targeted by the family as the ultimate destination for a new, and possibly improved, life (Cole & Siegel, 1990).

In contrast, refugee migration is an unplanned move, where people are forced from their homes with little notice. They have no target country nor opportunity to learn much about their new country and its culture. Rather than planning for a new life, refugees are simply trying to survive and protect their family members. They may have to travel to several different countries before one will allow them to stay on a permanent basis. During the migration, they may stay long enough in more than one country to bear children and have their children enter the school system, even on a temporary basis. Therefore, their children may begin to learn the languages of several host countries. However, it is also not uncommon for education to be interrupted and languages to be incompletely learned. Refugee children's histories may include information about disrupted lives, inadequate health care resulting in disease and malnutrition, social, emotional, and physical deprivation, significant losses, and educational gaps (Ajdukovic and Ajdukovic, 1993; Williams and Berry, 1991). There are serious cognitive and emotional implications in such situations.

In addition to the stressors discussed above, refugee families with a deaf member face yet another stressor while waiting for the immigration decision regarding the deaf member. Concern that a disabled person might cause undue strain on social and medical services can be cause for denying formal entry into a country. While waiting for this decision, the family remains in limbo.

Once a family has been granted entry into a new country, it must begin to build a new life. This involves learning the host country's language, enrolling the children in school, finding housing and employment, and creating a new identity and attachment to the new society.

Host communities tend to focus on the external separation from the home country by providing services within existing structures. However, an individual's emotional separation from the home country is a process that can begin before the actual move (as is usually the case with planned migration), or it may be prolonged due to traumatic events related to the relocation and sociocultural differences between the home and host countries (Cole and Siegel, 1990; Cole, 1996b).

Overlaid on the above-described difficulties for deaf children is the family's cultural perception of deafness (Christensen & Delgado, 1993). It is well-documented that specific family responses to deafness can impact on a deaf child's educational process and mental health (Akamatsu, 1993; Cheng, 1993; Cohen, 1993; Gerner de Garcia, 1993; Hammond & Meiners, 1993; Jackson-Maldonado, 1993). The immigrant or refugee deaf child's eventual acculturation to both North American society as well as to North American Deaf culture depends on the interaction among general migration factors. Those include personal and familial factors and the cultural views of deafness. Beiser and his colleagues conclude that the combination of supportive traditional cultural elements and new cultural norms allows for the maintenance of ethnic pride and contributes to good mental health (Beiser *et al.*, 1988, 1995; Edwards and Beiser, 1994). For deaf children, these factors are key to overall adaptation and development.

If deafness is perceived as a source of shame ("My wife's family has bad genes; therefore my child must have bad genes, too"), then building self-esteem in the deaf child will be a challenge. If deafness is perceived as the result of the parents' or the child's karma ("My child is deaf because I did something bad in a previous life, so I just have to accept this hardship"), then an attitude of helplessness may prevent proactive change from occurring. On the other hand, if deafness is perceived as an unavoidable but unfortunate event ("Allah ran out of parts for my child"), the family may either react with helplessness or may try to enable the child to do what he or she can. One common misperception is that a deaf child is incapable of much learning. Many families, especially from Third World countries, continue to confuse the ability to speak with the ability to learn. This is understandable, particularly in countries where special education services are unavailable or unheard of.

Whether a deaf child eventually assimilates within North American culture, becomes bi- or multicultural, or is marginalized depends on a complex interplay of the many factors discussed so far. A key factor in the deaf child's development is schooling and language development, which is discussed in the next section.

SCHOOLING AND LANGUAGE LEARNING

Approximately one-half of the world's children are refugees (United Nations High Commissioner for Refugees (UNHCR), 1994). Over half of these children come from single-parent, low-income families (Burke, 1992). Canada, which like the United States, is a nation of immigrants, experienced a doubling of in-migration during the late 1980s and early 1990s (Coelho, 1994), with three-quarters of the immigrant children of school age. This has presented schools with the tremendous challenge of meeting the educational needs of a rapidly changing population (Cole, 1996b).

Schools are the most significant change agent at the societal and the individual level. They are becoming the sites not only for academic learning, but also for acculturation, adaptation, remediation, and mental health provision. Therefore, effective interventions with immigrant and refugee children and their families must be founded upon knowledge and awareness of the kinds of issues and challenges that face them.

Fragmented schooling and gaps in children's education are all too common among immigrant and refugee children, whether they are deaf or hearing. While a family is in flight, survival takes precedence over education. Indeed, education may not even be available or accessible. Some refugee deaf children arrive in their host country many years after the optimal language development years and are permanently handicapped by not having had a language.

Educational opportunities for many refugee/immigrant children may contain gaps. For deaf children, adequate education may simply not have been available, even prior to leaving their home country. Their arrival in a North American school may be their first experience at formal schooling and their first experience with using technology such as hearing aids. For other children who were deafened, for example, by explosions during a war or by disease during migration, arrival at a school for deaf children will pose its own brand of "culture shock." That is, the need to learn visually, the need to learn to sign, and the need to learn to read and write a language they will not hear poses tremendous challenges to an already fragile child.

For deaf students, face-to-face communication in American Sign Language (ASL) and/or some form of signing in English becomes paramount. For some students this will be their first exposure to any language. For others, ASL functions as a second language, after some other signed language. Depending on the age of the student at the time they enter school in North America, first language acquisition may have been delayed to the point where complete acquisition is impossible, even under the best of conditions. This can have devastating consequences for subsequent cognitive and literacy development (Bonkowski *et al.*, 1991; Akamatsu, 1998).

Vygotsky (1978, 1987) argued that the communicative use of language in educational contexts is essential to cognitive development. This idea, explicated further by Wertsch (1985), points to the importance of society and "more knowledgeable others" in engaging a young person in the necessary interaction to generate higher psychological processes, such as intentional attention and memory, abstract thinking, and language. By understanding the nature of interaction (particularly language-based interaction), we can come to understand how an individual learns to think, use language, and learn.

Farah arrived from Somalia at the age of nine. She had never had a hearing aid and had never attended school. She spoke no Arabic or Somali and knew no sign language. Two years later, she was able to sign conversationally. When she was tested for nonverbal abilities, the examiner noted that she was able to demonstrate average abilities if time limits were not observed. Her verbal abilities were still limited.[2]

Deaf immigrant and refugee children often enter school without a language. The argument has been raised, somewhat simplistically, that these children are pedagogically little different from children born in North America, who also often enter school (or enter a signing program) with little or no language. However, the effects of the migration experience at both the individual and the familial level should not be ignored.

In Farah's case, she was fortunate to have a mother who attempted to teach her, using a combination of home signs, writing, and speech. Like most signing children, she became conversationally adequate in about two years' time. However, her ability to apply her native intelligence to learning, memory, and problem solving was affected because she was not able to think efficiently. That is, she was able to learn and solve problems correctly, but it took her somewhat longer to do so.

Signed language, while useful for interpersonal and instructional purposes, is but one language to learn in the acculturation process. English, at least in written form, must also be mastered. Given how difficult literacy acquisition is for native-born deaf children whose parents already speak, read, and write English, it requires little to imagine the daunting task facing refugee and immigrant children. As Humphries (1993) points out, "it hardly seems to be a matter of priorities" (p. 8).

Research studies have documented that there is great variability in the length of time that it takes hearing students to learn English and what kinds of instructional interventions promote this process (Wallace, 1986; Corson, 1993; Cole, 1996a), and there is little reason to expect the case for deaf children to be different (or easier). Because American schooling is inextricably linked to English proficiency, com-

---

[2] Throughout this chapter, "verbal" refers to all linguistic skills and abilities, regardless of specific language or modality.

municating in English is a prime goal for immigrant and refugee children. Difficulties with language acquisition tend to hamper education, social integration, and employment opportunities.

In recent years, much energy has been focused on the issue of English as a second language for all deaf students (e.g., Israelite *et al.,* 1992; Johnson *et al.,* 1989). Drawing on the work from bilingual hearing children, researchers have concluded that ASL should be the first and natural language for all deaf children in American schools. In the case of immigrant and refugee children, this conclusion must be challenged on several grounds. First, there are deaf families who use other signed languages as their home language. ASL would be a second language, or possibly a third language, if the family also knows their home country's spoken/written language. Second, there are families with deaf members who do not communicate with that deaf member in anything other than rudimentary gesture and speech. It must be remembered that the speech is in a language other than English. Therefore, even those children who do acquire some rudiments of spoken language, it is not English, nor is their home sign ASL. Third, immigrant and refugee parents are faced with the task of learning English themselves, and they often find it extremely difficult to learn to sign as well.

HEARING ESL LEARNERS VS DEAF CHILDREN LEARNING ENGLISH: SIGNING, SPEAKING, READING, AND WRITING

Hearing students who are learning English as a second language already possess a range of communication skills in their first language when they first arrive at school. Although some may have had little or no schooling, others may have come from communities with strong literate traditions and high educational standards. Thus, they come equipped to build a second language on the base of their first language. Students who are already literate in their first language may bring an additional foundation on which to build their English.

It is important to consider that some hearing students have weak language bases in several languages as a result of moves to more than one country. These students may not have had the opportunity to build a solid base in any one language or to become literate in any language.

For deaf children who arrive at school past the age of optimal language acquisition with no language at all, it is paramount to expose, indeed immerse, these children in an environment that is both language rich and accessible. For the majority of deaf children, this language would be ASL or some form of contact sign (Lucas and Valli, 1992). ASL appears to have a critical period similar to that of English, and therefore we can expect that children who arrive without a first signed language will be disadvantaged in ways similar to hearing children who have not acquired a solid first language (Fischer, 1994, 1997; Mayberry & Eichen, 1991). However, because ASL uses the visual modality, which can take advantage of visual iconicity and natural gesture, it has much in common with other fully developed natural signed languages, developing signed languages, and with home sign (Newport, 1996; Mylander & Goldin-Meadow, 1991), and skills developed even in home sign can be brought to bear on learning ASL and other natural sign systems (Fischer, 1997).

For the purpose of face-to-face conversation, especially when supporting context is available, it probably makes little difference whether this is accomplished in ASL or a signed form of English (Akamatsu, 1997; Mayer & Wells, 1996). Cummins (1984; 1989) refers to these communication skills as "basic interpersonal communication skills" (BICS). From a Vygotskian perspective, it is of these interpersonal skills that cognition is born.

However, more abstract language, which includes "cognitive/academic language proficiency" (CALP), takes five to seven years to develop and typically develops *through the acquisition of literacy* (Cole & Siegel, 1990; Cummins, 1984). This process becomes even more complex for deaf children who acquire their first language as a signed language relatively late in life and for whom literacy does not exist in this language. In such cases, they may have been exposed to other languages or dialects and may not have had time to consolidate even face-to-face communication skills. Upon arrival in Canada, students who appear to learn to sign rapidly within the first two years may be unreasonably expected to perform academically like their same-age peers who have had many years of signing.

Educators of deaf children have used information from hearing ESL learners to argue for the acceptance and use of ASL as a language of classroom instruction. Using Cummins' linguistic interdependence model, one argument that has been forwarded is that ASL, as the BICS language, provides an adequate base upon which to build English as a second language (Israelite *et al.*, 1992; Johnson *et al.*, 1989). Proponents of this argument believe that English can be learned through reading and writing, in the absence of speaking, listening, and signing in English.

Mayer and Wells (1996) have challenged this argument on several grounds. First, empirical research based on the linguistic interdependence model has found no correlation between the spoken form of a first language and literacy skills in a second language (Goldman, 1985; Cummins *et al.*, 1984). Second, it appears that the abstract *literacy* skills across languages are interdependent and relate to a "common underlying proficiency" (Cummins, 1991). The more similar the target language is to the home language, the easier it is for students to transfer language and literacy skills to the new language. Therefore, while first-language learning provides a foundation for English competence, it lays a general cognitive and perhaps metalinguistic foundation. It does not necessarily provide enough of a support for English literacy *unless literacy has already been achieved in the first language.* Furthermore, when the "first" language does not have a literate form, there are no academic language skills to transfer. Those cognitive skills that are language dependent may also be affected.

The implications for deaf children from disadvantaged living conditions and disruptive schooling are staggering (Thomas, 1992; Hafner and Ulanoff, 1994). Based on his research with hearing students, Cummins (1984, 1989) has called for a reexamination of pedagogical misconceptions which can lead to faulty decisions concerning school placement.

Fletcher and Cardona-Morales (1990) indicate that cooperative learning strategies in small groups allow for positive interdependence, individual and group accountability, and opportunities for social skills development. Fortunately for deaf children, they are usually placed in small classes where the teacher/student ratio is low. This advantage may be attenuated by the relatively few numbers of deaf children, thus limiting the opportunities they have for socialization and language development within the larger host country.

THE ROLE OF THE FAMILY

> Ahmed communicates animatedly with his family using "home sign." His family is very eager for him to learn sign language in school. However, although Minh lived with her extended family, only one cousin would try to communicate with her and was the "designated communicator." When that cousin's family moved out, Minh was left to cope with a family who did not communicate with her.

Misconceptions about sign language may inhibit parents from interacting with their children in sign, perhaps because their culture frowns upon overly expressive body language or because they feel that signing is a "lesser" form of language. The parents may also recognize that their deaf child has a greater command of sign than they do and feel powerless to interact with the child because they have no common language.

Although studies have concluded that parental involvement in school has a positive impact on children's academic achievement (Ziegler, 1987; Alter, 1992; Grace, 1993), parents may feel unempowered to work as partners with the school. As a result of linguistic barriers and adjustment difficulties, immigrant parents may feel misinformed or ill-informed about the school system and yet be reluctant or unable to approach the school system for help (Cole, 1996b).

> Thusyanthi is a conscientious student. Her widowed father finds it difficult to cope with the demands of work and parenting, a role he was never prepared for. He finds it difficult to prepare a nutritious lunch for Thusyanthi to bring to school and finds that no one will care for Thusyanthi while he works in the evenings because she is unmanageable at home. He cannot sign, which further complicates parenting.

In certain cultures, the schools are charged with the responsibility for educating as well as socializing the children. Parents, having provided for the basic needs of the child may feel that it is now solely the school's mandate to teach the child in order to become a functioning member of society. Because of their own limited education or inability to function in English or sign, parents may be unable to help their children with homework. They may find it difficult to participate in sign language classes because these classes are taught in English and/or because of their working conditions.

Spoken language interpreters are crucial in providing the link between the family and the school. Because finding interpreters can be difficult, particularly for languages with few local speakers, interpreters might be community social service providers, friends of the family, or family members of all ages who speak some English.

Using interpreters can be a complex process. Given the variety of English language skills to be found among users of this service, it is particularly important that the interpreter also be a cultural broker, able to interpret not only the verbal information of both parties, but also to interpret the intent of the message. Furthermore, because persons functioning in this role might be family members and therefore have a personal or vested interest in the target family, they should receive clear information about their role when functioning as interpreters.

Obviously, if there is no shared language, interpreters and their services are crucial to enhanced communication. Most schools and programs for deaf children are familiar with using signed language interpreters, but even so, difficulties tend to emerge. Often, two interpreters are needed if a teacher is deaf: ASL–English for the teacher and English–home language for the parents. Also key concepts related to education systems might not be clear to the parties involved. One is left to wonder what gets lost in translation.

Educators must remember that immigrant and refugee parents may not view themselves as equal partners in their children's learning. They will continue to require ongoing information and support in order to collaborate with the school and revalidate the value of the home language as well as sign language.

ASSESSMENT TRENDS IN DEAF EDUCATION

The role of assessment is an integral part of instruction and guided learning as well as accountability. Assessment should be a process of gathering information about a student in order to identify learning strengths and needs and to develop appropriate educational services (Cole, 1991). Concern about assessment practices for deaf children has largely revolved around two major issues: (1) validity and reliability of the measures and (2) subsequent educational practices that encourage maximal achievement. Many writers, educators, and researchers have noted the dangers of using verbal tests to measure intelligence in deaf and hard of hearing populations. These cautions have been raised with equal vehemence in the multilingual and multicultural literature (Cummins, 1994; Genesee & Hamayan, 1994).

The practice of restricting assessment to nonverbal measures may be sound in the early years of an immigrant child's experience. However, it is important to note that nonverbal measures may also be tainted by the child's lack of experience with the materials used in the assessment, or with being asked to solve problems that are decontextualized from the "real world." Furthermore, simply getting the child to understand what is expected can be problematic.

Given the degree of early deprivation, cultural background, and migration experience, the picture is understandably more complicated with deaf immigrant and refugee students. What holds true for assessing immigrant/refugee or language minority students holds doubly true for immigrant/refugee deaf students. Instruction in ASL as a language as well as opportunities to interact in ASL must be provided. However, the assessment of ASL is in its infancy, and formal curricula for ASL instruction are only now being developed for use in schools. The assessment of English has a large literature, but even here, debate continues to focus on fairness in testing, and the advisability of using assessments to continuously prove that even the most advantaged deaf students have enormous difficulty with English (King & Quigley, 1985; Luetke-Stahlman & Luckner, 1991; Paul, 1993; Vernon & Andrews, 1990.)

Standardized tests are highly correlated with English language proficiency and school learning (Cole, 1991). The literature on deafness is replete with warnings about the disadvantage at which deaf students find themselves when faced with measures that do not adequately differentiate between language-related difficulties and the actual level of knowledge or skill the students possess. Furthermore, it is important not to misperceive linguistic deficits as deficits in ability since de-contextualized language may present difficulties for children from culturally different homes (Royal Commission on Learning, 1994). However, there is some evidence that long-term language deprivation, such as that created by deafness and lack of access to language and education, can result in cognitive deficits that cannot be remediated solely by a few years' exposure to signed language (Akamatsu *et al.,* 1994).

Educators and parents must be aware of lowered expectations of immigrant or refugee deaf students, either because of their migration experience or because of their hearing status. While actual levels of achievement, particularly in the early years, may not accurately reflect their abilities, ongoing dynamic assessment can aid in setting *realistic* goals for these students.

Currently, assessment acts as a lightning rod for those who feel marginalized and disenfranchised (Cole, 1996a), including all deaf and hard-of-hearing children. However, indefinitely delaying or exempting these individuals from any kind of assessment of these students puts them outside the system of accountability, and can have serious implications for the provision of appropriate programs and services and the preparation of students who are self-sufficient and able to exercise the rights and responsibilities of citizenship (Samuda, 1990). Akamatsu (1998) has also called for ongoing measures of language-related abilities (whether in signed or printed language) in formulating a comprehensive view of a deaf immigrant or a refugee student.

When assessing deaf immigrant and refugee students, it is important to measure progress at four levels: (1) the individual, (2) deaf immigrant or refugee background, (3) other deaf peer groups, and (4) normally hearing peers. Normative data for deaf students is difficult enough to acquire due to the low incidence of deafness. This type of data on immigrant/refugee deaf students will be even more difficult to collect. One practical and immediately applicable solution to this difficulty is to perform dynamic assessments over a period of time, creating and analyzing portfolios of the student's work. Where appropriate, the "test–teach–test" method will yield information to allow educators and parents to understand what the student can do without help as well as what kinds of intervention/teaching create the most learning for the student. This information can be linked directly to instructional planning and to students' learning experiences (Cole, 1996b; Estrin, 1993; Gordon and Musser, 1992).

Alternative assessment procedures, such as "portfolio-based assessment," and the use of "authentic" or "performance-based" assessments, alone or in combination with "culture-free" or "culture-fair" tests, have been advocated because they provide information that can be applied directly to instructional planning. Concerns have been raised, however, that such evaluations are not equally valid measures for particular groups and may lead to unfair outcomes (Cole, 1996a; Lam, 1995).

It is important to keep the above-described assessment issues in mind, because assessment continues to be emphasized in school systems as a legislated requirement and as a valued service by teachers and parents. Psychologists trained in both deafness and multicultural issues bring many skills and areas of knowledge, including, among others, developmental, learning, and personality theories, individual differences; multilingual education, consultation, observation, and interview skills; selection and evaluation of appropriate measures; and skills for considering the effects of language, culture, and personality on adjustment and performance (Cole, 1991; Cole & Siegel, 1990; Martin, 1991; Vernon & Andrews 1990). This evolution toward comprehensive and equitable psychological assessment is timely in light of the diverse student population, the reform movement in education, and the reevaluation of special education services. Through consultation and assessment, which provide a comprehensive picture about "the child as a whole," parents are likely to be reassured that in spite of their child's early history, significant and relevant gains in language and learning can be made by their child and that favorable outcomes are possible.

MULTICULTURAL EDUCATION AND MENTAL HEALTH SERVICES

Six-year-old Farah and her three-year-old sister Naima need new earmolds and possibly new hearing aids. Their mother, who is deaf, speaks some Somali, but has great difficulty communicating with the Somali community liaison worker. She also cannot use the telephone. The mother finds herself cut off from both the local Somali community and from the local deaf community.

The education, health, and mental health service needs of deaf immigrant and refugee children are so complex that the education system alone cannot be expected to address all the needs of these children. Coordination must occur among several service provision (e.g., education, health, employment, resettlement, mental health, and ethno–cultural) systems with which the family comes into contact if effective, efficient, and culturally sensitive services are to be provided.

Families' frames of reference, in general and related to deafness, are culturally based and need to become familiar to the service providers (Turner, 1996). Without a cultural context, factors related to age, gender, education and family position may impact the counseling process, and professionals may incorrectly judge behaviors as symptoms of psychopathology (Cole, 1996a). Giordano (1994) has indicated helpful clinical guidelines for mental health professionals working in a multicultural milieu. His guidelines may be modified to include: (a) the assessment of behavior and learning in the context of cultural norms, the importance of ethnicity to the family, and the cultural implications of deafness to the family; (b) the validation and strengthening of the student's and family's ethnic identity and cultural background; (c) the assistance of identifying and resolving family value conflicts, particularly around deafness and the use of sign language; (d) the evaluation of the pros and cons of teacher/student ethnic and/or hearing status match, and (e) the teacher's ongoing self-assessment related to limits of knowledge about various ethnicities or about deafness itself.

Schools are often the first system that newcomers learn about, but special education services, under whose auspices deaf and hard-of-hearing children receive education, may be uncharted territory. Parents may not realize that special education services are available in North America or understand their rights and responsibilities regarding getting appropriate educational services for their children. Due to language, educational, and/or cultural barriers, they may be unable to advocate effectively for their children.

Because schools are perceived to be a trusted environment which facilitates education and eventual access to North American society, parent outreach is vital at point of contact with the education system. Given the ongoing emotional and social needs of immigrant and refugee children, it is important for schools to develop partnerships with external agencies and ethnic organizations. It is thus important for psychologists and social workers employed by school boards to develop multicultural and integrated service delivery models that can facilitate the coordination of prevention and intervention functions (Cole, 1996b; Hicks *et al.*, 1993).

One such vehicle for service delivery in many North American school boards is that of in-school multidisciplinary consultation teams, composed of educators, school psychologists, and social workers (Cole, 1992; Wiener & Davidson, 1990). Generally, these teams are designed to support teachers in providing appropriate interventions for students in need of assistance. Expanded team mandates can include consultative services to staff, parents, and community agencies. In their five-year follow-up study on school teams, Cole and Brown (1996) found that teams continue to be utilized for consultation about immigrant and refugee students, particularly around the common difficulties in coping with adjustment to a new language and culture. About a quarter of the staff surveyed saw refugee needs as an attribute that was most often related to student referral for team consultation.

Siegel and Cole (1990) developed a framework for organizing programs which link primary, secondary and tertiary prevention initiatives. This model provides both for direct intervention by mental health professionals as well as for preventive programs delivered by teachers and other in-school staff. For example, primary prevention programs focused on such subjects as anti-racist education, self-esteem, or social skills training can be provided by mental health staff in partnership with teachers. It is hoped that a broader role for mental health professionals in education will provide an avenue for advocacy about the provision of preventatively oriented services. Secondary prevention programs, formulated in consultation with schools, are directed toward students who are at risk emotionally or socially. Tertiary prevention programs should be directed to students and families in crisis. A schematic of this model, with examples for deaf children, is presented in Table 1.

Table 1.

Preventively Oriented Interventions for Immigrant and Refugee Deaf Students

Recipient and level of service	Primary prevention (Identify resources; provide and analyze information; program for all deaf students)	Secondary prevention (Program for students "at risk")	Tertiary Prevention (Programs for students whose problems significantly interfere with their adaptation to school)
Students or parents, direct service	Provide parents with information about the effects of deafness on development	Facilitate parenting group for new immigrants	Conduct individual assessment and/or counseling
Students or parents, mediated service	Consult with teachers as they assess student needs and develop individual educational plans	Consult with teachers on newly arrived students' learning needs	Consult with teacher prior to formal referral
School staff	Develop class profiles; discuss relevance of migration background with teachers	Invite community leaders to consult on specific ethnocultural issues	Liase between school and community service providers to provide services for those in need
School system	Present inservice workshop on refugee issues	Develop plan for identifying students at risk for adjustment difficulties	Develop plan for responding to needs of refugee students and their families

IMPLICATIONS FOR PROFESSIONAL DEVELOPMENT

Schools are complex organizations. Both preservice and in-service models of training must reflect a clear commitment to equity and multicultural issues. The profiles of communities dictate the need for better links between university trainers and supervising practitioners as well as deaf and underrepresented faculty and student recruitment. While efforts to include a culturally Deaf perspective in preservice training have become more common, it is important to remember that hearing status (or deafness status) alone does not confer the requisite knowledge for working in a professional capacity with nontraditional populations. Moreover, not all educational personnel (teachers, school psychologists, school social workers) feel competent to handle the increased demands for the variety of interventions required by these individuals. To facilitate increased participation in ongoing professional development, such training must be framed so that adult learners perceive that the learning is related to their needs, rather than an attack on their competence.

Substantive change in practice often takes several years to achieve. Cross-role participation is likely to stimulate shared understanding and new approaches to multicultural services. In line with the trend toward increased accountability in education and mental health, there seems to be a growing need to address outcome-based measures for training and practice in the field. Ecological models for multicultural services require conceptual knowledge and skills training. This, however, will require knowledge of multicultural education, anti-racist policies and programs, social skills training, crisis management, and violence prevention.

REFERENCES

Ajdukovic, M., & Ajdukovic, D. (1993). Psychological well-being of refugee children. *Child Abuse and Neglect,* **17,** 843–854.

Akamatsu, C.T. (1998). Thinking with and without language: What is necessary and sufficient for school-based learning? In A. Weisel (Ed.), *Issues unresolved: New perspectives on language and deaf education* (pp. 27–40). Washington, DC: Gallaudet University Press.

Akamatsu, C. T. (1993). Teaching deaf Asian and Pacific Island American children. In K. Christensen & G. Delgado (Eds.), *Multicultural issues in deafness* (pp. 127–142). White Plains, NY: Longman.

Akamatsu, C.T., Musselman, C., & Miller, A. (1994). *Using a language/communication proficiency interview as a form of dynamic assessment.* Paper presented at the American Educational Research Association, New Orleans, April 4–8.

Alter, R.C. (1992). Parent–school communication: A selective review. *Canadian Journal of School Psychology,* **8,** 103–110.

Beiser, M., Barwick, C., Berry, J.W., da Costa, G., Fantino, A.M., Ganesan, S., Lee, C., Milne, W., Naidoo, J., Prince, R., Tousignant, M., & Vela, E. (1988). *After the door has opened: Mental health issues affecting immigrants and refugees.* Ottawa, Canada: Ministries of Multiculturalism and Citizenship and Health and Welfare.

Beiser, M., Dion, R., Gotowiec, A.J., & Huyman, I. (1995). Immigrant and Refugee Children in Canada. *Canadian Journal of Psychiatry,* **40,** 67–72.

Benard, B. (1993). Fostering resiliency in kids. *Educational Leadership,* **November,** 44–48.

Bonkowski, N., Gavelek, J., & Akamatsu, C.T. (1991). Education and the social construction of mind. In D. Martin (Ed.), *Advances in Cognition, Education, and the Deaf* (pp. 185–194). Washington, DC: Gallaudet University Press.

Burke, M.A. (1992). Canada's immigrant children. *Canadian Social Trends,* **Spring:** 15–20.

Cheng, L. (1993). Deafness: An Asian/Pacific Island perspective. In K. Christensen & G. Delgado (Eds.), *Multicultural issues in deafness* (pp. 113–126). White Plains, NY: Longman.

Christensen, K., & Delgado, G. (1993). *Multicultural issues in deafness.* White Plains, NY: Longman.

Coelho, E. (1994). Social integration of immigrant and refugee children. In F. Genesee (Ed.), *Educating second language children* (pp. 301–327). Cambridge, UK: Cambridge University Press.

Cohen, O. (1993). Educational needs of African American and Hispanic deaf children and youth. In K. Christensen & G. Delgado (Eds.), *Multicultural issues in deafness* (pp. 45–68). White Plains, NY: Longman.

Cole, E. (1996a). Immigrant and refugee children and families: Supporting a new road traveled. In M. Luther, E. Cole, & P. Gamlin (Eds.), *Dynamic assessment for instruction: From theory to application* (pp. 35–42). Toronto: Captus University Publications.

Cole, E. (1996b). An integrative perspective on school psychology. *Canadian Journal of School Psychology,* **12,** 115–121.

Cole, E. (1992). Characteristics of students referred to school teams: Implications for preventive psychological services. *Canadian Journal of School Psychology,* **8,** 23–38.

Cole, E. (1991). Multicultural psychological assessment: New challenges, improved methods. *International Journal of Dynamic Assessment and Instruction,* **2,** 1–10.

Cole, E., & Brown, R. (1996). Multidisciplinary school teams: A five-year follow-up study. *Canadian Journal of School Psychology,* **12,** 155–168.

Cole, E., & Siegel, J. (1990). School psychology in a multicultural community: Responding to children's needs. In E. Cole and J. Siegel (Eds.), *Effective consultation in school psychology* (pp. 141–169). Toronto: Hogrefe.

Corson, D. (1993). *Language, Minority Education and Gender.* Clevedon, UK: Multilingual Matters.

Cummins, J. (1994). Knowledge, power, and identity in teaching English as a second language. In F. Genesee (Ed.), *Educating second language children* (pp. 33–58). Cambridge, UK: Cambridge University Press.

Cummins, J. (1991). Language development and academic learning. In L. Malave & G. Duquette (Eds.), *Language, culture and cognition.* Philadelphia: Multilingual Matters.

Cummins, J. (1989). *Empowering minority students.* Sacramento: California Association for Bilingual Education.

Cummins, J. (1984). *Bilingualism and special education: Issues in assessment and pedagogy.* Clevedon, UK: Multilingual Matters.

Cummins, J., Swain, M., Nakajima, K., Handscombe, D., Green, D., & Tran, C. (1984). Linguistic interdependence among Japanese and Vietnamese immigrant students. In C. Rivera (Ed.), *Communicative competence approaches to language proficiency assessment: Research and application* (pp. 60–81). Clevedon, UK: Multilingual Matters.

Edwards, G. J., & Beiser, M. (1994). Southeast Asian refugee youth in Canada: The determinants of competence and successful coping. *Canada's Mental Health,* **Spring,** 1–5.

Estrin, E.T. (1993). Alternative assessment: Issues in language, culture and equity. Knowledge Brief II. *Far West Lab for Education and Development* (pp. 1–8). San Francisco, CA: ERIC.

Fischer, S. (1998). Critical periods for language acquisition: Consequences for deaf education. In A. Weisel (Ed.), *Issues unresolved: New perspectives on language and deaf education* (pp. 9–26). Washington, DC: Gallaudet University Press.

Fischer, S. (1994). Critical periods: Critical issues. In B. Schick & M.P. Moeller (Eds.), *Proceedings of the 7th annual conference in issues in language and deafness: The use of sign language in educational settings: Current concepts and controversies* (pp. 1–11). Omaha: Boys Town National Research Hospital.

Fletcher, T.V., & Cardona-Morales, C. (1990). Implementing effective instructional interventions for minority students. In A. Barona and E. Garcia (Eds.), *Children at Risk*. Washington, DC: National Association of School Psychologists.

Genesee, F., & Hamayan, E.V. (1994). Classroom-based assessment. In F. Genesee (Ed.), *Educating second language children* (pp. 212–239). Cambridge, UK: Cambridge University Press.

Gerner de Garcia, B. (1993). Addressing the needs of Hispanic deaf children. In K. Christensen & G. Delgado (Eds.), *Multicultural issues in deafness* (pp. 69–90). White Plains, NY: Longman.

Giordano, J. (1994). Mental health and the melting pot. *American Journal of Orthopsychiatry, 64*, 342–345.

Goldman, S.R. (1985). *Utilization of knowledge acquired through the first language in comprehending a second language: Narrative composition by Spanish-English speakers*. Report submitted to the U.S. Department of Education.

Gordon, E.W., & Musser, J.H. (1992). *Implications of diversity in human characteristics for authentic assessment* (CSE Technical Report 341). Los Angeles: Centre for Research on Evaluation, Standards, and Student Testing, ERIC.

Grace, C. (1993). A model program for home–school communication and staff development. In K. Christensen & G. Delgado (Eds.), *Multicultural issues in deafness* (pp. 29–42). White Plains, NY: Longman.

Hafner, A.L., & Ulanoff, S.H. (1994). Validity issues and concerns for assessing English learners. *Education and Urban Society, 26*, 367–389.

Hammond, S.A., & Meiners, L. (1993). American Indian deaf children and youth. In K. Christensen & G. Delgado (Eds.), *Multicultural issues in deafness* (pp. 143–166). White Plains, NY: Longman.

Hicks, R., Lalonde, R.N., & Pepler, D. (1993). Psychosocial considerations in the mental health of immigrant and refugee children. *Canadian Journal of Community Mental Health, 12*, 71–87.

Humphries, T. (1993). Deaf culture and cultures. In K. Christensen & G. Delgado (Eds.), *Multicultural issues in deafness* (pp. 3–16). White Plains, NY: Longman.

Israelite, N., Ewoldt, C., & Hoffmeister, R. (1992). *Bilingual–bicultural education for deaf and hard-of-hearing students.* Toronto, Ontario: MGS Publication Services.

Jackson-Maldonado, D. (1993). Mexico and the United States: A cross-cultural perspective on the education of deaf children. In K. Christensen & G. Delgado (Eds.), *Multicultural issues in deafness* (pp. 91–112). White Plains, NY: Longman.

Johnson, R., Liddell, S., & Erting, C. (1989). *Unlocking the curriculum: Principles for achieving access in deaf education.* Gallaudet Research Institute Working Paper 89–3. Washington, DC: Gallaudet University Press.

King, C., & Quigley, S. (1985). *Reading and deafness.* San Diego: College Hill.

Lam, T. (1995). Fairness in performance assessment. *Eric Digest,* **EDO-CG-95-25,** 1–2.

Lucas, C., & Valli, C. (1992). *Language contact in the American Deaf community.* Washington, DC: Gallaudet University Press.

Luetke-Stahlman, B., & Luckner, J. (1991). *Effectively teaching students with hearing impairment.* New York: Longman.

Martin, D. (Ed.) (1991). *Advances in cognition, education, and deafness.* Washington, DC: Gallaudet University Press.

Mayberry, R., & Eichen, E. (1991). The long-lasting advantage of learning sign language in childhood: Another look at the critical period for language acquisition. *Journal of Memory and Language,* **30,** 486–512.

Mayer, C., & Wells, G. (1996). Can the linguistic interdependence theory support a bilingual–bicultural model of literacy education for deaf students? *Journal of Deaf Studies and Deaf Education,* **1,** 93–107.

Mylander, C., & Goldin-Meadow, S. (1991). Home sign systems in deaf children: The development of morphology without a conventional language model. In P. Siple & S. Fischer (Eds.), *Theoretical issues in sign language research: Psychology.* Chicago: University of Chicago Press.

Newport, E. (1996). *Sign language research in the Third Millennium.* Paper presented at the Theoretical Issues in Sign Language Conference, Montreal, Canada, September 19–22.

Paul, P. (1993). Deafness and text-based literacy. *American Annals of the Deaf,* **138**, 72–75.

Royal Commission on Learning (1994). *For the love of learning.* Ontario, Canada: Queen's Printer of Ontario.

Samuda, R.J. (1990). *New approaches to assessment and placement of minority students.* Toronto, Canada: Ministry of Education.

Siegel, J., & Cole, E. (1990). Role expansion for school psychologists: Challenges and future directions. E. Cole and J. Siegel (Eds.), *Effective consultation in school psychology* (pp. 3–17). Toronto, Canada: Hogrefe.

Thomas, T.N. (1992). Psychoeducational adjustment of English-speaking Caribbean and Central American immigrant children in the United States. *School Psychology Review,* **21**, 566–576.

Turner, S. (1996). Meeting the needs of children under five with sensory-neural hearing loss from ethnic minority families. *Journal of the British Association of Teachers of the Deaf,* **20**, 91–100.

United Nations High Commissioner for Refugees (1994). *Refugee children.* Geneva: UNHCR.

Vernon, M., & Andrews, J. (1990). *The psychology of deafness.* New York: Longman.

Vygotsky, L. (1987). Thought and word. In R. W. Rieber and A. S. Carlton (Eds.), *The collected works of L. S. Vygotsky* (Vol. 1). New York: Plenum.

Vygotsky, L. (1978). *Mind in society: The development of higher psychological processes.* Cambridge, MA: Harvard University Press.

Wallace, C. (1986). *Learning to read in a multicultural society.* Oxford: Pergamon.

Wertsch, J. (1985). *Vygotsky and the social formation of mind.* Cambridge, MA: Harvard University Press.

Wiener, J., & Davidson, I. (1990). The in-school team experience. In E. Cole & J. Siegel (Eds.), *Effective consultation in school psychology* (pp. 19–32). Toronto: Hogrefe.

Williams, C.L., & Berry, J.W. (1991). Primary prevention of acculturative stress among refugees. *American Psychologist, 46,* 632–641.

Ziegler, S. (1987). *The effects of parent involvement on children's achievement* (Research Services Report 185). Toronto: Toronto Board of Education.

On the Border: Cultures, Families, and Schooling in a Transnational Region

Claire L. Ramsey

Mata más una esperanza que un desengaño (Hope is more destructive than truth.)

A Mexican proverb

Mrs. Lyons, a hearing, Anglo-American teacher of deaf children in Southern California, comments, "Marisol Hernandez was absent last week. Her mother took her to the interior of Mexico to visit a curandero, to cure her deafness. Why would she do such a thing? Why don't the Mexican American parents have faith in what we teachers can do at school for their children?"

Another day Ms. Ralstad, a colleague of Mrs. Lyons, helps one of her 5th graders, Miguel Angel, with a worksheet. She turns from him to take me aside. "You know," she says seriously, "His parents are still in denial. He'll never start improving in school until they accept his deafness."

Mrs. Lyons and Ms. Ralstad are two of the teachers I met during a period of field work in an elementary school program for deaf children where the majority of the children were of Mexican heritage.[1] To illuminate the multicultural world in which the children lived and went to school, this chapter will describe several salient features of the educational context of Anglo teachers who teach in a densely populated and very active transnational region and of Mexican heritage families with deaf children who reside in this area. I use the term "transnational" advisedly, primarily to avoid the unsavory connotations of the term "border." The U.S./Mexico border came into existence after the region's ways of life were established. As others argue (e.g., Gandara, 1993), Mexican communities in the Southwest and California can be considered indigenous, since they existed before this region became part of the United States. Since the United States/Mexico border was established, these communities have received constant linguistic replenishment and cultural maintenance via movement north from the Republic of Mexico (of both immigrants and short-term visitors). This reason, among others, accounts for the resilience of Spanish among second- and third-generation U.S. citizens. Additionally, Mexican values about family life and childrearing retain a role in these communities and among well-assimilated U.S.-born citizens of Mexican heritage.

Controversies about Mexican immigration to the United States over the border near San Diego, California, obscure the fact that this transnational region, the cities and towns that lie on the U.S./Mexico border, as well as those near the border to the north and south, is intriguing for educators interested in issues of language and culture. De-

[1] I am grateful for two grants that supported this study. The Spencer Foundation funded a study of teachers, children, and classroom language. The University of California Linguistic Minority Research Institute funded a study of the children's community and their families. In addition, Celia Gonzalez and Maribel Paredes of UC San Diego served as research assistants, and Leticia Lares Ortega facilitated work in Mexico. Les agradezco a todas. All names of children, teachers and schools have been changed, as have some details about the school, in order to protect the privacy of participants.

spite news reports, it is worth noting that transnational movement is overwhelmingly legal and orderly. Mexican citizens who reside in Tijuana and its suburbs cross daily to work legally in the United States. Residents and citizens of the United States who live in San Diego cross into Mexico for the same reason. Americans married to Mexicans may live in Mexico, while Mexicans married to Americans may live in the United States. Thousands of people move north and south to shop, attend school, meet friends, and visit family members every day. Families often extend over the border, with Mexican citizen members living in Baja California and the interior of Mexico, and U.S. citizen members living in California or other parts of the United States. In the greater San Diego/Tijuana metropolitan area both English and Spanish are spoken, and both appear in print and on television and radio. On the Mexican side, English is widely used, just as Spanish is common on the U.S. side. The border constitutes a political and bureaucratic boundary, but many residents of this area, Mexicano, Chicano, and Anglo, live transnational, bilingual lives.

Although deaf children in most communities occupy a complicated linguistic and cultural niche, deaf children of Mexican heritage potentially move among several worlds, the bilingual world of their homes and community where Spanish and English are the dominant languages, the world of school, where English and a signed language are dominant, and the larger community, where English is dominant. Deafness, however, can mask the reality of the many borders deaf children may cross. In a recent discussion of deaf students from ethnic and linguistic "minority" communities, Cohen *et al.* (1990) note that it is not uncommon for educators of deaf students to work from the assumption that the status of "deaf" precludes a child's membership in an ethnic group and effectively wipes out his or her ethnic identity. The myth that "disability eliminates ethnicity," coupled with conflicts between parents and educators described by Bennett (1988) and Harry (1992) motivated the study reported here. By examining the social context of education among a group of Mexican heritage families with deaf children in Southern California, I hoped to illuminate the relationship between the status of "deaf child" and the status of Mexican or Mexican American child. It is clear that deaf children who are born into the transnational communities are raised as deaf children of Mexican heritage.

BACKGROUND

Latino Families with Deaf Children

For Mexican-heritage deaf children, the notion that a disability like deafness strips them of their family's ethnic identity may be based on the lack of knowledge about the meaning of deafness and disability in the Mexican American belief system as well as about childrearing and language socialization in Mexican American families with deaf children. In general, little is known about Latino families who have deaf children (Rodriguez & Santiviago, 1991). Even less is known about Mexican families with deaf children in the western United States. Bennett (1987) and Gerner de Garcia (1993) have conducted ethnographies of Central and South American and Caribbean families with deaf children in the northeast United States, but advise that their findings cannot be generalized to Mexican heritage families in the west.

The generalization about young deaf children from hearing families of any ethnicity is that when they enter school they have had little or no access to their family or community's language and literacy practices, and that they have "no language." Although recognition of deaf students' home cultures is now promoted (e.g., Janesick & Moores, 1992, MacNeil, 1990), there remains a pronounced belief, as well as anecdotal and empirical evidence, that deafness itself erects a barrier that interferes with transmission of family cultural practices and language to the deaf child.

However, closer examinations of Latino families (with both deaf and hearing children), their language and literacy practices and their interactions with schools, suggest that deaf children are as genuinely

Colombian, Dominican, or Mexican as the rest of their families, even though they may not speak Spanish. Bennett (1988) found that the Caribbean and Central American parents he worked with were well informed about deaf education, and determined to raise their deaf children as Colombian-, Dominican-, or Mexican American children in the United States. He describes tensions between teachers and parents over their children's ethnic identities, as well as over the control of the rearing of their deaf children.[2] Ramsey *et al.* (1995) report a case study of one well-assimilated California Mexican family with a deaf child. The mother in this family, who was deeply involved in the pursuit of a signing education for her son, nevertheless regretted that he could not speak or understand Spanish well enough to speak with his father, who was Spanish-dominant. She also expressed dismay that her son, because of the strained communication with other family members, was considered neither a competent member of the family nor a satisfactory Mexican heritage boy by the grandparent generation.

Research on language socialization and literacy practices in Mexican communities with hearing children in California encourages a closer look at the everyday lives of Mexican families with deaf children. Anderson and Stokes (1984) suggest that minority families provide a range of language and literacy practices that anticipate their children's participation in school. Vasquez *et al.* (1994) describe the ways that families "interpret, explain and debate" the significance of their interactions with the Anglo world and suggest that adult discussions help children in these families learn analytic and reflective skills that contribute to school literacy. Although deaf children do not have complete, unimpeded access to their family's heritage, they are still being raised by their parents, often with close contact to their extended family. However, these family members may have incomplete

---

[2] Harry (1992) describes similar phenomena among Puerto Rican families, whose children had been diagnosed as "learning disabled." Many of these children were regarded as unimpaired and progressing normally in Puerto Rican schools. Parents in this community viewed the stateside schools as improperly using racial and ethnic stereotypes to "invent" this diagnosis for their children. They were offended by school personnel and mistrusted them.

information with which to guide their childrearing decisions and to interpret the world in which their children grow up.

The Latino Deaf Population and Schooling Problems

The traditional low achievement of Latino deaf students highlights the need for a clearer understanding of this group. There is an increasing population of deaf students from Latino homes in the United States, and they face greater schooling difficulties than both their Anglo deaf counterparts and their hearing Latino peers. Deaf students of Latino heritage constitute 13% of the U.S. hearing impaired school age population and at least 40% of the population in school programs for deaf students in the western United States (Center for Assessment and Demographic Studies, 1988–1989). Latino students represented 61% of the California deaf student population in 1989, with increases projected in this group.

Latino deaf students face even greater difficulties than deaf students of other ethnicities. They have significantly lower scores on reading comprehension and mathematics computation than their white and African American peers (Allen, 1986; Holt, 1993). They are less likely to be offered opportunities for integration with nondisabled peers (Rodriguez & Santiviago, 1991). They are also less likely to be placed in academic courses and more likely to drop out of school than their Anglo, African American, and other peers (Allen *et al.*, 1989).

The School

Flores Elementary School is a public elementary school. Nearly all of the hearing children (over 90%) who attend the school come from Mexican heritage homes, as do many of the general education teachers. It is a bilingual school for hearing children with a "maintenance" rather than a "transitional" focus. Both English and Spanish are spoken in classrooms in all grades, and environmental print around the school as well as in general education classrooms appears in both languages. The principal, Dr. Plummer, is an Anglo bilingual educator, fluent in English and Spanish, and well regarded by the surrounding community. The school, in fact, is unusually accessible to parents and grandparents, who often meet the children and walk them home for lunch or after school. In the surrounding neighborhood, Flores School plays an important role, offering English, parenting, and citizenship classes, as well as serving as a site of several parent support groups. Dr. Plummer has also learned ASL, since the district's elementary deaf and hard-of-hearing program (called the DHH Program at the school) is located in her building.

The DHH program offers preschool through 6th-grade classes in both self-contained and integrated settings. The students regularly write and distribute a newsletter, reporting on activities among the DHH classes and publishing student reports, drawings, and stories. Most DHH students are eligible for "extended school year" services as well. The program offers sign language and deaf culture courses for parents. In addition, there is a parent group that meets about once a month for a social and a program, although attendance at parent meetings fluctuates.

DEAF CHILDREN OF MEXICAN-HERITAGE AND SCHOOLING

Three major questions organized the study. The first question was about the mix of languages in classrooms with Mexican heritage deaf children and the interactions of American Sign Language, English, and Spanish. The second question asked about teachers and school staff perspectives on teaching Mexican heritage deaf children, especially any unique problems associated with teaching non-Anglo deaf children. Accordingly, I focused on the ways that teachers account for students' successes and failures. I was especially interested in the contrast between schooling problems assigned to deafness and those attributed to coming from a Mexican heritage home. Finally, the third question asked about parent and community perspectives about raising and educating deaf children.

METHOD

I employed several qualitative methodologies in this study, including participant observation in classrooms and at parent meetings, individual interviews, and interview/discussion groups of parents and other family members. I received permission to observe in two classrooms and I visited for several hours a week over a five-month period. The classes were a mix of 4th- through 6th-grade children, each with a total of between 17 and 20 students. Two teachers, three instructional assistants, two interpreters, and a speech communication specialist worked with this group. For some activities, groups of children rotated, and for others the adults switched rooms. Several children were "mainstreamed" for much of the school day. In each room, I sat in a corner or at the side to observe as teachers, instructional assistants, and specialists directed instruction. When students were doing seat work or reading, I assisted as needed. I participated as a visitor when children or teachers drew me in to conversations or asked for help. In addition, I spent two days at "outdoor school" with the 6th-grade students in the group. "Outdoor school" consists of a week-long stay at a camp in the nearby mountains. Students study plants and animals, the environment, and other science topics with their teacher and with special outdoor school teachers.

At the request of the teachers, classroom observations were not videotaped. Instead, I developed a sampling protocol and coded language changes during ongoing teacher-led classroom activities. I recorded on a chart changes in language (among ASL, English, and Spanish) as they occurred, noting who initiated the discourse, to whom it was directed, what language was in use, what the topic and function of language was when the changes occurred, and any juxtapositions of two languages. These language shifts are noticeable, especially since a shift from ASL to English means a change from a relatively silent classroom, with no audible speech, to one where spoken language suddenly intrudes. I missed some shifts in language while I was coding, a typical sampling problem. I believe, however, that any sampling effects were minor. Structure, patterns, and rules underlie language and discourse so powerfully that, as often occurs in observations of language, patterns began to take shape in a relatively small corpus of data of teacher–student interaction. The most recurrent patterns were confirmed during interviews with teachers and instructional assistants.

I also interviewed teachers and other school personnel, conducting one formal interview with each, as well as a series of conversations over the period of the study and succeeding months. I participated in scheduled parent group meetings and also invited parents and families to several events that were social as well as research oriented. The U.S. events included potluck meals, a children's program with a deaf leader, and a parent/family member discussion group. The Mexico events consisted of several morning-long discussion groups with refreshments, to which parents and extended family members were invited. Parent meetings were both videotaped and audiotaped and transcribed later by native speakers of Spanish and English. U.S. meetings were held in English, Spanish, and American Sign Language. Mexico meetings were held in Spanish. Five parent meetings were held (two in the United States and three in Mexico), each lasting between 90 minutes and 2 hours.

PATTERNS OF LANGUAGE USE AND LANGUAGE SHIFT IN THE CLASSROOMS

The specific schooling needs of Mexican American deaf children may or may not be distinct from those of all deaf children. However, one area that has been especially confusing has been the role of Spanish in classrooms for deaf children who come from (or are assumed to come from) Spanish-dominant homes. Teachers often fear they will need to use Spanish with Mexican-heritage deaf children, or that parents will request Spanish-language speech lessons, although there is no such explicit requirement with respect to deaf children. California guidelines (1986) for deaf education state that the special needs of "minority hearing impaired students should be recognized." For example, if there are indications that a student speaks a language other than English, initial assessments must include evaluation of speech communication skills in that language. However, the guidelines also acknowledge that many deaf children enter school unable to "demonstrate evidence of language acquisition." In this case, a plan to develop "appropriate" language skills must be put in place. Hence, there is no requirement to use Spanish unless a child already speaks Spanish. Since most profoundly deaf children do not fluently speak the language of their families, this is an uncommon circumstance. This does not mean, however, that the children are not "Mexican American," and the assumption that the primary marker of Mexican American ethnicity is the use of fluent Spanish is an oversimplification of life in the transnational San Diego–Tijuana region.

It is worth noting some obvious facts before describing patterns of language use. First, interactions of ASL, English, and Spanish operate in two dimensions. English and Spanish are spoken languages with print variations available, while ASL is a signed language with no spoken form and no widely available print form. Second, only a few staff at the Flores School DHH program are trilingual, and know English, Spanish, and ASL. Only these adults, then, have the option of choosing between two spoken languages, as well as one signed language. The majority of the DHH teachers, who know English and ASL, have only one spoken language option and one signed language option.

Profoundly deaf students at Flores School either know ASL or are acquiring it. Their command of English, and their literacy skills vary, as does the intelligibility of their speech. The DHH student body is heterogeneous, and hard-of-hearing children are placed in classes with deaf students. Hard-of-hearing students also know, or are in the process of acquiring, ASL, the primary medium of instruction. In addition, most of these children could depend to some degree on hearing to comprehend and speak English. These children, then, are the group who might also comprehend and speak Spanish. During the study, only one deaf child, Lourdes, knew Spanish fluently. She was a nonsigning newcomer, previously educated via oral methods in southern Mexico. ASL classes were provided for her and her family, and by the end of the school year she had begun to sign at school.

Mary McCormick, the 5th–6th-grade teacher, is a hearing English–ASL bilingual. She does not speak Spanish. Her instructional assistant, Mrs. Simmons, is a monolingual hearing speaker of English who is learning ASL. Mary's primary language in the classroom is ASL. Two hard-of-hearing boys in her class, Antonio and Bernardo, speak and understand Spanish. These two sometimes spoke Spanish to each other, both during class and in underground, nonpublic conversations. During seat work, Antonio also spoke Spanish aloud to himself, in off-hand comments about the class. He mumbled comments like "dificíl" (difficult) or "¿que hacemos?" (what are we doing). He demonstrated the same kind of "self-talk" in English. Mary knew that these two boys had Spanish abilities and believed that her other students did not.

Caroline Ralstad-Salcedo, the 4th–5th-grade teacher, is a hearing English–ASL–Spanish trilingual. She speaks English natively, and speaks Spanish well, and she and her husband are raising their children in an English–Spanish bilingual household. The instructional assistant in Caroline's room, Mrs. Lamb, is a native speaker of Spanish, a balanced Spanish–English bilingual who also has ASL proficiency. Like Mary, Caroline's preferred medium of instruction is ASL. Two hard-of-hearing boys in her class, Joey and Michael, speak Spanish. Michael, whose minor hearing loss has a very minimal educational impact, is a very fluent speaker of Spanish. Joey had less usable hearing and less obvious facility with Spanish.

Caroline uses Spanish from time to time in her classroom. Importantly, all instances of spoken Spanish coded during visits to her class were limited to one language function, directives. Although she uses ASL and spoken English for a full range of classroom functions, it appears that she uses spoken Spanish only to get students' attention or to utter imperatives, e.g., "Michael, siéntate" (Michael, sit down) or "Joey, por favor, atención" (Joey, please, attention).

Mrs. Lamb worked individually with Lourdes, the newcomer from Mexico. Lourdes' speech (spoken Spanish) was intelligible. She used speech-reading to follow spoken Spanish and did not have strong English or ASL skills.

While the two teachers' language repertoires contrasted, both used ASL as their preferred medium of instruction. In each class, spoken Spanish appeared among students, but neither class exhibited environmental print in Spanish although print Spanish was common in the rest of the school. Only in Caroline's class was Spanish used as a medium of instruction for a range of instructional and social functions with Lourdes, who had not learned either ASL or English yet.

Despite the characteristics of the two classrooms, an underground multilingual world existed in the DHH program among the children and another staff member, Mr. Montemayor. His official capacity at Flores School was to serve as the interpreter for deaf students in mainstream settings, deaf staff during meetings, and Spanish speaking parents during conferences. He is a very balanced bilingual, who speaks Spanish natively and unaccented English. (This set of capacities is not uncommon in the transnational region.) He is active in several deaf communities in Mexico and the United States. When he was not interpreting, he circulated through the DHH classrooms, assisting teachers as needed. Often, he used Spanish with the Spanish-speaking hard-of-hearing boys and with Lourdes in casual conversations. Since he was known to the children as a Mexican who knew Spanish, children sometimes engaged him in "unofficial" Spanish lessons. He reported that some students (Michael, Joey, Antonio) asked him to tell them how to pronounce Spanish words or how to say something properly in Spanish. Other students, who teachers believed did not know Spanish, asked him to teach them vocabulary, and kept written artifacts in Spanish in their desks. In addition, the children were all aware of the fact that he knew Mexican Sign Language (LSM) and sometimes asked him for LSM lexical items.

In sum, then, the following facts characterize distribution of languages at the Flores School DHH program:

- ◆ All teachers used ASL and all students used ASL or were acquiring ASL abilities;

- ◆ Some students had sufficient hearing to detect spoken language. Teachers often spoke with these students, sometimes accompanying their speech with signing and sometimes using speech alone;

- ◆ Only if a teacher knew Spanish, and knew her student interlocutor was likely to hear and understand it, did she use Spanish.

The language situation at Flores School's DHH program was a bit more complex than DHH programs in other parts of the country. Although Spanish was not used as a medium of instruction, it was certainly present in the atmosphere of Flores School, as it was in the community and the homes of the children. Indeed, it was clear that the deaf and hard of hearing students were interested in Spanish, just as any children might be. (Ramsey (1997) describes a group of deaf children who were also very interested in languages, although they did not live in a transnational area.) In addition many parents of the DHH students preferred to use Spanish for their everyday interactions at home, community settings, and meetings with school personnel. The DHH program was also unique in that ASL was the primary language for face-to-face interaction and for instruction. English was used primarily in its print form. This pedagogy, termed "bi–bi" or "bilingual–bicultural" education for deaf children, is spreading among residential schools for deaf children but is not yet common in public school programs for deaf children. However, the pedagogy and its ideological underpinnings are well-known among California educators of deaf students, and the California community of deaf people is highly sophisticated and visible. The Flores School staff had decided to adopt ASL as the medium of instruction, and successful efforts have been made to hire deaf teachers and staff. The use of ASL in the classrooms was not particularly controversial among Mexican heritage parents.

The transnational location of Flores School also contributed to the distribution of languages at the DHH program. In this area, families live in communities where bilingualism is common and where younger generations often have a distribution of language skills that is distinct from that of the older generation (as in families where grandparents and even parents are monolingual Spanish speakers, and children are Spanish/English bilinguals). It is possible that using an ASL/English bilingual approach to deaf children's education is rendered less controversial and more acceptable to parents under these circumstances than it might be in other communities. (Parents on both sides of the border were taking sign language classes to facilitate communication with their deaf children, even though the use of signing with deaf children is a relatively new idea in Mexico. Most schools still use oral methods or "Español Signado" (a "signed Spanish" system similar to Signing Exact English) in conjunction with Total Communication. See Noriega (1996) for a discussion of current issues and trends in education for deaf children in Mexico.) Finally, only in a transnational region will another country's indigenous sign language be in use. Again, LSM was not used formally in the education program, but children and some staff used some Mexican signs, and one family used LSM at home. This range of languages is certainly the outcome of the location of the program, and was unusual in the number of languages, as well as the ways that signed and spoken languages were distributed among deaf, hard-of-hearing, and hearing people.

TEACHER VIEWS ON MEXICAN PARENTS

In formal, scheduled interviews, as well as informal conversations, I discussed the school experiences and achievement of the students in the Flores School DHH program with instructional personnel. Repeatedly I was told by Anglo staff that the problems experienced by their Mexican American students were rooted in their parents' lack of participation in the school program. Linguistic interference from Spanish was never cited as a problem, although teachers believed that a few students knew Spanish. Among the teachers, a deaf or hard-of-hearing child's fluent knowledge of spoken Spanish was considered neither an achievement, nor as evidence of potential for achievement, but merely part of a common repertoire of languages in the community. In contrast, knowing only spoken Spanish was considered a problem, and the Mexican newcomer, Lourdes, was provided with a great deal of support as she added ASL and print English to her skills. Further, after the study was completed, a group of children who already had strong literacy skills in Spanish were enrolled in the DHH program. Their Spanish skills were considered the basis for developing English literacy skills, and they were placed for part of the day in Spanish-language reading classes so they could maintain and increase their Spanish literacy.

The Flores School DHH program had both unusual language resources, and a well-grounded bilingual methodology for both hearing and deaf children. However, these features do not necessarily add up to a complete understanding of multicultural issues. One teacher told me that her students were "just like other deaf kids, except they have Mexican parents." While this is a blunt statement, it is a very clear statement of reality. Anglo teachers of the deaf feel very confident in their training and their methods for dealing with deaf children. They have much less training for working with non-Anglo parents. Hence, for them, the most serious confusion (bordering on despair at times) rested in their inability to make sense of the students' parents.

In several ways, Anglo teachers had difficulty interpreting Mexican parents' actions with regard to the school. Often, they resorted to a common myth about Mexican culture—that it is highly traditional— which places their children at a great disadvantage. Some teachers felt that Mexican heritage people in the United States have not adapted well to the modern world and do not understand the importance of education and that parents of deaf children are not sophisticated enough to understand what teachers ask of them or expect of them. If parents are not highly educated themselves, they are virtually incapable of engaging with the school or helping their children with homework.

Teachers were especially mystified by traditional non-Western treatments for deafness and by parents' seeming lack of interest in their children's educational rights. Several Anglo staff reported feeling insulted and deeply puzzled to learn that parents either "prayed" over their deaf children or took them to *curanderos* or *naturistas* (faith healers or natural healers) in Mexico for cures. Although some of the treatments were exotic and loaded with symbolism (e.g., a treatment where a priest places a key under the deaf child's tongue), the teachers' most common assumption was that Mexican heritage parents did not have faith that the school program could help their children and did not believe strongly enough in the benefits of special education for deaf children. The teachers perceived that when parents sought help outside the official world of the school program, they were "in denial" about their child's deafness.

Teachers of the deaf demand a lot from the parents of deaf children. Not only are parents expected to compliantly involve themselves with the teachers' program of instruction and rehabilitation, parents should show their good faith by learning to sign, and, critically, by indicating their process of struggling with the grief and shock of having a deaf child. It is not uncommon to hear a teacher link the struggle and eventual acceptance of deafness with a child's school achievement. The "grieving process," in particular the popularized Kubler-Ross (e.g., 1969) "stages" of grieving play an important role in teacher mindsets about hearing parents of deaf children. The expected stages of grieving figured prominently in the Flores School teachers' accounts of their students' school achievement. Many Mexican heritage parents were "in denial," I was told. In addition, many of them continued to "bargain" with God in the hopes their children would become hearing people. Some Anglo staff expressed the strong belief that as long as parents are "in denial," their deaf and hard-of-hearing children cannot make progress in school. In their worldview, only deaf children whose parents have completely accepted their deafness will do well in school. Only parents who exhibit, name, and pass through the "stages" of grieving can be said to have truly accepted their child's deafness.

Although Mexican heritage parents are often considered "passive," several teachers were still surprised and upset that Mexican heritage parents were reluctant to attend Individualized Education Program (IEP) conferences. When they did attend, they were reluctant to "demand their rights" and to participate as fully in the discussion (including reports of current growth and plans for future educational goals) as teachers expected them to.

In sum, in part because they were unable to make sense of the Mexican heritage parents' actions on behalf of their deaf and hard of hearing children, some of the teachers of the deaf had constructed a nearly impossible situation for themselves. Their students' progress was almost completely out of their hands, since parents' failings, their seeming lack of interest in their "rights," their denial and presumed stubbornness about truly accepting their children, and their perceived inability to help their children with homework were at the root of the students' difficulties with school.

BEING MEXICAN PARENTS

Not surprisingly, people who had the experience of being Mexican heritage parents had different accounts of the school setting. First, Mr. Montemayor commented that while the Anglo DHH teachers could sign well, and appeared to communicate with the students, he often felt that they did not really understand the Mexican American children, especially the family relationships and values that structured their lives away from school. For example, in general, Mexican child-rearing is supposed to take place in the home. Sending a child away from home to attend school, even if it makes educational sense to a teacher, is a difficult choice for Mexican heritage parents to make. Since children who are sent to residential schools are seen as children who "don't have any family to take care of them" parents send their children away from home for education only under very special or extreme circumstances. Yet several teachers at Flores School had told parents that their children would be educationally better off living at and attending a residential school for deaf students a 3- to 4-hour drive away from home. Mr. Montemayor understood that such suggestions insulted parents, as though teachers believed the parents were not doing their best to take care of their deaf children.

Most importantly, neither Mr. Montemayor nor the Mexican American and Mexican parents used the lexicon of grieving in either English or Spanish. Mr. Montemayor recognized this vocabulary, but commented that "We (i.e., Mexicans) don't talk that way." Indeed, when asked to tell their "diagnosis narrative" and to talk about their emotional response to the diagnosis of deafness, Mexican parents on both sides of the border made comments like "Well, we love our son very much." or "Of course we were surprised (or saddened) by the diagnosis, but we will do anything we can to help our child." They all framed their approach to deaf children as motivated by love, affection, and obligation, e.g. "I'm not very good at signing yet, but I'm learning because I am her mother. I must communicate with her, and how else, except to sign?" (Anglo parents, in contrast, might say that they would like to learn to sign better, but they "aren't good with languages" or that they "don't have time" to take a class).

Mexican parents hold a very non-Anglo view of teachers. Parents on both sides of the border expressed the belief that teachers, by virtue of their training, knowledge, and long years of education, are the experts in helping their children with school learning. A teacher's status is to be respected, and respect is bestowed upon the role of teacher more than it is on the person who occupies the role. Parents speak of making sacrifices to find a school for their children (and for many the sacrifices are genuine), and they acknowledge with grace the important role teachers play in schooling their deaf children. Not surprisingly, this set of values about teachers, which differs from the values of many Anglo middle-class parents, generates distinct parental responses to school as well. As a mother in Mexico told me, "Parents here expect to obey the teachers." Teacher training and teacher practical knowledge, in the abstract at least, exist in a domain that parents do not claim for their own. Hence, the idea of participating in an IEP conference as a peer of the teacher and other professional participants, is alien to many Mexican parents. However, this behavior is not simply "passivity." Rather, like some Anglo parents, they assume that teachers are experts. Parents place their children in the hands of teachers during the school day precisely because teachers are seen as responsible for the school learning that parents value deeply, which they feel they cannot provide themselves. This is in striking contrast to Anglo parents, who not only participate in IEP conferences as peers of the teachers, but expect to be highly involved in the educational lives of their deaf children. Where Mexican parents express their desire to "do what is best for my child," Anglo parents are more likely to view the process of participating with teachers in educational decisions as "asking for (or demanding) what my child has a right to receive."

This is not to say that Mexican heritage parents do not grieve or that they do not understand their children's right to educational services. Nor do I imply that Anglo parents do not hold love, affection, and obligation as important values with regard to their children. However, in my data, Mexican heritage parents simply did not manifest the specific kinds of behavior and emotions that Anglo teachers expect parents to display, and this led teachers to regard them as less-than-compliant clients of the school. This fact—that one group of parents has adopted the framework of grieving and its lexicon, as well as the legalistic vocabulary of "rights," and the other has not—illuminates to some degree the Anglo teachers' irritation and disappointment with Mexican heritage parents as well as Mr. Montemayor's abstract belief that the Anglo teachers were not "communicating" well with the Mexican heritage parents.

Just as Mexican parents place school responsibilities in the hands of trained teachers, they keep home and community activities distinct from school-like activities. This contrast illuminates the extent to which deaf children of Mexican heritage parents are not only deaf but Mexican as well and illustrates one way in which this dual identity is manifested. Several of the children in the U.S. group were receiving instruction from a local priest for their First Communion. Their mothers were very pleased to report that the priest knew American Sign Language and conducted their deaf children's instruction in a way the children could understand.

In previous years the First Communion ceremony itself included both deaf and hearing children, the priest spoke and an interpreter was present to sign the mass for the deaf children. In the year of the study, the mothers of the current group of deaf children explained to me that the interpreted mass did not seem right to them. They felt that having an interpreter made their children stand out too much and that the interpreter distracted the hearing people in attendance. As a result, the mass lost some of its solemnity, and this important event was reduced to a kind of showiness that they felt was insufficiently religious. They approached the priest, and requested a separate First Communion event for the deaf children where he would sign, in order to avoid using an interpreter and creating the distraction and distance they had felt in previous years.

These parents did not object to sending their deaf children to a public school with hearing children, and they knew that some of their school activities were integrated and that the deaf children depended on interpreters. However, for an intimate occasion like a First Communion, integration was seen as a problem, not as evidence of their children's "normalcy" or ability to interact with hearing people. Instead, the fact that their children were deaf and Mexican heritage Catholics was foremost. Again, this is in contrast to the widely held Anglo-American yearning for integration of able-bodied and disabled people at any cost and the companion norm of the "melting pot."

Mexican heritage families in the transnational region can experience intense pressure from extended family (and sometimes from others in their community) on matters of childrearing. They feel deeply their obligation to produce children who are "bien educados," that is, well-raised, decent, honest, polite, and civil. To have a child who is less than "bien educado" is to have created a "mal educado," a descriptor that says more about the parents than it does about the child. This value has several manifestations, which are magnified in families where the older generation resides in or still feels very tied to Mexico and the younger parent generation is American-born or resident on the north side of the line.

Several participants (mothers and fathers, as well as aunts and uncles) reported their families' responses to the diagnosis of their deaf child and to the decisions they had made on their behalf. First, they reported the drawn-out process of deciding to send a deaf child to a residential school. They wrestled with their own sadness and guilt about sending a child away from home. They also were on the receiving end of heavy criticism from their own parents and from neighbors and other Mexican heritage parents of deaf children. They all reported that their extended families were furious at them (even ashamed of them) for sending sons and daughters to live away from home at the residential school. In addition to violating the taboo against sending children away, one mother was criticized for giving in to her daughter's request to transfer and for not acting correctly and sufficiently parental. Sending a child away is a sign of incompetence, weakness, and not behaving like a proper Mexican parent, a serious evaluation for a mother or father with Mexican childrearing values.

When extended family, especially the grandparent generation, learned that their grandchild was deaf, many tended to assume that the child would be forever incompetent, unable to grow up properly, understand the world and his or her place in it, and unable to take care of him- or herself. A mother in Mexico reported that her parents' knowledge of deaf people was limited to observations of a young deaf woman who sold candy outside an office building. Another reported that the older generation in her family claimed to know of "country people" who simply kept their deaf child hidden away, because deaf children require lifelong protection from the world. Finally, more than one parent (on both sides of the border) reported that they knew of "older people" or "country people" who still believed that giving birth to a deaf child was a sign of divine punishment, the cause of which was left to the imaginations of neighbors and friends. Each of the parents reported that some members of their family assumed that their deaf child was "retarded" or *"flojo"* (roughly, lazy, intentionally disengaged with the world, unwilling to apply oneself). Almost all of the parents shared their families' concerns about speech, despite the fact that many of them were learning to sign and understood that an American Deaf Community exists. Some had taken their children to Deaf Community events in San Diego. Like Anglo parents they worried that their children's opportunities would be limited, and their aspirations (which ranged from finding a good spouse and raising children to attending medical school) would be difficult to achieve if their children did not acquire the ability to speak. However, the older generation included an additional concern, which placed pressure directly on the parents. A truly "well educated" Mexican heritage child speaks Spanish. Grandparents and members of their generation routinely criticized parents of deaf children for not adhering to their responsibility to make sure their deaf children comprehend Spanish and speak it properly. One U.S. mother reported that her mother routinely asked her why she had not "taught" her deaf son to speak Spanish, since her three other children spoke and understood Spanish well. The problem of not speaking was not seen as an outcome of profound deafness from birth, but of an inadequate mother who stubbornly did not comply with cultural norms.

Although it was a proscribed topic, all of the parents knew of other parents who had taken their deaf children to Mexico for a variety of "cures" for deafness. The treatments ranged from religious—prayer ceremonies organized by priests known for their deep faith and healing abilities—to heavily symbolic nonreligious treatments—placing a small bird in the deaf child's mouth until it sings three times—to the exploitative—taking a child to an isolated hut at midnight for an expensive but unknown treatment. (The mother who participated in the latter left as soon as the "healer" demanded more money.) These were the activities that mystified the Anglo teachers. Although very few parents admitted that they had sought such cures, those who did explained that they did so at the request of extended family members who lived in Mexico. Family members often arranged for cures or sent information about cures. Others bombarded parents with magazine clippings about cochlear implants, a "cure" of another sort that is only a bit less fantastic than the laying on of hands or the use of singing birds.

INTERACTIONS OF DEAFNESS AND MEXICAN HERITAGE

The point of this discussion is not to draw Anglo teachers as thick-headed or overeducated professionals, nor is it to portray Mexican and Mexican heritage parents as exotic. Rather, I report these data to illuminate the context of teachers and parents who are different from one another in profound ways that can affect the children whose development they all care about.

Patterns of language use at school reveal only a fraction of the ways that Mexican heritage deaf children live with their dual status. Although some of the Flores School adults and children knew Spanish, there was no pedagogical role for Spanish in the DHH program. Indeed, the challenges of fostering deaf children's learning are great, and most teachers believe that fostering English acquisition, and perhaps ASL acquisition, are difficult enough. Conventional wisdom holds that deaf children have a linguistic disability. Rightly or wrongly, they are rarely considered genuine candidates for spoken language multilingualism. Although teachers as well as the general public (especially in Southern California) tend to equate Mexican heritage or a Spanish surname with Spanish language dominance, clearly the deaf students at Flores School were not Spanish-dominant. In fact, except for one student who was raised in Mexico, none of the DHH children were Spanish dominant, although some knew Spanish.

Accordingly, to assume that the Spanish language (teaching and using it and confronting the possible effects of interference) is the most problematic issue in educating Mexican heritage deaf students is to miss more serious issues. Despite the fact that the Flores School children did not use Spanish, they were children who were both Mexican American and deaf, a fact that was implicitly recognized by the teachers.

Ironically, however, the statement that deaf students are just like other deaf students except for their Mexican parents precisely captures the situation at Flores School. Although the Spanish language may be the primary external marker of Mexican ethnicity, as the teachers at Flores School described their worldview it became clear that speaking Spanish was not the most important characteristic of their parents. Rather, from the teachers' point of view, the problem was that Mexican parents were less than skilled at participating in their parent roles in relation to the school. It is not difficult to make the leap from not participating in parental roles at school to not participating in parental roles at home, and this is the logic that several DHH teachers followed.

In reality, however, although deaf children's childhoods are often atypical, their language acquisition delayed, and their communication with their families distorted, they are not completely adrift in their families and communities in a culture-free state. The Mexican heritage deaf children in this study were very much a part of their parents' community and raised according to their parents' heritage. Often, teachers' perceptions (whether confused, irritated, or sympathetic) of the effects of parents' heritage structured the ways that the children and their school achievement were perceived. This created for some teachers a situation where very little of their work would make a difference in the children's learning, since their parents' presumed "alien" culture interfered.

One of the burdens that modern institutions of schooling place upon parents of deaf children is the expectation that they will adopt the behavior, beliefs, and values of the "textbook" Anglo, middle-class parent of a deaf child. Although the preferred beliefs and values may differ, it is not uncommon for teachers to expect parents to adopt their professional stance toward deaf education. Naturally this convergence does not always occur, and in these cases teachers sometimes claim that parental weaknesses are at the root of deaf children's school problems. One of the many tensions that the deaf education field will confront and need to work through is the nature of the linguistic, cultural, and professional gaps that exist between teachers and parents, especially in areas where the multicultural and multilingual are routine features of life for both deaf and hearing people. School and classes for deaf children are not rendered bilingual, bicultural, multilingual, or multicultural simply because of their location or their student population. Rather, the task is to adapt and alter schooling practice in order to find meaningful ways to engage both children and their parents. Teachers of the deaf are indeed highly educated and overwhelmingly well-intentioned. Many have every reason to feel confident in the classroom. The challenge for the field is to turn attention back to classrooms and to face the reality that not all parents of deaf children will adopt the vocabulary, behavior, and values expected of them by school personnel.

References

Allen, T. (1986). Patterns of academic achievement among hearing impaired students: 1974–1983. In A. Schildroth & M. Karchmer (Eds.), *Deaf children in America.* San Diego: College Hill.

Allen, T., Rawlings, B., & Schildroth, A. (1989). *Deaf students and the school to work transition.* Baltimore, MD: Paul H. Brookes.

Anderson, A., & Stokes, S. (1984). Social and institutional influences on the development and practice of literacy. In H. Goelman, A. Oberg & F. Smith (Eds.), *Awakening to literacy.* Portsmouth, NH: Heinemann Educational Books.

Bennett, A. (1987). *Gateways to powerlessness: Incorporating Hispanic deaf children and families into formal schooling.* Unpublished manuscript. Jackson Heights, NY: The Lexington Center.

California State Department of Education (1986). *Program guidelines for hearing impaired individuals.* Sacramento, CA: Office of State Printing.

Center for Assessment and Demographic Studies (1988–1989). *The annual survey of hearing-impaired children and youth 1988–89 school year.* Unpublished report. Washington, DC: Gallaudet University Press.

Cohen, O., Fischgrund, J., & Redding, R. (1990). Deaf children from ethnic, linguistic and racial minorities: An overview. *American Annals of the Deaf,* 135, 67–73.

Gandara, P. (1993). Language and ethnicity as factors in school failure: The case of Mexican-Americans. In R. Wollons (Ed.), *Children at risk in America.* Albany, NY: State University of New York.

Gerner de Garcia, B. (1993). Addressing the needs of Hispanic deaf children. In K. Christensen & G. Delgado (Eds.), *Multicultural issues in deafness.* White Plains, NY: Longman.

Harry, Beth. (1992). *Cultural diversity, families and the special education system.* New York: Teachers College Press.

Holt, J. (1993). Stanford Achievement Test, 8th Edition: Reading comprehension subgroup results. *American Annals of the Deaf,* 138, 172–175.

Janesick, V., & Moores, D. (1992). Ethnic and cultural considerations. In T. Kluwin, D. Moores & M. Gaustad (Eds.), *Toward effective public school programs for deaf students.* New York: Teachers College Press.

Kubler-Ross, E. (1969). *On death and dying.* New York: Macmillan.

MacNeil, B. (1990). Educational needs for multicultural hearing-impaired students in the public school system. *American Annals of the Deaf,* 135, 75–82.

Noriega, J. A. (Ed.) (1996). *El silencio del sordo/La cultura del sordera.* Psicologia Iberoamericana, 4. Mexico DF: Universidad Iberoamericana.

Ramsey, C. (1997). *Deaf children in public schools: Placement , context and consequences.* Washington, DC: Gallaudet University Press.

Ramsey, C., Padden, C., & Sterne, S. (1995). *Deafness, ethnicity and learning to write.* Working paper, Research Program in Language and Literacy. La Jolla, CA: UCSD Center for Human Information Processing.

Rodriguez, O., and Santiviago, M. (1991). Hispanic deaf adolescents: A multicultural minority. *Volta Review,* 93, 89–97.

Vasquez, O., Pease-Alvarez, L., & Shannon, S. (1994). *Pushing boundaries: Language and culture in a Mexicano community.* Cambridge, UK: Cambridge University Press.

Meeting the Needs of Hispanic/Latino Deaf Students

Barbara Gerner de García

"We need to model for our children the compassion, the love, the kindness, the understanding, and the wisdom they deserve. I ask you to listen with your hearts and respect the voices here before you. We have a responsibility to make sure that education reflects compassion and humanity."

Lourdes Dias Soto,
*Language, culture, and power:
Bilingual families and the struggle for quality education*

Hispanic/Latino students are the largest racial/ethnic minority in deaf education, yet resources to meet their needs are limited. Many of these students are from Spanish-speaking homes, and live in trilingual/multicultural worlds. The academic achievement of these students is lower than their Anglo and African American peers, and they are less likely to leave school with a high school diploma. In order to improve educational outcomes for Hispanic/Latino deaf students, educators must learn more about language diversity issues, least-biased assessment practices, culturally appropriate teachings and curriculum, and working with Latino parents.

As we enter the 21st century, many issues face the future of education in the United States. One of the real challenges for many schools and programs serving deaf and hard-of-hearing students is the growing number of students from Spanish-speaking families and/or Hispanic/Latino backgrounds. Professionals in such programs—teachers, administrators, and support personnel—are often at a loss as to how to meet the needs of deaf and hard-of-hearing Hispanic/Latino children. They find that they have limited resources, in the form of either personnel or materials.

Hispanic/Latino students continue to have limited educational success in general education, as well as in deaf education. The dropout rate for Hispanic/Latino students continues to be alarmingly high, robbing the Hispanic/Latino community of future leaders and our society of productive citizens. Calculating dropout rates is complex. Different approaches to calculating figures and determining who is a dropout lead to variations in figures reported (Rodriquez, 1989; García, 1995). Hispanic/Latino deaf students drop out at a higher rate than African American (Schildroth & Hotto, 1995). Hispanic/Latino deaf and hard-of-hearing students may also become "internal dropouts," failing to participate in class, cutting classes, and attending school primarily for social reasons.

The concerns and problems of Hispanic/Latino deaf students parallel what we see in general education. A study by the NCES (National Center for Education Statistics) in 1991 found that in grade three there is little difference in the educational achievement of Hispanic/Latino students and Anglo students. By grade eight academic achievement drops off significantly for Hispanic/Latino students, leaving approximately 40% one or more grade levels below normal achievement levels (García, 1995). Studies over a period of 20 years have found that the achievement of Hispanic/Latino deaf children is lower than that of their Anglo and African American deaf peers (Allen, 1986; Jensema, 1975; Kluwin, 1994). In describing deaf school leavers age 14 and over, Schildroth and Hotto (1995) found 55% of deaf students of color, compared with 45% of White deaf students, left school with certificates rather than high school diplomas. More Hispanic/Latino than African American deaf students got certificates, and schools in the South were more likely to give certificates than other regions of the United States (Schildroth & Hotto, 1995).

In the past, immigrants with limited literacy skills in English were able to support a family (López, 1995). In the 19th century, the United States was an agricultural society, with an increasing industrial base. As we approach the 21st century, we are no longer an agricultural or an industrial economy, but a service economy. Service sector workers may be low-skilled minimum wage workers or highly skilled technicians and professionals. The world of work has dramatically changed with markedly less job stability and security. These are challenges for deaf education which make our least prepared students most vulnerable. The social safety net is shrinking, compelling the need to better prepare our students for skilled jobs.

THE HISTORY OF HISPANICS/LATINOS IN THE UNITED STATES

Today, close to 63% of the U.S. Hispanic/Latino community is of Mexican descent, over 11% are Puerto Rican, close to 14% are of Central American origin, almost 5% are Cuban, and the remaining 7% include South Americans and Dominicans (Campbell, 1996). The largest Hispanic/Latino populations are found on the coasts and southern border of the United States. The vast majority of Caribbean origin Latinos are on the east coast (Puerto Ricans, Dominicans, and Cubans), and most Mexican Americans live on the west coast and in the Southwest. Large communities of Central Americans are found in urban areas of Washington, DC, Los Angeles, and Miami.

It is not possible to truly understand the Hispanic/Latino community of the United States without understanding the history of this country. After the Native Americans, the Mexicans were the "first" Americans. Enslaved Africans were brought to the Caribbean a century before their arrival in Jamestown, making the African presence in the Hispanic/Latino world the oldest in the Western Hemisphere (de Varona, 1996).

In the early 19th century, American westward expansion threatened the Mexican territories of California, the Southwest, and Texas, leading to over a decade of warfare beginning in 1835. In 1845, Texas was annexed after Sam Houston defeated the Mexican General Santa Ana and despite the fact that Mexico renounced the resulting treaty. In 1848, the United States paid $15,000,000 for the Mexican Cession consisting of over one million square miles of territory including the modern states of California, New Mexico, and Nevada, and parts of Utah, Arizona and Colorado. The cession of these states and the annexation of Texas cost Mexico over half of its territory (de Varona, 1996; Takaki, 1993).

For much of the following century, Mexicans were allowed to cross the Rio Grande and California border with no need of passports. At the beginning of the 20th century, a series of revolutions and upheavals in Mexico, the extension of the railroad 900 miles into Mexico, the lack of work in rural Mexico, and a demand for labor on the other side of the border fueled Mexican migration and immigration (Takaki, 1993). Latinos in the Southwest remind us that this territory was once Mexico when they say, "We didn't cross the border. The border crossed us."

In 1898, after the Spanish–American war, Puerto Rico became a territory of the United States. Currently a Commonwealth, the debate continues whether Puerto Rico should become the 51st state. Puerto

Ricans, who are citizens of the United States, often migrate back and forth from the island they love to the mainland, where economic and educational opportunities are available (de Varona, 1996). This "circulatory migration" leads to a need for maintenance of the Spanish language, and migration becomes a way of life (Cohen, 1987). As a result, many Puerto Ricans do not expect to assimilate and demand accommodation from schools for the protection and maintenance of their language and culture (Diaz Soto, 1997; Nieto, 1995, pp. 391–392).

Many Cubans fled their country after the Cuban Revolution in 1959. Subsequent waves of refugees in 1965 and 1973 were made up primarily of upper- and middle-class members of Cuban society. The Mariel boatlift in 1981 and rafters escaping in the early 1990s included poorer, less educated, and more often Black Cubans. Many of the earliest Cuban refuges saw themselves as exiles who would someday return to live in the homeland, but increasingly younger generations consider the United States their permanent home. Cuban Americans are concentrated in southern Florida but are also found in large numbers in New York, New Jersey, the Washington, DC, area, and Los Angeles (de Varona, 1996).

The largest and longest established Hispanic/Latino groups are the Mexican, Puerto Rican, and Cuban communities. However, since the mid-1960s and 1970s, immigrants from the Caribbean (primarily Dominicans), Central America, and South America have arrived in increasing numbers (de Varona, 1996). Though often seen as economic refugees, many have also fled their countries as a result of political conflicts and upheavals.

The Dominican exodus to New York began after the assassination of the dictator Trujillo in 1961 and the U.S. invasion in 1965 during a popular uprising following a coup d'etat (Ferguson, 1992; Szulc, 1965). A worsening economy in the 1980s and 1990s fueled immigration (de Varona, 1996, Ferguson, 1992). The neighborhood of Washington Heights, in the borough of Manhattan, in New York City, is home to the largest Dominican community outside Santo

Domingo, the capital city of the Dominican Republic. With almost a million Dominicans in the United States, over 400,000 are found in New York City (Ferguson, 1992).

Three decades of unrest in Central America and the subsequent upheaval have created thousands of refugees. With Central and Latin American countries frequently characterized as "banana republics," many Americans tend to view Latin Americans as adverse to democracy with a tendency to military dictatorships, coup d'etats, and revolutions. However, in many cases U.S. involvement (covert, as in the case of the Nicaraguan Contras, as well as overt as in Santo Domingo, 1965, and Panama, 1989) has been involved. A civil war in El Salvador beginning in 1979 and ending in 1992, as well as political changes in Nicaragua and activities of the Contras, created many refugees (Novas, 1994; Winn, 1992). Military counterinsurgency campaigns, carried out in the countryside of Guatemala for over 18 years, were aimed primarily at indigenous Indians. Rigoberta Menchu, a Guatemalan Quiché Indian and the winner of the 1992 Nobel Peace Prize, lost her entire family to army atrocities and brought the plight of Guatemalan Indians to the attention of the world (Ohrn, 1995). The internal warfare ended and resulted in over a million refugees, some of whom fled to the United States (Winn, 1992).

THE HISTORY OF EDUCATION OF HISPANICS/LATINOS IN THE UNITED STATES

The history of the education of Hispanic/Latino students in the United States reveals a legacy of discrimination, segregation, and underachievement. However, much of this history has been ignored. As a result, the active resistance of Mexican Americans to discrimination and their struggles for educational reform are often unacknowledged (Donato, 1997). In the 19th century, in Texas, Arizona, and California, instruction in English in public schools was mandated, leading to a lack of participation by, and lack of success for, Mexican American children. Although segregation of Mexican American children was not legislated as it was for African American students, it was common practice until the 1940s, particularly in the southwest (Meier & Stewart, 1991). García (1995) describes the goal of "Americanization" that has long been and continues to be expressed by educators working with Mexican American students—U.S.-born as well as immigrant. Americanization, García argues, means the elimination of cultural and linguistic differences, with the home culture of Mexican Americans considered inferior and a target for elimination.

In 1898, when the United States took over Puerto Rico as a territory, only 8% of the island's children, primarily upper class, were enrolled in school. Spain had considered education a threat to their domination of the island; thus no public education was provided until the U.S. arrival (Walsh, 1991). For forty years from 1909 to 1949, English was the mandatory language of instruction in schools on the island of Puerto Rico despite the fact that at the time this policy was implemented only 3.6% of the population spoke English (Crawford, 1992). The purpose of this education was to instill American ideals and Americanization through the teaching of English (Walsh, 1991).

Rodriquez (1989) describes three historic periods in the struggles for educational change on behalf of Puerto Rican students in U.S. mainland schools. Initially, the struggle focused on raising awareness of the problems Puerto Rican students experienced in school. During the 1960s, community agencies were established to deal with these issues. The 1970s saw the Puerto Rican community turning to the courts for legal remedies (Rodriquez, 1989, pp. 139–140). Nieto (1995, p. 388) argues that the characterization of Puerto Rican students in numerous reports as "problems," "losers," "dropouts," "culturally deprived," "disadvantaged," or "at risk" fails to consider what schools can and must do in conjunction with families and communities to improve educational outcomes for Puerto Rican students (see Nieto (1995) for an extensive review of the literature on the education of Puerto Rican students).

Upper- and middle-class Cubans arrived in record numbers after the 1959 Cuban revolution, many settling in southern Florida. Many, not trusting U.S. schools, sent their children to private and parochial schools, while the less affluent used public schools (Meier & Stewart, 1991). This large community of educated parents pushed for the establishment of bilingual education in Dade county, and with a Ford Foundation grant, established the first modern public bilingual programs in 1963 (Arias & Casanova, 1993).

Limited data are available regarding the educational experiences of more recent arrivals from Central America, Latin America, and the Dominican Republic. An ethnographic study of Central American high school students in northern California (Suarez-Orozco, 1987) found that these students, despite the trauma they had experienced as refugees from war, were experiencing success. Their teachers described them as more motivated, more respectful, and earning better grades than their peers of other ethnicities. Suarez-Orozco concludes that these students, like many new immigrants, believed that if they studied and worked hard, they would get ahead in this society. In contrast, their African American and Mexican American peers were more cynical about the possibilities for success. Coming from communities that have experienced "depreciation" (p. 168) in this society, the psychological barriers (both within these communities as well as on the part of educators) are formidable. The psychology of school failure and alienation found among too many Mexican American and Puerto Rican students makes their school experiences markedly different and much more negative than recent arrivals such as the Central American students described (Suarez-Orozco, 1987).

THE GROWTH OF LINGUISTIC DIVERSITY

Linguistically diverse groups make up the largest segment of the multicultural population of this country. Linguistic diversity is narrowly defined by the federal government as (persons with) "non-functional English." A more encompassing definition includes any person whose native language is a language other than English, regardless of their proficiency in English (Trueba, 1989). The overwhelming majority of linguistically diverse individuals are Spanish-speaking. In California and the Southwest, Spanish-speakers make up 73% of those who do not speak English (Olson, 1988, cited in Campbell, 1996).

Although the first modern public bilingual programs for Cuban refugee students began in the 1960s, bilingual education has been practiced in the United States since the 18th century (Crawford, 1992). Communities of European immigrants maintained numerous native language institutions, including schools, libraries, publications, and social institutions into the 20th century (Arias & Casanova, 1993). The rise of nativism, xenophobia, and immigration at the beginning of this century occurred in reaction to increasing numbers of immigrants from Southern and Eastern Europe. Anti-immigrant organizations, Americanization campaigns, and the idea that speaking English equaled being a loyal American grew (Arias & Casanova, 1993; Crawford, 1992). President Theodore Roosevelt declared that "A hyphenated American is not an American at all" (Crawford, 1992, p. 7). During World War I, speaking German was banned in many U.S. cities, and the Russian Revolution led to a widespread fear of "Bolsheviks." People who spoke other languages were not trusted, an attitude that is reflected in current efforts opposing bilingual education and the use of languages other than English in public life (Crawford, 1992).

It is important to understand the history of language policy in the United States as well as the histories of racial/ethnic groups. This history has resulted in a legacy of negative attitudes toward immigrants and their languages. These attitudes, long dormant, resurged in the 1990s and influence our own attitudes toward students and families from language diverse backgrounds. These prejudices about language have been labeled *linguicism* by Skutnabb-Kangas (Nieto, 1996) and are infrequently challenged. Nevertheless, these negative attitudes do affect our view of Hispanic/Latino deaf students and their parents, a point that will be discussed later in this chapter.

MEETING THE NEEDS OF HISPANIC/LATINO DEAF CHILDREN

Programs and Personnel

Over 40% of the school-age deaf and hard-of-hearing population is from racially, ethnically, and culturally diverse backgrounds, with Hispanic/Latino, and Asian/Pacific Islanders being the fastest growing groups (Schildroth & Hotto, 1995). Delgado's 1984 book, *The Hispanic Deaf*, first described the needs of this population, as well as the best practices at that time. Since the time of the study conducted in 1979–1980, "A Survey of Non-Native Homes," the first nation-wide study looking at deaf children from language diverse families (Delgado, 1984b), the Hispanic/Latino deaf school-age population has increased dramatically. In the 1973 Annual Survey of Hearing-Impaired Children and Youth,[1] Hispanic/Latino students made up 7% of the school-age population (Schildroth & Hotto, 1995). In 1983, they were 11%, and in 1993, 16% (Schildroth & Hotto, 1995). Figures from the 1996–1997 Annual Survey indicate that Hispanic/Latino deaf students are now 18% of all deaf and hard-of-hearing students (Center for Demographic Studies, 1997). Unfortunately, awareness of the needs and best approaches to meet the needs of these students has not kept pace.

In numerous school districts, urban and increasingly suburban, students of color are the majority. In schools for the deaf, residential schools tend to have fewer students of color than local programs

---

[1] The name of this survey has changed over the years from Annual Survey of Hearing-Impaired Children and Youth to the Annual Survey of Deaf Children and Youth.

(Cohen *et al.,* 1990). Among the 10 schools for the deaf participating in a three-year grant for preparing multicultural school leaders,[2] the three local programs were 96.2, 79, and 74.3% students of color in 1994. The residential schools ranged from a low of 11% students of color to 50.5% (Gerner de García, 1997a). Hispanic/Latino deaf populations of their schools range from 3.7% in a Midwestern residential school to as high as 56% in an urban Eastern school.

Looking at the student demographics at postsecondary institutions provides a graphic illustration of the failure of deaf education to adequately prepare Hispanic/Latino students. Less than 7% of the deaf students at California State University, Northridge (CSUN), near Los Angeles were Hispanic/Latino, and approximately 5% at Gallaudet in 1996 were Hispanic/Latino (Gallaudet University, 1996).

At a time when the number of Hispanic/Latino deaf children is increasing, educators are not well prepared to meet their needs. The lack of professionals prepared to work with Hispanic/Latino deaf children was addressed as long ago as 1981 by the Conference of Educational Administrators Serving the Deaf[3] (CEASD). Noting increasing numbers of Hispanic deaf children and their unique needs, this resolution called for the hiring of Hispanic/Latino professionals. In 1978–1979, only 0.6% of teachers of the deaf were Hispanic/Latino. In the next 10 years, this increased to only 1.3% (CEASD, 1989). A 1993 study of deaf and hearing minority professionals in the field (Andrews & Jordan, 1993) reported 2% of teachers (104) and 4% of administrators (35) were Hispanic/Latino. As this study included postsecondary professionals, the number of K–12 professionals was actually lower.

Efforts to meet the needs of Hispanic/Latino deaf students have been concentrated in the Northeastern states. As the states and cities

---

[2] Project THREADS (Transformations for Humanistic and Responsive Education for All Deaf Students) funded by the Department of Personnel Preparation, Office of Special Education and Rehabilitation, U.S. Department of Education.

[3] The name has since been changed to Conference of Educational Administrators of Schools and Programs for the Deaf.

involved in these projects and programs for Hispanic deaf students were in jurisdictions with legislatively mandated bilingual education programs, there was more awareness of the needs of Hispanic/Latino students, deaf and hearing. The attention given the needs of deaf children from language diverse backgrounds has also been the result of legal actions. In New York City, three court cases, *José P. v. Ambach* (1983), *United Cerebral Palsy (UCP) of New York v. Board of Education of the City of New York* (1979) and *Dycia, S. v. Board of Education of New York City,* resulted in a consolidated judgment which provided for bilingual special education programs, outreach, evaluation, and due process assurances (Baca, 1990, pp. 251–252).

In 1975, Projecto Opportunidad at Rhode Island School for the Deaf was funded by Title VII to provide support for deaf students from Spanish-speaking and Portuguese-speaking families (Blackwell & Fischgrund, 1984). That same year, the State of New York and 11 schools for the deaf and blind funded CREED VII (Cooperative Research Endeavors in the Education of the Deaf), including 5 schools for the deaf in New York City, for the support of Hispanic deaf students (Lerman, 1984). In 1979, staff from Opportunidad and CREED were funded by the Office of Special Education and Rehabilitation Services (OSERS) for Project LISTO—Latino In Service Training and Orientation (Lerman & Vilá, 1984). Project LISTO provided training for schools and programs for the deaf throughout the northeast and planted the seeds for the Hispanic Deaf Program, founded at the Horace Mann School for the Deaf, Boston, in 1988, as well as efforts in other schools to meet the needs of this population.

A series of conferences from 1989 to 1992 addressed meeting the educational needs of Hispanic/Latino and other multicultural deaf children. These conferences received funding from OSERS and support from CEASD, Gallaudet, and other institutions. The first conference Meeting the Needs of Black and Hispanic Deaf Children was held at Gallaudet in April 1989. This was followed by a conference held on the west coast in San Diego, California, in April 1990, Meeting the Needs of Multicultural Deaf Children, which also addressed the needs of Asian/Pacific Island and Native American deaf children. In November 1992 the Hispanic Deaf Experience in San Antonio, Texas, focused on educational as well as community issues. Lamar University, Beaumont, Texas, the home of the Hispanic Deaf Teacher Education Program, hosted a conference The Hispanic Deaf Child in the Classroom in November 1996, primarily drawing participants from the state of Texas.

During the 1990s as the Hispanic/Latino deaf population grew, school and programs across the United States for deaf and hard-of-hearing students worked to develop new projects and programs. In places including Florida, California, the Southwest, and the Mid-Atlantic, pre K–12 schools and higher education institutions are introducing English as a Second Language programs, trilingual programs, research projects, trilingual interpreting, Latino parent outreach, and multicultural training. These pioneering efforts must expand and be replicated to ensure better education for Hispanic/Latino deaf and hard-of-hearing students.

Language Needs

As previously stated, the educational outcomes for Hispanic/Latino deaf students are poor. Since the 1988 report from the Commission on Education of the Deaf, *Toward Equality,* as well as the paper, "Unlocking the Curriculum" (Johnson *et al.,* 1989), there is growing awareness that the educational outcomes achieved by most deaf school leavers are unsatisfactory and unacceptable.

For years, deaf education has struggled with the issues of language, although this has been stated in terms of "communication mode." While the oral vs manual debate in this country has gone on for over 100 years, the debate over language of instruction, American Sign Language (ASL) or English, has intensified in the past 20 years (Johnson *et al.,* 1989; Lane *et al.,* 1996). *In the current debate over bilingual/bicultural education for deaf children, the needs and realities of deaf children from language diverse families are frequently overlooked.*

Some educators and parents may believe that three languages will confuse a deaf or hard-of-hearing child (Kopp, 1984). However, research indicates that this is not the case (Gerner de García, 1993, 1995a). The opposition to bilingual education and trilingual education for deaf children may be more political than pedagogical. It may be the result of linguicism, as well as, in the case of Hispanic/Latino deaf students, the low status of the Spanish language and Spanish speakers. Humphries argued (1993) that a society that has not accepted people who are deaf as bilingual and bicultural is unlikely to accept deaf people as multicultural.

Hispanic/Latino deaf children and adults who communicate using signed languages that are not ASL may be labeled as having "no language" when they enter U.S. schools. They may use their country of origin's signed language, e.g., Puerto Rican Sign Language (PRSL), or home signs (idiosyncratic signs created to use with friends and/or family) and gestures. However, frequently their language is not seen as a different language (Gerner de García, 1998). In a description of a large group of Mexican deaf men from rural Oaxaca gathering to tell stories and reminisce, they are described a "languageless clan" (Schaller, 1991, p. 184) and having the "ability to communicate without language" (p. 186). This description shows the linguicism that colors the widespread view of Hispanic/Latino deaf children and adults. It is based in the racism that permeates this society that holds some languages and cultures as more valuable.

The language diversity of Hispanic/Latino deaf students is characterized as a "problem." There is a widespread view of language diversity in U.S. schools which characterizes "language as a problem" rather than seeing different languages as resources (Ruiz, 1990; Ruiz & Nover, 1992). For many years (and often still) ASL was viewed as inferior to spoken languages or not a language at all (Maher, 1996; Lane *et al.*, 1996). With negative views of ASL still common, it is not surprising that unfamiliar sign languages used by immigrant deaf children and adults would be stigmatized.

It may be the case that some oppose a multilingual/multicultural representation of the Deaf experience in this country because it upsets the popular paradigm of a hearing/deaf dichotomy. A multicultural Deaf Community is harder to describe, answers are not as readily available, and changes will be more difficult to implement. However, by denying the realities of Hispanic/Latino deaf students who live in a trilingual/multicultural world, we contribute to their failure. Their complete, complex identities must be accepted.

Educational and Cultural Traditions

When working with deaf children from Spanish-speaking families, schools and staff must recognize that language and culture are inextricably linked. The relationship between language and culture is so deeply entwined, it is difficult to consider language and culture separately (Baker, 1993). However, the accommodation for the language needs of Spanish-speaking families is limited. The Individuals with Disabilities Education Act (IDEA) requires that Individualized Education Plan (IEP) meetings be in the home language and related paperwork such as parental notification and the IEP be translated, meeting mandated timelines. Beyond mandated translation, often little is done in many schools to meet the linguistic and cultural needs of Hispanic/Latino families with deaf children.

Once an Hispanic/Latino deaf child enters school, the child's unique cultural and linguistic needs may be ignored. This occurs because intake personnel and many teachers and administrators lack awareness of these unique needs as well as information on meeting these needs.

The first contact between Hispanic/Latino families and service providers may result in cultural conflict. Parents and school professionals have differing perspectives and expectations regarding roles. In traditional Hispanic/Latino values the teacher is accepted as the authority figure (Scarcella, 1990). American educators, as well as the IDEA, expect that parents be partners, but some culturally diverse parents need guidance in taking on this role. Spanish-speaking families may also be concerned about integrating their child into the family and Hispanic/Latino community. Trilingual and multicultural staff are essential for the inclusion of Hispanic/Latino families, but

multicultural competence is the responsibility of all school staff—
hearing, or deaf, Anglo, or non-Anglo (see Sass-Lehrer *et al.,* 1997).
*Every member of the school staff can learn respect and sensitivity, as well
as a few words in Spanish to make Latino families feel welcome.*

All hearing families with deaf children need early intervention and
support. Unfortunately, many programs may be inaccessible to
Spanish-speaking families, who may have difficulty getting to the clinic
or school due to work schedules and/or lack of transportation and
childcare and who may face language and cultural obstacles. Deaf
adults, particularly those from Hispanic/Latino backgrounds, are important role models for parents. However, such individuals should be
culturally sensitive, as well as prepared to work in early intervention.
Being deaf and/or Hispanic/Latino does not automatically make a person suited to the work. All early intervention with culturally diverse
families must consider cultural and linguistic differences, and differing
perspectives of the school and professionals' roles and the families' roles.

Hispanic/Latino parents may not be empowered even in schools
with trained staff. Bennett (1987, 1988), a sociolinguist and researcher at the Center for Puerto Rican Studies at Hunter College,
carried out an in-depth ethnographic study of the formal intake
process (assessment, evaluation, and placement) of Hispanic/Latino
deaf preschool children. In a case study focusing on a middle-class
Hispanic mother, Bennett found that despite the fact that the mother
shared the educational values of the school and had some rapport with
the school's professionals, her input was limited. This occurred in spite
of legal guarantees in special education laws protecting the participation of the parents. Despite the mother's repeated efforts, an open discussion of the effect of classroom organization, pedagogy, and
curriculum on her son's perceived behavior problems did not occur.

Bennett interviewed more marginalized Hispanic/Latino parents,
those who were poorer, less educated, and less acculturated, and found
them to be critical of the school. He observed in their interactions
with staff, these same parents were very passive. They resisted building
bridges with a school that claimed to want more parental participation

but had proven untrustworthy. Bennett concluded that their lack of involvement may have served to help the Hispanic/Latino parents to preserve their cultural integrity.

When a child is discovered to be deaf or hard of hearing, parents must decide, with the advice of various professionals, what type of educational program is best. This decision often must be made when parents are coping with complex feelings including loss, grief, and bewilderment. Hispanic/Latino deaf children may be identified later than is typical. This may be due to a lack of Spanish-speaking professionals, including health care providers, and limited access to health care. Late diagnoses also occur when doctors dismiss the concerns of mothers, and Latina mothers feel this occurs because they are not seen as capable or competent in child development (Gerner de Garcia, 1993). Some diagnoses cannot be verified until migration to the mainland or an urban area or immigration to the United States (Gerner de García, 1993).

LANGUAGE DOMINANCE AND LANGUAGE PROFICIENCY

Determining the dominant language and language proficiency of deaf and hard-of-hearing children who are from Spanish-speaking families and/or immigrants is a complex process. This is difficult to do without the help of professionals who are culturally sensitive and trilingual. There are no standardized instruments that are normed for children who are both deaf and Hispanic or Spanish-dominant. In school jurisdictions without Spanish-speaking professionals, resources, and appropriate programs, these children's language needs may not be met. Despite legal requirements to assess a special needs student in the home language, it is often assumed that a deaf child from a hearing family entering school has little or no "language." Because of the hearing loss, it is further assumed that the child has learned little of the home language and is not affected by the language difference between home and school.

There is research that indicates that these assumptions are often incorrect. A study of Hispanic/Latino deaf and hard-of-hearing preschoolers (Luetke-Stahlman & Weiner, 1984) found that the children varied in their language preferences. Some children did best with signed input only, and others benefited from the use of Spanish paired with signs. The degree of hearing loss alone did not determine whether a child benefited from Spanish input.

A study of Spanish-speaking families with deaf children (Gerner de García, 1993, 1995a) found that the communication in these families was quite complex. Siblings were often trilingual, and the deaf children used a variety of strategies in order to communicate at home. The deaf children codeswitched using spoken Spanish, gestures, non-ASL signs (either home signs or signs from their country of origin), and ASL. In the families studied, the deaf children worked hard to communicate using their codeswitching repertoire. However, at school, they were described as children who had little or no communication at home, despite the fact that they had never been observed in their home environments.

A deaf child who has begun school in a Spanish-speaking country most likely has some Spanish language and literacy skills. Some children may have minimal skills due to factors such as the predominance of oral education, lack of trained teachers of the deaf, or varying quality of deaf education programs. Children new to the United States probably do not know much, if any, ASL or English. They may use a signed language such as PRSL or Dominican Sign Language (DRSL) that is not familiar to their American teachers (who may be hearing, as well as unfamiliar with Latin America). Perhaps they use home signs and gestures as they attempt to communicate in a new and unfamiliar environment.

Too often, schools label immigrant deaf students as having "no language," rather than seeing them as using a different language. When immigrant deaf and hard of hearing students are labeled by U.S. schools this way, they may be placed in special classes for deaf children with multiple disabilities. Their language differences are seen as a disability. They are not provided with appropriate educational programs that introduce them to ASL and English as new languages. This is an example of the tendency to characterize language diversity as a problem (Ruiz, 1990; Ruiz & Nover, 1992).

In the case of deaf and hard-of-hearing children from Spanish-speaking families who are U.S.-born, some may suppress their knowledge of Spanish in formal testing situations (Lerman & Vilá, 1984). If Spanish-speaking deaf and hard-of-hearing children do not use their Spanish in the school environment, it may be because they think they will not be understood. They see that Sign Language and/or English are the languages for school and Spanish is the language of the home. These children's language abilities in Spanish remain hidden from their teachers. Unless observations are carried out in the home and community with the children's families, their true language capabilities may not be revealed (Gerner de García, 1993; Lerman & Vilá, 1984).

Determining language dominance of many Hispanic/Latino children is difficult. It is more useful to determine what the child knows in each language. Trilingual deaf and hard-of-hearing children often have overlapping language knowledge. However, a concept or word known in one language may not be there in another language. Bilinguals and trilinguals are rarely equally fluent across languages. Their languages may have specific domains, such as social language, home language, or field-or discipline-specific language. Some concepts may not be expressed as easily in another language or in the same way.

LEP DEAF STUDENTS

The federal government defines which students labeled "language minority" fall within the category of Limited English Proficient (LEP) within Title VII—The Improving of Schools Act of 1994—Public Law 103–382. According to this definition a student is LEP if he/she "has sufficient difficulty speaking, reading, writing or understanding the English language and whose difficulties may deny such individuals the opportunity to learn successfully in classrooms where the language of instruction is English...due to the following reasons:

◆ was not born in the United States or whose native language is a language other than English *and* [author's emphasis] comes from an environment where a language other than English is dominant;

◆ is native American or Alaskan native and who is a native resident of the outlying areas and comes from an environment where a language other than English has had significant impact on such individual's level of English language proficiency, or

◆ is migratory and whose native language is other than English and comes from an environment where a language other than English is dominant (sec. 7501)" (Anstrom, 1996, pp. 1–2).

Assessment and the determination of language dominance is crucial in meeting the legal requirements that mandate services for children who are labeled LEP. The legal requirements that pertain to LEP children were outlined in the Lau Remedies (or guidelines). The Lau Remedies were developed after the Supreme Court, in 1974, ruled in favor of Chinese-speaking parents who brought a class action suit against the San Francisco public schools on behalf of their Chinese-speaking children who were educationally disadvantaged because they were not receiving either bilingual or ESL services (Lyons, n.d.).

After the favorable ruling, the Department of Health, Education, and Welfare, in 1975, announced the Lau Remedies, which specified "approaches, methods, and procedures" for (Lyons, n.d., p. 11):

◆ identifying and evaluating national origin-minority students' English language skills;

◆ determining appropriate instructional treatments;

◆ deciding when LEP children were ready for mainstream classrooms;

◆ determining the professional standards to be met by teachers for language minority children.

In deaf education, it is often argued that *all* deaf children are LEP. This is most often heard from supporters of bilingual–bicultural deaf education who support the development of ASL as a first language and English as a second language.[4] Therefore, many educators of the deaf believe that all deaf children are limited English proficient and need instruction in English as a Second Language.

There is another perspective on the issue of whether most deaf students are "ESL students" (Livingston, 1997, p. 13). This view argues that most deaf students come to school without a first language, while ESL students have a first language and are learning an additional language. Most American deaf students have to learn two languages when they enter school—English and ASL.

Those educators who are familiar with both second language research and deaf education make a distinction between deaf children of hearing parents who speak a language other than English and those from families who speak English. Additionally, if a deaf child was born outside of the United States, on an Indian reservation, or in Puerto Rico, they would fit the federal description of children more likely to be LEP. Immigrant deaf children have had less exposure to English, either spoken or in print. They may have difficulty in the classroom due to lack of familiarity and experience with the English language, especially print, and they would be at a greater disadvantage than their deaf and hard-of-hearing classmates who have been exposed to English (visually or auditorially) their entire lives. However, as is the

---

[4] There is some confusion surrounding the meaning of the term English as a Second Language in deaf education. Those unfamiliar with the field of ESL interpret it to simply mean learning English after learning a first language, ASL. They may not be aware that there is ESL pedagogy and ESL is a field and a profession. Increasingly, the term ESOL, English for Speakers of Other Languages, is used when talking about hearing LEP students. However, the word "speakers" may not be a term to use to describe deaf learners. For many deaf immigrant children and adults, English will be their third or fourth language. Therefore, I use the term ESL and mean English as a second or additional language, as well as the related field and pedagogy.

case for hearing children, deaf children from families that speak a language other than English are not necessarily LEP unless they meet criteria established by the federal government.

Identification of deaf children from families that speak languages other than English is crucial in order to comply with IDEA, and federal laws requiring special services for LEP students. Schools should complete a Home Language Survey for each student entering school, and each school/district/jurisdiction may determine how the Home Language Survey will be conducted. It may be a written form completed by parents, or answers to a question or series of questions asked to parents at a student's intake that are recorded and kept on file. This survey is the first step to determining which students are LEP, information that must be taken into consideration when doing intake assessments, and deciding what services the student will receive. LEP deaf students are those who lack knowledge of U.S. culture and English to the extent that they will have difficulty learning in classes with their deaf peers and should receive instruction that addresses these gaps. This specialized instruction may include ESL, instruction in ASL (or the sign language used in the school), and/or adapted content instruction.

LIMITATIONS OF FORMAL ASSESSMENTS

The purpose of assessment should be to provide information about what the student is capable of doing and how the student learns (learning style and preferences, as well as rate of learning). Assessment should not focus on deficits and what the child cannot do and does not know. In addition to standardized assessments, naturalistic or dynamic assessments should be part of the evaluation of deaf children, particularly those from culturally diverse backgrounds. Naturalistic or ethnographic assessment methods (Cheng, 1987, Christensen, 1993) include observations by teachers and specialists in the classroom, the school environment, the home, and the community. Naturalistic assessment allows the evaluator to observe and document how the child uses communication in various contexts and settings, and how the child uses language to learn, grow, and experience the world.

Culturally diverse and immigrant children may not have experience with formal testing situations (Erickson *et al.,* 1983). Some immigrant children may have had little or no formal education and in these cases formal testing is unlikely to yield much information. Ethnographic, naturalistic, and dynamic assessments are more appropriate.

Most standardized tests present information that is decontextualized or context-reduced. This makes testing tasks more difficult for children who depend on contextualized information in order to access the knowledge that they have. Decontextualized tasks can be very unfair tests for children who are culturally different and bring different backgrounds to the situation (Cheng, 1987). Furthermore, evaluators who do not share the culture of the child may not be able to adequately interpret his or her performance. The evaluator may have difficulty judging when a test item is confusing or unclear because it is culturally unfamiliar to the child. If the evaluator is not trilingual and/or bicultural or assisted by someone who is, the results of the evaluation are likely to be biased (Cummins, 1984; Erickson *et al.,* 1983; Figeroa *et al.,* 1984).

When using standardized Spanish language instruments, it is important to take dialectical differences into consideration. Many tests used in the United States are designed with specific Spanish-speaking populations in mind, such as Mexican American or Puerto Rican. Dialects of Spanish vary from country to country. The word for terms such as mommy, baby, ball, car, and other vocabulary used in everyday life can vary widely from country to country. Recent immigrants and children who have not been exposed to varieties of Spanish other than the dialect used in their home, such as younger children who have not been to preschool, are least likely to know standard terms. Word lists providing alternative terms can be created for use by Spanish-speaking evaluators with specific tests. The evaluator chooses the term the child is expected to understand, substituting another if the child does not respond.

Many instruments widely available in English have been translated into Spanish. However, the quality of translation varies (Erickson & Omark, 1981; Gelatt & Anderson, 1983). While the English versions usually have norms available, they are often not available for the Spanish versions. Even if Spanish norms are available, they do not apply to children who are deaf. Deaf norms for certain instruments may also not be applicable because they do not apply to children who are from racially and culturally diverse backgrounds. The WISC-R (Wechsler Intelligence Scale for Children-Revised) has been replaced by the WISC III (1991) which is one of the most commonly used psychological tests for deaf children. The WISC-R (1974) did have deaf norms but as they were developed in 1977, they are not considered to apply today. The Center for Assessment and Demographic Studies at Gallaudet is in the process of developing deaf norms for WISC III (Traxler, 1997). There is a Spanish language version, dating back to 1983, although there are no norms that apply to deaf children (Educational Testing Service, 1993).

A Team Approach to Assessment

Schools use standardized instruments to assess Hispanic/Latino deaf children, despite the limitations of such tests, when intaking students, as well as for schoolwide testing. In order to expedite initial evaluations and to determine student progress from year to year, schools often need to use closed-ended instruments.

Trilingual personnel must be part of the team for individual assessments that occur at the initial and triennial evaluations. The lack of Spanish-speaking professionals in deaf education can make this more difficult. Schools and programs for the deaf should learn about community resources and establish liaisons in order to ensure that Hispanic/ Latino deaf children receive the most appropriate assessments.

Spanish-speaking professionals in related fields are valuable contacts who can help identify deaf children who may not be appropriately placed or served. Spanish-speaking audiologists and bilingual speech and language pathologists may come in contact with deaf and hard-of-hearing children who have not been formally identified. Sometimes these children have been placed in bilingual or bilingual special education programs, where they do not receive the services that they need as deaf or hard-of-hearing students.

Psychological evaluation of Spanish-dominant deaf and hard-of-hearing children requires a psychologist who is experienced in testing deaf children. Often the choice is to have a child evaluated by a psychologist fluent in Spanish and experienced in testing Hispanic/Latino students or a psychologist trained in deafness. Although often only nonverbal sections of psychological tests are administered to deaf students, skills in using visual–gestural communication[5] are essential when evaluating children who do not know Sign Language (ASL or the system used in the school), or oral Spanish may be required to test the child. The psychologist can work with a trilingual interpreter, a trilingual teacher, or, if trilingual personnel are not available, a Spanish language interpreter. Because some Spanish language psychological tests may not be appropriate for deaf children, the need for collaboration between bilingual psychologists and psychologists trained in deafness is important.

Language Assessment Instruments

The Rhode Island Test of Language Comprehension has been translated and adapted for use with Spanish-dominant deaf children but has not been published (Santiviago, n.d.). This test consists of 100 items—50 simple sentences and 50 complex sentences—that test the receptive comprehension of a variety of grammatical structures in

---

[5] Nonverbal communication through gestures without reliance on a lexicon of ASL or other sign language.

Spanish. It can be used with Hispanic/Latino deaf children who are five to six years old and older with receptive language at the sentence level. There are deaf norms available for the English version of the test but no norms for the Spanish version. This test can be used with children who are Spanish-dominant and know ASL (or the sign system used in the school) to measure the child's receptive language in the stronger language. Used this way, it is assumed that the child requires Spanish to maximize comprehension.

If a child is trilingual, this test can be administered orally without the use of sign language to determine the extent of the child's knowledge of spoken Spanish. This is most appropriate for children who use spoken Spanish at home with their families, or know no sign or English. The results will indicate to what extent the child understands simple and complex sentences in oral Spanish.

The Rhode Island Expressive Language Test consists of 50 pictures that are shown to the child to elicit language. The elicited language is evaluated for the range of vocabulary, sentence structure, and length of utterance. However, a testing situation may not elicit a child's true capabilities. If this test is used in a school or program to evaluate deaf students, it can be used for limited and cautious comparison of Spanish-dominant deaf students with deaf peers.

PROGRAMMATIC CONSIDERATIONS

Once assessment is completed, placement and program recommendations must be made. The first decision that must be made is whether placement in a school or program for deaf and hard-of-hearing or a bilingual program for hearing students is most appropriate. This determination should depend on the resources available in each setting. It should not be assumed that hard-of-hearing students can function equally well in either setting.

The notion of least restrictive environment has been debated in the field of deafness, with greater focus since the 1988 Commission on

Education of the Deaf report *Toward Equality.* Mainstreaming has been considered less restrictive than substantially separate education for all disabled children. However, in the case of deaf children, it has been argued that access to communication and a deaf peer group are essential elements.

All of the limitations and problems that exist for deaf students placed in mainstreamed classrooms exist for a deaf or hard-of-hearing Hispanic/Latino student placed in a bilingual (Spanish/English) class-room or bilingual special education class. Because communication is oral, the student misses a great deal, if not most, of the classroom in-teraction. Students I have observed in such settings did not have in-terpreters or accommodations except for amplification systems. Their teachers were not oriented to deafness, and had been led to believe that the deaf or hard-of-hearing student using amplification could function in the classroom without additional support.

Failure in such a situation is likely when the student is not pro-vided with the support and accommodations needed. Sometimes the student, who does not know English or Sign Language, is main-streamed into a classroom with an interpreter. In this situation, the student cannot understand the teacher or the interpreter, and is un-likely to progress.

ENGLISH AS A SECOND LANGUAGE FOR DEAF LEP STUDENTS

Immigrant deaf students who require ESL services are sometimes re-ferred to the regular ESL program. The ESL teacher, often with a heavy student load, does not know what to do with a deaf student. These referrals may be made because the student's language needs are seen as beyond the realm of deaf education, or in an attempt to meet legal requirements for LEP services. However, it is unlikely that the needs of LEP deaf students can be met in regular ESL programs, even with a sign language interpreter. Instruction in a class for hearing ESL

students includes emphasis on the development of auditory comprehension and oral production of English. This emphasis is most
intensive at the elementary grade levels and would not meet the
English language learning needs of most deaf and hard-of-hearing
students.

Unfortunately, there are very few teachers of the deaf who are
trained in ESL methods. When (and if) immigrant deaf students receive ESL support, the support provided may be minimal and from an
untrained teacher. In this situation, which unfortunately dominates
deaf education, immigrant students are left to learn English and ASL,
Signed English, or the sign system their school uses through submersion. Submersion is described by Nieto (1992) as "sink or swim"
approach to educating children whose first language does not match
the language of the school. In the United States this would mean a totally English language environment. In schools and programs for the
deaf, ASL or a form of Signed English would usually be used, as well
as English, without any use of the children's native language(s) for
instruction.

Another obstacle immigrant deaf students face is a lack of awareness on the part of teachers of the difference between social language
and academic language. Basic interpersonal communication skills
(BICS), or social language skills, develop more rapidly than cognitive
academic language proficiency skills (CALPS) or academic language
skills (Cummins,1984). The age that the immigrant student enters
U.S. schools is also crucial and students entering high school are faced
with more cognitively demanding academic language (Brisk, 1998).

Immigrant deaf students may quickly learn the ASL they need for
interacting with their peers. However, just as hearing children learning English, the ability to use ASL or Sign Language in face-to-face
conversation does not mean that the student is able to use ASL or Sign
Language for academic tasks. Learning to use language for academic
purposes is a much longer process than learning to use a language for
social interaction. While conversational skills develop rapidly (two
years or so to become fluent), academic language takes from five to
seven years or more to fully develop (Collier, 1989; Krashen, 1996).

In schools and programs for deaf students that use manual or visual–spatial language, instruction in classrooms may be done primarily "through the air" with the teacher signing ASL or a form of manual English and using written English. In some settings, the teachers speak English while trying to simultaneously sign what they are saying. However, in both situations, immigrant students are depending on the input of two languages they do not know. They do not know the visual–spatial language (ASL or the Manual English system) or English (presented orally and/or in written form). Because they do not understand the written English used in the classroom and are unable to read their textbooks, homework assignments, or the written English presented by the teachers, these students fail. They are failing because they are being taught in languages they do not know. Their failure may then be used as continued justification for their placement in the lowest functioning groups.

Teachers of the deaf who provide ESL to LEP deaf students are exploring new territory (see Gerner de García, 1995b). A few pioneers teaching ESL to deaf immigrant students have made tremendous efforts to educate themselves by studying bilingual/ESL education in addition to deaf education. They have few models to follow (for a description of a university level ESL program for deaf students see Cordero-Martinez, 1995). There are not many materials designed for deaf LEP students available, although many of the commercially available ESL materials can be used with deaf students or can be adapted. However, without an appropriate background in both deaf education and ESL/bilingual education theories and pedagogies for K–12 students, most teachers are not adequately prepared to educate LEP deaf students.

IMMIGRANT STUDENTS WITH LIMITED SCHOOLING

Some immigrant Hispanic children come to U.S. schools with only the most basic alphabet and number skills. Although they may have attended school in their home countries, the school curriculum was not fully accessible to them because of their deafness. Many schools in Latin America and the Caribbean still adhere to an oral philosophy and use of sign language is minimal or sporadic.[6] In U.S. schools, special programs are needed to adequately service older immigrant deaf students with limited literacy. An 8-year-old immigrant deaf student could be placed in a 1st-grade class, but what should be done with an 11-year-old or an 18-year-old who does not read?

Too often, immigrant deaf students are placed with the lower functioning deaf students, who often have multiple disabilities. Placement in classes for multiply disabled students is a result of seeing the language differences of the immigrant Hispanic/Latino deaf students as a disability. Rather than providing special programs for the LEP students, they are placed in these classes. However, in these classes, the immigrant deaf students have limited exposure to age-appropriate peer language, desirable school behaviors, or stimulating curriculum. Teachers and administrators may justify these placements by saying that the newly arrived students would find the regular program frustrating because they do not have adequate knowledge of ASL and English. However, it may be the teachers who are avoiding frustration, because they are unprepared to deal with the needs of immigrant deaf students.

Separate classes for multiply disabled deaf students are a form of special education within deaf education. The placement of LEP deaf students in these classes, regardless of the rationalization of such placements, is inappropriate and may be illegal. If these students are LEP, under federal law they should receive specialized instruction (described previously). If they do not have additional disabilities, their placement in classes with multiply disabled deaf students could be legally challenged. These students are unlikely to make satisfactory progress or reach their maximum potential. The school has failed to

---

[6] A number of Latin American countries such as Venezuela, Uruguay, Argentina, Chile, and Columbia have instituted bilingual programs for the deaf, using the Sign Language of the local Deaf Community and written Spanish (Claros-Karchner, 1997).

provide the appropriate programs to develop ASL and teach English as a Second Language, which the student needs in order to learn alongside his/her peers.

STUDENTS WITH SPANISH LITERACY

How can schools and programs for deaf students best serve Hispanic/Latino students who read and write in Spanish? As previously stated, students with basic literacy skills in Spanish often may be reading below their age and grade level. Most deaf students read at levels significantly lower than their grade level, yet some teachers seem to expect deaf students who read Spanish to be at or near grade level. Whether deaf students are learning to read English, Spanish, or any other language, they find learning to read challenging.

It is also important to recognize that students who have not become literate in Spanish are unlikely to become skilled readers in English. It may be important to continue to develop reading skills in Spanish until the student knows how to read. Once someone knows how to read, he or she does not have to learn to read again when learning a new language. The reading skills transfer to the new language. It can be difficult to define what "knowing how to read" means for a deaf student. However, a Hispanic/Latino student who is still reading below a 3rd-grade level should be considered for continued literacy development in Spanish.

A LITERATURE-BASED APPROACH

Whole language strategies and thematic teaching are excellent approaches to use with deaf students (Perspectives, 1991) and may be particularly successful with Hispanic/Latino deaf students, including newly arrived immigrant students. These methods are widely used in bilingual and ESL classrooms (Crawford, 1993; Heard-Taylor, 1989; Hudelson, 1989; Peregoy & Boyle, 1993). Books that describe the use of children's literature written in Spanish include *A Magical Encounter* (Ada, 1990), *Experiences with Literature: A Thematic Whole Language Model for the K–3 Bilingual Classroom* (Nevárez et al., 1990), and *Contemporary Spanish-Speaking Writers and Illustrators for Children and Young Adults: A Biographical Dictionary,* (Schon, 1994).

Using children's literature brings beautiful picture books into the classroom. When teachers make these books available to their students, the students feel special. Picture books appeal to all ages and should not be limited to Pre-K to 3rd-grade students. Initially, older students may see them as "kids books" but there are creative ways that teachers can engage older learners in these books (see Benedict & Carlisle, 1992).

Teachers also find it more motivating to work with children's literature. Teaching thematic units is very rewarding. While it may seem difficult to teach using units when you see students only one or two periods a day (as may be the case when providing ESL or bilingual reading services), teaching thematically provides more continuity for both students and teachers. Whole language strategies and thematic teaching can be extremely productive for all ESL teachers, including teachers of deaf and hard-of-hearing students who are learning ASL and English.

When using a literature-based approach with students who are deaf, reading for discovery, for pleasure, and for the joy of the story should be emphasized. There should be a reduced emphasis on the mechanics of reading, which a traditional basal reader may stress. Furthermore, the use of multicultural children's literature makes it possible to bring in the experiences and the stories that are more meaningful to Hispanic/Latino deaf students.

If bilingual literacy is the goal, children's literature in Spanish is increasingly available. Students who are dominant in English can be introduced to familiar stories and books in Spanish language editions. Students who are biliterate can be given both the Spanish and the English version of a story or book and read the version they prefer.

Finally, teachers should take care to evaluate carefully books that they choose to use with Hispanic/Latino themes to make sure that the books do not perpetuate stereotypes about the cultures they claim to portray. In a case study of Puerto Ricans in children's literature, Nieto (1993) describes the invisibility of Puerto Ricans, negative views of the use of Spanish, and the reliance on stereotypes. A study of the portrayal of Mexican American girls and women in books written for early elementary grades found while the use of stereotypes had decreased since the 1970s, there was still a lack of "authentic representation" of Mexican American females (Rochoa & Dowd, 1993, p. 63). The Council on Interracial Books for Children (1994) has produced a guide called "Ten Quick Ways to Analyze Children's Books for Racism and Sexism," which is a good starting point for teachers evaluating materials.

CONCLUSION

Educational outcomes for Hispanic/Latino deaf students will not improve until educators of the deaf recognize the unique needs of this population. Rather than viewing the education of Hispanic/Latino deaf students as problematic, educators must consider how to retool themselves to meet the challenges. Educators cannot afford to allow these students to fail. With the rapid growth of the Hispanic/Latino deaf population, commitment to these students cannot remain the work of the small number of Hispanic/Latino professionals in the field.

Educators must make the effort to learn more about the communities of their Hispanic/Latino students. Educators must recognize the tremendous diversity in the Hispanic/Latino population and understand the ethnic backgrounds of their students. In addition to learning some basic Spanish, educators should learn about the history of Latinos in the United States, as well as the broader history and cultures of Latin America. They should do this not only through formal means, such as reading books and taking courses and workshops, but through direct interaction with the parents of their students and with their communities. Latino festivals, theater productions, exhibits, and conferences provide direct experience and are a meaningful way of connecting to our students' lives and enriching our own knowledge base (Gerner de García & Leone, 1997).

Teacher education programs should prepare students in deaf education to work with a widely diverse student population. While CED standards require a multicultural education course or curricular infusion of multicultural concepts (Christensen, 1993), this is clearly not enough to meet the complex needs of many Hispanic/Latino deaf students. In 1992, the state of California adopted a new system of credentialing that prepares teachers to work with linguistically and culturally diverse students known as the CLAD (Cross-Cultural Language and Academic Development) and BCLAD (Bilingual Cross-Cultural Language and Academic Development). Knowledge is developed in areas including first and second language acquisition, bilingual and ESL pedagogies, culture and learning, language, and literacy in the primary language (Barreto, 1997). Teachers of the deaf would benefit from developing this knowledge base (Gerner de García, 1997b).

The educational, as well as social–emotional needs of Hispanic/Latino deaf students will be better met when all educators of the deaf recognize that we are *all* responsible for *all* our students. Each of us can begin to accept that responsibility by trying to become more culturally competent teachers. We must continue to expand our knowledge base—adding information about new cultures, learning a new language, becoming more skilled in ASL, involving ourselves in the diverse Deaf Community and the communities of our students and our families. There are no simple answers or ready-made curricula that will meet the diverse needs of the students we will face. However, the greatest resource we have may be ourselves and our willingness to teach anyone who comes to our door. That is what makes a true teacher, and above all, a teacher who is prepared to meet the needs of Hispanic/Latino deaf students.

REFERENCES

Allen, T. E. (1986). Patterns of academic achievement among hearing impaired students: 1974–1983. In A. Schildroth & M. Karchmer (Eds.), *Deaf children in America.* San Diego: College Hill.

Andrews, J. F., & Jordan, D.L. (1993). Minority and minority-deaf professionals: How many and where are they? *American Annals of the Deaf,* **138**(5), 388–396.

Anstrom, K. (1996). *Defining the limited-English proficient student population: Directions in language and education.* National Clearinghouse for Bilingual Education (Vol. 1, No. 9). Internet WWW page at <http:www.ncbe.gwu.edu/ncbepubs/directions/09.htm> (version current January 2000).

Arias, M. B., & Casanova, U. (1993). Contextualizing bilingual education. In M. B. Arias & U. Casanova (Eds.), *Bilingual education: Politics, practice, research.* (pp.1–35). Chicago: University of Chicago Press.

Baca, L.M. (1990). Theory and practice in bilingual/cross cultural special education: Major issues and implications for research, practice, and policy. In *Proceedings of the First Research Symposium on Limited English Proficient Students' Issues* (U.S. GPO: 1991-306-379-50546, pp. 247–280). Washington, DC: Government Printing Office.

Baker, C. (1993). *Foundations of bilingual education and bilingualism.* Philadelphia: Multilingual Matters.

Barreto, R.M. (1997). Reform in teacher education through the CLAD/BCLAD policy. *Multicultural Education, 5*(2), 11–15.

Benedict, S., & Carlisle, L. (1992). *Beyond words: Picture books for older readers and writers.* Portsmouth, NH: Heinemann.

Bennett, A. (1988). Gateway to powerlessness: Incorporating Hispanic deaf children and families into formal schooling. *Disability and Society,* **3** 119–151.

Bennett, A. (1987). *Schooling the different: Ethnographic case studies of Hispanic deaf children's initiation into formal schooling.* Final report to the Office of Special Education and Rehabilitation. Washington, DC: U.S. Department of Education.

Blackwell, P., & Fischgrund, J. (1984). Issues in the development of culturally responsive programs for deaf students from non-English speaking homes. In G.L. Delgado (Ed.), *The Hispanic deaf: Issues and challenges for bilingual special education* (pp. 154–166). Washington, DC: Gallaudet College Press.

Brisk, M. E. (1998). *Bilingual education: From compensatory to quality schooling.* Mahwah, NJ: Erlbaum.

Campbell, D. E. (1996). *Choosing democracy: A practical guide to multicultural education.* Englewood Cliffs, NJ: Prentice Hall.

CEASD (Conference of Educational Administrators Serving the Deaf) (1989). *National survey of teachers of the deaf.* Unpublished paper, Gallaudet University, Washington, DC.

Center for Assessment and Demographic Studies (1997). *Annual survey of deaf and hard of hearing children and youth.* Unpublished raw data, Gallaudet University, Washington, DC.

Center for Assessment and Demographic Studies (1989). *Annual survey of hearing-impaired children and youth.* Washington, DC: Gallaudet College.

Cheng, L. (1987). *Assessing Asian language performance: Guidelines for evaluating limited-English proficient students.* Rockville, MD: Aspen.

Claros-Kartchner, R. (1997). *Deaf education in Hispanic America: A historical analysis of theory and practice.* Unpublished manuscript, University of Arizona.

Christensen, K.M. (1993). Looking forward to a multicultural commitment. In K.M. Christensen & G.L. Delgado (Eds.), *Multicultural issues in deafness* (pp. 179–183). White Plains, NY: Longman.

Cohen, O. (1987, March). *Current and future needs of minority hearing impaired children and youth.* Testimony before the Commission on the Education of the Deaf.

Cohen, O., Fischgrund, J., & Redding, R. (1990). Deaf children from ethnic, linguistic, and racial minority backgrounds: An overview. *American Annals of the Deaf, 135,* 67–73.

Collier, V.P. (1989). How long? A synthesis of research on academic achievement in second language. *TESOL Quarterly,* **23,** 509–531.

Commission on Education of the Deaf (1988). *Toward equality: Education of the deaf.* Report to the President and Congress of the United States.

Cordero-Martinez, F. (1995). A visual–spatial approach to ESL in a bilingual program with deaf international students. *Bilingual Research Journal,* **19**(3 & 4), 469–482.

Council on Interracial Books. (1994). Ten quick ways to analyze children's books for racism and sexism. *Rethinking our classrooms: Teaching for equity and justice* (pp. 14–15). Milwaukee, WI: Rethinking Schools.

Crawford, J. (1992). *Hold your tongue: Bilingualism and the politics of "English Only".* Reading, MA: Addison-Wesley.

Crawford, L.W. (1993). *Language and literacy learning in multicultural classrooms.* Needham Heights, MA: Allyn & Bacon.

Cummins, J. (1989). *Empowering minority students.* Sacramento, CA: California Association for Bilingual Education.

Cummins, J. (1984). *Bilingualism and special education: Issues in assessment and pedagogy.* San Diego: College Hill.

de Varona, F. (1996). *Latino literacy: The complete guide to our Hispanic history and culture.* New York: Henry Holt.

Delgado, G.L. (1984a). *The Hispanic deaf: Issues and challenges for bilingual special education.* Washington, DC: Gallaudet College Press.

Delgado, G.L. (1984b). Hearing-impaired children from non-native-language homes. In G. L. Delgado (Ed.) *The Hispanic deaf: Issues and challenges for bilingual special education* (pp. 28–37). Washington, DC: Gallaudet College Press.

Diaz Soto, L. (1997). *Language, culture and power: Bilingual families and the struggle for quality education.* Albany, NY: State University of New York.

Donato, R. (1997). *The other struggle for equal schools: Mexican Americans during the Civil Rights era.* Albany, NY: State University of New York.

Educational Testing Service (1993). *Escala de Inteligencia Wechsler para Ninos: Wechsler-David.* ERIC Clearinghouse on Assessment and Evaluation-Test Locator. Internet page at URL <http://ericae.net/tc2/tc000415.htm> (version current January 2000).

Erickson, J. D., Anderson, M. P., & Fischgrund, J. (1983). *Bilingual language learning system.* Rockville, MD: American Speech and Language Association.

Erickson, J. D., & Omark, D. R. (1981). *Communication assessment of the bilingual bicultural child.* Baltimore, MD: University Park Press.

Ferguson, J. (1992). *Dominican Republic: Beyond the lighthouse.* London: Latin American Bureau.

Figueroa, R., Delgado, G., & Ruiz, N. (1984). Assessment of Hispanic children: Implications for Hispanic hearing-impaired children. In G.L. Delgado (Ed.), *The Hispanic deaf.* Washington, DC: Gallaudet College Press.

Gallaudet University (1996). *Hispanic/Latino Task Force.* Unpublished notes, Gallaudet University, Washington, DC.

García, E. E. (1995). Educating Mexican American students: Theory, research, policy, and practice. In J. A. Banks (Ed.) & C.A. McGee Banks (Assoc. Ed.), *Handbook of research on multicultural education* (pp. 372–387). New York: Macmillan.

Gelatt, J., & Anderson, M.P. (Eds.) (1983). *Bilingual language learning system.* Rockville, MD: American Speech and Language Association.

Gerner de García, B.A. (1998). Lenguaje e identidad: El latino sordo en los Estados Unidos. *El Bilingüismo de los Sordos.* 1(3). Bogota, Colombia.

Gerner de García, B.A. (1997a). *Project THREADS (Transformations for Humanistic and Responsive Education for All Deaf Students).* Unpublished raw data, Special Projects for Preparation of Personnel for Careers in Special Education (84.029k).

Gerner de García, B.A. (1997b) Multicultural education applications for teachers of the deaf: Creating culturally responsive curriculum. In J. Egelston-Dodd (Ed.), *Monograph of Collected Papers from the 23rd Annual Conference, Association of College Educators Deaf and Hard of Hearing* (pp. 46–54). Rochester, NY: National Technical Institute of the Deaf.

Gerner de García, B. A. (1995a). Communication and language use in Spanish-speaking families with deaf children. In C. Lucas (Ed.), *Sociolinguistics in deaf communities* (Vol. 1). Washington, DC: Gallaudet University.

Gerner de García, B. A. (1995b). ESL applications for Hispanic deaf students. *Bilingual Research Journal, 19*(3&4), 452–467.

Gerner de García, B.A. (1993). Language use in Spanish-speaking families with deaf children. Doctoral dissertation, Boston University, 1993. *Dissertation Abstracts International, 53,* 12-A, order No. GAX93-17684.

Gerner de García, B., & Leone, B. (1997, February/March). Multicultural education: Getting started with self-education. *TESOL Matters, 7*(1).

Heard-Taylor, G. (1990). *Whole language strategies for ESL students.* San Diego, CA: Dormac.

Humphries, T. Deaf culture and cultures. In K.M. Christensen & G.L. Delgado (Eds.) *Multicultural issues in deafness* (pp. 3–15). White Plains, NY: Longman.

Jensema, C. (1975). *The relationship between academic achievement and the demographic characteristics of hearing impaired youth.* Office of Demographic Studies. Washington, DC: Gallaudet College.

Johnson, R.E., Lidell, S., & Erting, C. (1989). *Unlocking the curriculum: Principles for achieving access in deaf education* (Gallaudet Research Institute Working Paper 89-3). Washington, DC: Gallaudet University.

Kluwin, T. N. (1994). The interaction of race, gender, and social class effects in the education of deaf students. *American Annals of the Deaf,* **139**(5), 465–471.

Kopp, H.G. (1984). Bilingual problems of the Hispanic deaf. In G. L. Delgado (Ed.), *The Hispanic deaf: Issues and challenges for bilingual special education* (pp. 69–78). Washington, DC: Gallaudet College Press.

Krashen, S.D. (1996). *Under attack: The case against bilingual education.* Culver City, CA: Language Education Associates.

Lane, H., Hoffmeister, R., & Bahan, B. (1996). *A journey into the deaf-world.* San Diego, CA: Dawn Sign.

Lerman, A. (1984). In G. L. Delgado (Ed.), *The Hispanic deaf: Issues and challenges for bilingual special education* (pp. 38–56). Washington, DC: Gallaudet College Press.

Lerman, A., & Vilá, C. (1984). A model for school services to Hispanic hearing-impaired students and their families. In G.L. Delgado (Ed.) *The Hispanic deaf: Issues and challenges for bilingual special education* (pp. 167–179). Washington, DC: Gallaudet College Press.

Livingston, S. (1997). *Rethinking the education of deaf students: Theory and practice from a teacher's perspective.* Portsmouth, NH: Heinemann.

López, R.V. (1995, September). Bilingual education: Separating facts from fiction. *NABE Report.* Washington, DC: National Association of Bilingual Education.

Luetke-Stahlman, B., & Weiner, F. (1984). Language and/or system assessment for Spanish/Deaf preschoolers. In G.L. Delgado (Ed.), *The Hispanic deaf: Issues and challenges for bilingual special education* (pp.106–121). Washington, DC: Gallaudet College Press.

Lyons, J.J. (n.d.) *Legal responsibilities of educational agencies serving national origin language minority students* (National Origin Desegregation Assistance Technical Series). Washington, DC: The Mid-Atlantic Equity Center.

Maher, J. (1996). *Seeing language in signs: The work of William Stokoe.* Washington, DC: Gallaudet University Press.

Meier, K. J., & Stewart, J. (1991). *The politics of Hispanic education: Un paso pa 'lante.* Albany, NY: State University of New York Press.

Nevárez, S., Mireles, R., & Ramírez, N. (1990). *Experiences with literature: A thematic whole language model for the K–3 bilingual classroom.* Reading, MA: Addison-Wesley.

Nieto, S. (1996). *Affirming diversity: The sociopolitical context of multicultural education* (2nd ed.). White Plains, NY: Longman.

Nieto, S. (1995). A history of the education of Puerto Rican students in U.S. mainland schools: "Losers," "outsiders," or "leader"? In J. A. Banks (Ed.) & C.A. McGee Banks (Assoc. Ed.), *Handbook of research on multicultural education* (pp. 388–411). New York: Macmillan.

Nieto, S. (1993). We have stories to tell: A case study of Puerto Ricans in children's books. In V.J. Harris (Ed.), *Teaching multicultural literature in grades K–8* (pp. 171–201). Norwood, MA: Christopher Gordon.

Novas, H. (1994). *Everything you need to know about Latino history.* New York: Penguin.

Ohrn, D. G. (1995). Rigoberta Menchu. In R. Ashby & D. G. Ohrn (Eds.), *Herstory: Women who changed the world.* (pp. 291–293). New York: Viking.

Perspectives in education and deafness (1991). *Whole language— A folio of articles.* Washington, DC: Precollege Programs Outreach Services, Gallaudet University.

Rochoa, O.J., & Dowd, F. S. (1993). Are Mexican-American females portrayed realistically in fiction for grades K–3?: A content analysis. *Multicultural Review, 2*(4), 60–69.

Rodriquez, C.E. (1989). *Puerto Ricans: Born in the U.S.A.* New York: Unwin Hyman.

Ruiz, R. (1990). Official languages and language planning. In K. Adams & D. Brink (Eds.), *Perspectives on official English*. Berlin: Mouton de Gruyter.

Ruiz, R., & Nover, S. (1992). ASL and language planning in deaf education. In D.S. Martin & R.T. Mobley (Eds.), *Proceedings of the First International Symposium on Teacher Education in Deafness* (pp. 153–171). Washington, DC: Gallaudet University.

Santiviago, M.I. (n.d.) *The Rhode Island Test of Language Comprehension: Spanish version*. Unpublished manuscript, Rhode Island School for the Deaf.

Sass-Lehrer, M., Gerner de García, B.A., & Rovins, M. (1997). *Creating multicultural environments for deaf children and their families* (Sharing Ideas Series). Washington, DC: Gallaudet University Pre-College National Mission Programs.

Scarcella, R. (1990). *Teaching language minority students in the multicultural classroom*. Englewood Cliffs, NJ: Prentice Hall.

Schaller, S. (1991). *A man without words*. New York: Summitt.

Schildroth, A.N., & Hotto, S.A. (1995). Race and ethnic background in the Annual Survey of Deaf and Hard of Hearing Children and Youth. *American Annals of the Deaf,* 140(2), 96–99.

Schon, I. (Ed.) (1994). *Contemporary Spanish-speaking writers and illustrators for children and young adults: A biographical dictionary.* Westport, CT: Greenwood.

Schon, I. (1993). Good and bad books about Hispanic people and culture for young readers. *Multicultural Review,* 2(1), 28–31.

Schon, I. (1980–1991). *A Hispanic heritage: A guide to juvenile books about Hispanic people and cultures* (Series I–IV). Metuchen, NJ: Scarecrow Press.

Suarez-Orozco, M. M. (1987). Towards a psychosocial understanding of Hispanic adaptation to American schooling. In H. T. Trueba (Ed.), *Success or failure: Learning and the language minority student* (pp.156–168). Cambridge, MA: Newbury House.

Szulc, T. (1965). *Dominican diary.* New York: Dell.

Takaki, R. (1993). *A different mirror: A history of multicultural America.* Boston: Little, Brown.

Traxler, Carol. *Carol Traxler's Assessment Page.* Internet WWW page at URL <http://gri.gallaudet.edu/~catraxle/INTELLEC.HTM# wechsler> (version current January 2000).

Trueba, H. (1989). *Raising silent voices: Educating the linguistic minorities for the 21st century.* Cambridge, MA: Newbury House.

Walsh, C.E. (1991). *Pedagogy and the struggle for voice: Issues of language, power, and schooling for Puerto Ricans.* New York: Bergin & Garvey.

Winn, P. (1992). *Americans: The changing face of Latin America and the Caribbean.* New York: Pantheon.

READINGS AND RESOURCES

While this section divides books into professional and student resources, many listings are suitable for both. Grade levels are based on interest level as well as the reading level of most deaf students in those grades. Notations are added when the title does not clearly indicate a specific focus on group or region.

SUGGESTED READINGS FOR PROFESSIONALS

Culture and History

Alvarez, J. (1994). *In the time of the butterflies.* Chapel Hill, NC: Algonquin Books. (fiction, Dominican history, women)

Anaya, R. (1972). *Bless me Ultima.* New York: Time Warner. (fiction by the "father of Chicano literature," New Mexico)

Augenbraum, H., & Stavans, I. (Eds.) (1993). *Growing up Latino, Memoirs and stories: Reflections on life in the United States.* Boston: Houghton Mifflin.

de Varona, F. (1996). *Latino literacy: The complete guide to our Hispanic history and culture.* New York: Henry Holt.

Meier, M.S., & Ribera, F. (1993). *Mexican Americans/American Mexicans: From conquistadors to Chicanos.* New York: Hill & Wang.

Novas, H. (1994). *Everything you need to know about Latino history.* New York: Penguin.

Olmos, James Edward *et.al.,* (1999). *Americanos: Latino life in the United States.* Boston, MA: Little Brown.

Rivera, E. (1982). *Family installments: Memories of growing up Hispanic.* New York: Penguin.

Rodriques, L.J. (1993). *Always running, la vida loca: Gang days in L.A.* New York: Simon & Schuster.

Santiago, R. (Ed.) (1995). *Boricuas: Influential Puerto Rican writings: An anthology.* New York: Ballantine.

Santiago, E. (1993). *When I was Puerto Rican.* New York: Vintage.

Shorris, E. (1992). *Latinos: Biography of the people.* New York: Norton.

Stavans, I. (1995). *The Hispanic condition: Reflections of culture and identity in America.* New York: Harper.

Suro, Roberto (1999). *Strangers Among Us: Latino lives in a changing America.* New York: Vintage.

Bilingual Special Education

Baca, L., & Cervantes, H. (Eds.) (1998). *The bilingual special education interface* (3rd ed.). Columbus, OH: Charles E. Merrill.

Cummins, J. (1984). *Bilingualism and special education: Issues in assessment.* San Diego: College Hill.

Gonzalez, V., Brusca-Vega, R., & Yawkey, T. (1997). *Assessment and instruction of culturally and linguistically diverse students with or at risk of learning problems.* Needham Heights, MA: Allyn & Bacon.

Grossman, H. (1995). *Special education in a diverse society.* Needham Heights: Allyn & Bacon.

Winzer, M., & Mazurek, K. (1998). *Special education in multicultural contexts: From theory to practice.* Columbus, OH: Charles E. Merrill.

Bilingual Education and Language Diverse Students

Baker, C. (1993). *Foundations of bilingual education and bilingualism.* Clevedon, UK: Multilingual Matters.

Brisk, M.E. (1998). *Bilingual education: From compensatory to quality schooling.* Mahwah, NJ: Erlbaum.

Costigan, S., Muñoz, C., Porter, M., & Quintana, J. (1989). *El sabelotodo: The bilingual teacher's best friend.* Carmel, CA: Hampton Brown.

Crawford, J. (1995). *Bilingual education: History, politics, theory & practice.* (3rd edition). Los Angeles, CA: Bilingual Educational Services.

Cummins, J. (1989). *Empowering minority students.* San Diego: California Association for Bilingual Education.

Cummins, J., & Sayers, D. (1997). *Challenging cultural illiteracy through global learning networks* (Updated). New York: St. Martin's Press.

Darder, A. (1991). *Culture and power in the classroom: A critical foundation for bicultural education.* New York: Bergin & Garvey.

Darder, A. & Torres, R. (Eds.) (1996). *Latinos and Education: A critical reader.* New York: Routlege.

Genesee, F. (Ed.) (1994). *Educating second language children: The whole child, the whole curriculum, the whole community.* New York: Cambridge University Press.

Tinajero, J.V., & Ada, A.F. (Eds.) (1993). *The power of two languages: Literacy and biliteracy for Spanish-speaking students.* New York: Macmillan/McGraw-Hill.

Literacy for Language Diverse Students

Ada, A.F. (1990). *A magical encounter: Spanish language children's literature in the classroom.* Compton, CA: Hampton Brown.

Crawford, L.W. (1993). *Language and literacy learning in multicultural classrooms.* Needham Heights, MA: Allyn & Bacon.

Day, F. A. (1994). *Multicultural voices in contemporary literature: A resource for teachers.* Portsmouth, NH: Heinemann.

Day, F.A. (1997). *Latino and Latina voices in literature.* Portsmouth, NH: Heinemann.

Faltis, C.J. (1997). *Joinfostering: Adapting teaching for the multilingual classroom.* Prentice Hall.

Freeman, Y.S., & Freeman, D. E. (1996). *Teaching reading and writing in Spanish in the bilingual classroom.* Portsmouth, NH: Heinemann.

Freeman, Y.S., & Freeman, D. E. (1994). *Between worlds: Access to second language acquisition.* Portsmouth, NH: Heinemann.

Gibbons, P. (1991). *Learning to learn in a second language.* Portsmouth, NH: Heinemann.

Harris, V. J. (Ed.) (1993). *Teaching multicultural literature in grades K–8.* Norwood, MA: Christopher Gordon.

Heard-Taylor, G. (1990). *Whole language strategies for ESL students.* San Diego, CA: Dormac.

Nevárez, S., Mireles, R., & Ramírez, N. (1990). *Experiences with literature: A thematic whole language model for the K–3 bilingual classroom.* Reading, MA: Addison-Wesley.

Schon, I. (Ed.) (1994). *Contemporary Spanish-Speaking Writers and Illustrators for Children and Young Adults: A Biographical Dictionary.* Westport, CT: Greenwood.

Schon, I. (1980–1991). *A Hispanic heritage: A guide to juvenile books about Hispanic people and culture I–IV.* Metuchen, NJ: Scarecrow Press.

Textbooks and Curricular Resources

Banks, J. A. (1997). *Teaching strategies for ethnic studies* (6th ed.). Needham Heights, MA: Allyn & Bacon.

Christiansen, P., & Young, M. (1996). *Yesterday, today & tomorrow: Meeting the challenge of our multicultural America & beyond.* San Francisco: Caddo Gap.

Delacre, L. (1990). *Las navidades: Popular Christmas songs from Latin America.* New York: Scholastic.

Hoobler, D & T. (1994). *The Mexican American family album.* New York: Oxford. (also available, *The Cuban American family album* (1996).

Martinez, E. (Ed.) (1991). *500 años del pueblo Chicano: 500 years of Chicano history in pictures.* Albuquerque, NM: Organizing Project.

National Latino Communications Center (1996). *¡ Chicano! The history of the Mexican American civil right movement—Teaching and resource guide.* Los Angeles: NLCC Educational Media.

Ramírez, G., & Ramírez, J.L. (1994). *Multiethnic children's literature.* Albany, NY: Delmar.

The people's voice: Cuba: Culture and history. Maywood, NJ: The People's Publishing Group and the Rochester City School District. (other titles, *The people's voice: Dominican Republic* and *The people's voice: Puerto Rico).*

Perez-Selles, M.E., & Barra-Zuman, N.C. (1990). *Building bridges of learning and understanding: A collection of classroom activities on Puerto Rican culture.* Andover, MA: The Regional Laboratory for Educational Improvement of the Northeast and Islands.

Rosales, F. A. (1997). *¡ Chicano! The history of the Mexican American civil right movement.* Houston, TX: Arte Publico Press.

Schwartz, L. (1994). *The Hispanic question collection.* Santa Barbara, CA: The Learning Works.

Sinnott, S. (1991). *Extraordinary Hispanic Americans.* Chicago: Children's Press.

Wilson, C., & Fleig, W. A. (1997). *Un paso al día: 180 daily brain teasers about Hispanic cultures.* Scott Foresman

Suggested Readings for Students

Ada, A.F. (1998). *Under the Royal Palms: A childhood in Cuba.* New York: Atheneum Books. (grades 6–8, nonfiction, Cuban American)

Ada, A.F. (1997). *Gathering in the Sun: An alphabet in Spanish and English.* New York: Lothrop, Lee, and Shepard. (grades 1–4, fiction, Migrant families)

Anaya, R. (1999). *Farolitos for Abuelo.* New York: Hyperion. (grades 1–4, fiction, New Mexico)

Anaya, R. (1987, 1995). *The farolitos of Christmas.* (grades 4–8, fiction, New Mexico)

Bunting, E. (1996). *Going home.* New York: Harper Collins. (grades 1–3, nonfiction, Migrant family)

Bunting, E. (1994). *A day's work.* New York: Clarion. (grades 1–3, nonfiction, Mexican American)

Dávalos, F. (1998). *The secret stars.* Tarrytown, NY: Marshall Cavendish. (grades 1–5, fiction, Three Kings Day in New Mexico)

Gonzales Bertrand, D. (1999). *Family, familia.* Houston, TX: Arte Publico Press. (grades 1–4, fiction, Mexican American)

Gordon, G. (1993). *My two worlds.* New York: Clarion. (grades 3–8, nonfiction, Dominican, New York)

Hoyt-Goldsmith, D. (1996). *Migrant worker: A boy from the Rio Grande valley.* New York: Holiday House. (grades 4–8, nonfiction, Texas)

Hoyt-Goldsmith, D. (1994). *Day of the Dead: A Mexican-American celebration.* New York: Holiday House. (grades 4–8, nonfiction, California)

King, E. (1999). *Quinceanera: Celebrating fifteen.* New York: Dutton. (grades 5–8, nonfiction)

López, T.A. (1993). *Growing up chicano/a: An anthology.* New York: William Morrow. (grades 9–12, nonfiction)

Mohr, N. (1986). *El Bronx remembered.* Houston: Arte Publico. (grades 7–12, fiction, Puerto Rican)

Mohr, N. (1986). *Going home.* New York: Bantam. (grades 6–8, fiction, Puerto Rican)

Mohr, N (1979, 1990). *Felita.* New York: Bantam. (grades 4–8, fiction, Puerto Rican)

Presilla, M. E. (1994). *Feliz nochebuena, feliz navidad: Christmas feasts of the Hispanic Caribbean.* New York: Henry Holt. (grades 4 and up, nonfiction)

Soto, G. (1997). *Snapshots from the wedding.* New York: Putnam. (grades 1–4, fiction, Mexican American)

Thomas, J.R. (1994). *Lights on the river.* New York: Hyperion. (grades 4–8, fiction, Mexican American, migrant farmworkers)

Westridge Young Writers Workshop (1992). *Kids explore America's Hispanic heritage.* Santa Fe, NM: John Muir. (grades 3–8, Mexican American focus, nonfiction)

Zapater, B. M (1992). *Three Kings' Day.* Cleveland, OH: Modern Curriculum. (grades 2–6, nonfiction, Puerto Rican)

Bilingual (English/Spanish) Books

Cisneros, S. (1994). *Hairs/Pelitos.* New York: Knopf. (K–4, fiction)

Delacre, L. (1993). *Vejigante/Masquerader.* New York: Scholastic. (grades 3–8, fiction, Puerto Rico)

Garza, C.L. (1996). *In my family/En mi familia.* San Francisco, CA: Children's Book Press. (grades 3–8, nonfiction, Mexican American, Texas)

Garza, C.L. (1990). *Family pictures/Cuadros de familia.* San Francisco, CA: Children's Book Press. (grades 3–8, nonfiction, Mexican American, Texas)

Gonzalez, R. & Ruiz, A.(1995). *Mi primer libro de dichos: My first books of proverbs.* San Francisco, CA: Children's Book Press. (grades 4–8, nonfiction, Mexican American)

Books in English and Spanish

These titles have separate English and Spanish editions

Ada, A.F. (1993). *My name is María Isabel* (Spanish edition: *Me llamo María Isabel*). New York: Simon & Schuster. (grades 3 and up, fiction, Puerto Rican)

Ancona, G. (1998). *Barrio: José's neighborhood.* San Diego, CA: Harcourt Brace. (grades 5–8, nonfiction, San Francisco's Mission District)

Ancona, G. (1995). *Fiesta U.S.A.* New York: Dutton. (grades 3–8, nonfiction)

Cisneros, S. (1984, 1994). *The house on Mango Street* (Spanish edition: *La casa en Mango Street*). New York: Vintage. (grades 9–12, fiction)

Delacre, L. (1996). *Golden tales: Myths, legends and folktales from Latin America* (Spanish edition: *De oro y esmeraldas: Mitos, leyendas, cuentos populares de Latinoamérica*). New York: Scholastic Press. (grades 4 and up)

Dorros, A. (1995). *Isla.* New York: Dutton. (K–4, fiction)

Dorros, A. (1991). *Abuela.* New York: Dutton. (K–4, fiction)

Garza, C.L. (1999). *Ventanas magicos—magic windows.* Danbury, CT: Children's Book Press. (grades 1–6, fiction, Mexican American)

Mohr, N. (1995). *The magic shell* (Spanish edition: *El regalo mágico*). New York: Scholastic. (grades 5–8, fiction, Dominican, New York)

Rodriguez, L. (1998). *America is her name.* Williamantic, CT: Curbstone Press. (grades 3–5, fiction, Mexican American)

Rodriques, L.J. (1993). *Always running, la vida loca: Gang days in L.A.* (Spanish edition: *La vida loca: El testimonio de un pandillero en Los Angeles*). New York: Simon & Schuster. (grades 9–12, Chicano, nonfiction)

Santiago, E. (1993). *When I was Puerto Rican* (Spanish edition: *Cuando era Puertorriqueña*). New York: Vintage. (grades 9–12, nonfiction)

Santiago, E. & Davidow, J. (Eds.) (1999). *Las Christmas: Favorite Latino authors share their holiday memories.* New York: Vintage. (grades 6–12, fiction)

School Support Services for Hispanic Deaf Children and Families in Southern California School Settings

Kevin Struxness

Differences in language, cultural background, and socio-economic level help create barriers to participation in the educational system for the Hispanic deaf student. The system must do its part in adapting to these differences...

Alan Lerman

In recent years, educators of the Deaf have noticed that more and more students with Hispanic surnames have enrolled in southern California classrooms. Yet, the school support services for Hispanic Deaf students and their families have not been addressed seriously in the educational setting.

The mission of the research project detailed here was to identify the existing support services and resources being delivered to Hispanic Deaf students and their families in four selected school sites in southern California. The project was also intended to investigate the communicative relations between the families and their Hispanic Deaf students as well as relations between school professionals and the families.

The research was conducted in southern California, specifically, in four school programs for the Deaf in cities which have large Hispanic populations. All four schools had Hispanic Deaf student populations. Code names for the participating schools were given to provide anonymity as follows: Oak School, Central School, North School, and Lassen School. Oak School serves middle school and high school students on its campus, Central School is a high school, North and Lassen Schools are both elementary schools. Two-page surveys printed in English and Spanish were employed to reach families through the cooperation of the participating schools.

There were two categories of subjects in each of the participating schools in southern California. The first category consisted of the families of Hispanic Deaf students. The students ranged in grade from preschool through 12th. The other category included four school administrators and/or teachers who represented or worked with Hispanic Deaf students at their schools. They were also asked to identify the absence or presence of certain school support services for both the students and the families as well as to note special arrangements, if any.

SURVEY RESPONSES FROM FAMILIES

Responses to the first question disclosed that the students ranged in age from 2 to 22 years. Educators and therapists widely accept that identification of deafness should be as early as possible for early intervention (Bowe, 1991; Ogden & Lipsett, 1982; King & Quigley, 1985; Grant, 1984). Examination of the survey data demonstrated that the mode age (most common age) of identification of deafness across all subjects was between soon after birth and under 1 year. Of 86 subjects, 69 were identified as Deaf or Hard-of-Hearing prior to the age of 3. Eight were deaf at birth. The mode age appears to be contrary to observations of Christiansen (1987) and Gerner de Garcia (1993), which stated that multicultural children's deafness tended to be identified later than in their European American counterparts. One explanation for this phenomenon may be that many of the children in this study were born in the United States and had access to professional intervention.

The corpus revealed that the most common age for first-time school enrollment among the subject children was between 2 and 4. This age is consistent with that of European Americans. Again, these subjects may have been born in or came to the United States in their early years. However, there were 10 cases where Hispanic Deaf students were not enrolled until after the usual kindergarten age of 5. Three were enrolled at age 6, two at 7, two at 8, one at 9, one at 10, one at 12, and one at 13.

The most common language spoken at home among the subject families was Spanish. Based on the returned surveys, North School had the largest group (16 of 20) that spoke only Spanish at home. Lassen School had fairly even numbers across six individual and combined languages utilized at home. The most frequent combination was English and Spanish. The next most frequent combination was English and sign language. There were four subject families that used three languages (English, sign language, and Spanish) for communication. One family stood apart from the others by the virtue of their unique combination, American Sign Language and Mexican Sign Language; everyone in the family was Deaf.

Sixty-five subject families used their home languages with everyone in their families, including Deaf siblings. Taken together from four school sites, 30 subject families stated that they knew sign language while 41 families did not. Another 15 families indicated that they knew a little sign language. Overall, 84% of all subject families used some kind of manual means of communication (signing, finger-spelling, and/or pad and pen). This result supported that of Lerman's study, that 75% of Hispanic parents use manual communication to some extent (1984).

The most frequently cited sources for families to learn sign language were adult/college classes and self-study with books and/or videos at home. The families who studied at home reported that their Deaf child also helped them.

Forty-one survey respondents, however, reported that they had not learned how to sign. They explained that they had no opportunities to study sign language. This explanation was found to be the most common reason among the subject families. Some respondents cited classes being taught in English instead of Spanish, their language of preference. Still others claimed the lack of free time to pursue knowledge of basic signing. Some pointed out that sign language classes were not available in their neighborhood. This significant finding with Spanish-speaking respondents reinforces the need for schools to provide sign classes taught in Spanish. Christensen (1986) reported at the end of her study that 95.5% of the participating families that learned to sign felt the quality of communication with their Deaf child had improved greatly. Further, parents' attitudes toward the school and their child's deafness became more positive as the parents gained elementary skills in sign language.

Regarding family communication styles employed with Deaf children, the survey listed six different methods that might be used at home: (1) spoken Spanish, (2) spoken English, (3) sign language, (4) fingerspelling, (5) home signs, and (6) pad and pen. Analysis of the data for this question showed varying usage of different individual methods or combinations thereof. The most commonly used methods at Oak School were sign language (70%) and home signs (68%); at Central School spoken English (62%), home signs (54%), and finger-spelling (46%); at North School spoken Spanish (70%) and home signs (60%); and at Lassen School sign language (62%), spoken

English (38%), and spoken Spanish (38%). The least used method at Oak School was spoken Spanish (18%); pad and pen was the least used method at Central School (15%), North School (10%), and Lassen School (8%).

Oak and North Schools stand at opposite ends of the continuum on the usage of spoken Spanish. Oak School reported a low of 18%, while North School reported a high of 70% on the utilization of spoken Spanish between hearing and Deaf family members. The mode of all families at the four school sites was home signs, with 48 of 86 subject families or 56%. Sign language came a close second at 46 families (53%). Spoken English (42%) was the third most used method. Pad and pen proved to be the least used method among the families (20%).

Parent support groups and educators recognize that the importance of contact between families and schools cannot be overemphasized. The surveys indicated that all of the families except for two have visited their child's school more than once. For the four schools combined, 35% of the families visited a few times, 34% visited sometimes, and 29% visited often. The data appear to show that the families made an effort to visit their children's school on a regular basis.

A significant finding regarding the parents' attitude toward their child's education was that they placed a premium on the education of their children. Eighty-seven percent of the respondents showed strong support for Deaf children's education. Twelve percent rated Deaf children's education as fairly important. Not one respondent judged education of little value for his/her Deaf child. This finding confirmed that of Weston's study (1992), that the majority of parents, regardless of their own educational background, support their children's education.

Parents of newly identified Deaf children often have little or no knowledge of the Deaf Community and/or professional intervention for Deaf children. Some families receive referrals for assistance quickly while other families wait longer to receive referrals. The surveys revealed that parents have many different sources for assistance and referral, with 17 sources identified. The most frequent sources were school districts (39%), hospitals (10%), and family friends (9%).

Some subjects credited hospitals and still others speech and hearing clinics. The hospitals and speech and hearing clinics are often in proximity; these institutions, combined, represented 13% of the referrals.

In the public education system, a hearing student often attends three or four schools prior to his/her graduation from high school. Based on 81 responses, Hispanic families with Deaf children exhibited a similar rate. At the high school level of Oak and Central Schools, 26% of the students had attended three schools, while 21% had attended four schools. At North and Lassen Schools, elementary schools, 61% of the students had attended one school, 30% two schools, 6% three schools, and 3% four schools. The largest number of school changes was six for a high school student at Central School.

Eighty-five percent of Spanish-speaking parents were aware of their right to Spanish-speaking interpreters for business with the school personnel. Fifteen percent claimed no knowledge of such a right.

The next question on the survey asked the Spanish-speaking respondents if they were aware of school staff members who could speak Spanish. Again, 85% percent of the families expressed their awareness of that. The remaining 15% percent had no idea that any staff members at their child's school could speak Spanish.

On communication with school, the most frequently used method by far was telephone—79% of the respondents. The method second in frequency was classroom or office visit. The third most frequent method involved written notes. Only seven reported communication books, the least used medium.

It is essential for parents to know what services their child's school has to offer for the students as well as the parents. In Deaf education, school support services run the gamut of sign language interpreters, sign language classes, parent support groups, remedial services, bilingual education, counseling, speech therapy, health care, and other services. Oak and North Schools had eight (24%) and seven (35%) respondents, respectively, who were not aware of the school support services for the students. The administrators at Oak and North Schools need to take action to rectify this communication gap. On the same topic, parents were asked to list what school support services were available at their child's school. Across the four school sites, the support services mentioned in order of decreasing frequency were sign language classes (42), sign language interpreters (37), parent support groups (28), bilingual education (18), remedial services (15), counseling (3), and speech therapy (1).

In order to understand Deaf children's afterschool activities, parents were asked to select from a list possible activities and to list other activities. Upon analysis of 86 surveys, different home activities totaled 16. Unfortunately, watching TV was listed as the most frequent response (79). It is not known how many of these televisions were equipped with closed caption technology. In order of frequency, the list also included completing homework assignment (66), helping with housework (56), playing with neighbors (50), sports activities (45), playing video games (38), working part-time (9), reading (3), arts and crafts (2), hanging out with friends (2), listening to music (2), and spending time on the computer (2). Surprisingly, about half of the respondents indicated that their child had video games. Only three respondents added that reading was another home activity for their children.

Of 84 respondents who answered the question on knowledge of Spanish, 35 reported that their Deaf children had no knowledge of spoken Spanish. Twenty-two determined their children to have a limited command of Spanish. Sixteen respondents judged their children to have some proficiency in Spanish. The remaining 11 respondents judged their children's proficiency in Spanish to be advanced. Two respondents did not answer the question. Further, close examination of the surveys revealed that 44 families speak only Spanish at home. In Spanish-speaking families, 37% of the Deaf children displayed no Spanish proficiency, 18% had little proficiency, 30% had some proficiency, and the remaining 14% had good proficiency.

The last question on the survey asked the respondents if they had met a Deaf adult. Of 82 responses to the question, the results were 32% never, 16% once, 21% a few times, 9% sometimes, and 22% often.

SURVEY RESPONSES FROM SCHOOL PROFESSIONALS

Another questionnaire was designed to solicit information from the school programs that serve Deaf students, including those of Hispanic background. The questionnaire was three pages long and requested information which is different from that which was requested of the families. As previously stated, Oak School served students in the 6th grade and beyond, Central School was a high school, and North and Lassen Schools were elementary schools. North School had an infant program that admitted enrollees as young as 18 months old.

The first item on the school questionnaire solicited numerical information on the educational programming for Deaf and Hard-of-Hearing students of all ethnic backgrounds on their school site. As a combined middle school and high school, Oak School reported an enrollment of 320 students ranging in age from 12 through 22. As a high school, Central School reported a total of 40 students ranging in age from 14 through 20. North School, an elementary school, had 156 students from infants through 13 years of age. Also an elementary school, Lassen School had 47 students ages 3 to 12 in its Deaf and Hard-of-Hearing program. All schools indicated that most of their Hispanic students stay in their Deaf education programs throughout all grades.

Oak School had, by far, the largest group of credentialed teachers of the Deaf, with 59 on its payroll. Central School had 5 teachers for its Deaf/Hard-of-Hearing (DHH) program. North and Lassen Schools reported 18 teachers and 5 teachers, respectively. Of 87 teachers at the four southern California school sites, only one teacher was Hispanic. The Hispanic teacher was employed at Oak School. The single Hispanic teacher represents 1% of the teachers in this study. This troubles the investigator since the four school sites were located in a geographical area with a large Hispanic population. Even worse, the 1% is still smaller than the quoted 2% of 5166 teachers with Hispanic background in the field across the nation, according to Andrews and Jordan (1993). Andrews and Jordan also stated that California was fifth in the employment of Hispanic educational pro-

fessionals. Yet, Oak School complained that they have had little success in the recruitment of more teachers from underrepresented ethnically and linguistically diverse groups. Most applicants continued to be European Americans. In view of the ongoing situation, the proposal from Cohen *et al.* (1990) needs to be under advisement for the establishment of a national clearinghouse to assist programs and schools for the Deaf with the recruitment of qualified multicultural professionals and paraprofessionals.

The number of teachers who could speak Spanish at the schools looks a little more encouraging. Oak, Central, and North Schools each reported one teacher with fluent Spanish. Lassen School had two teachers with intermediate skills. The principal at Lassen School happened to be fluent in Spanish as well. All schools had a few school support staff members who could converse with Spanish-speaking parents. Oak, North, and Lassen Schools had students who used Spanish upon entry into their programs. In these cases, the schools did not employ the students' dominant language to facilitate second language acquisition of English. This finding is significant.

Central School had no instance of students who used facile Spanish upon admission. However, Oak, North, and Lassen Schools all reported that they employ any or a combination of American Sign Language, English, and Spanish for assessment. Oak School had two Deaf members on its assessment team; one of the two was Hispanic and could speak Spanish. North School had a Deaf specialist for assessment. Lassen School felt it was also important to pay attention to the nonverbal aspects as an important part of assessment for a truer representation of the students' abilities. Central School used American Sign Language, English, and gesture to assess its students.

North and Lassen Schools provided speech and/or auditory services for Spanish-speaking Deaf students. Lassen School made it clear that the service was rendered for Hard-of-Hearing students whose language was Spanish. On the other hand, Oak and Central Schools did not provide such service for their Spanish-speaking students; they provided therapy in English only.

The 1990 study by Cohen *et al.* revealed that only 27% of schools polled across the nation provided multicultural awareness seminars for their staff members. In the present study, three of the four schools provided such training. Oak, North, and Lassen Schools underwent sensitivity training as part of professional development in response to the increasing diversity of the communities. Central School reported no such training despite the fact that 26 of 40 of its students were Hispanic. Oak School reported 152 Hispanic students, which represented 48% of the entire student body. At North School, Hispanic children accounted for 20%. Lassen School had the highest proportion of Hispanic students—70%. All schools experienced an increase in the Hispanic student population. Oak School expects Hispanic student enrollment to continue to increase for the foreseeable future.

All schools embraced Total Communication as their communication policy. North School also had a separate oral program for a smaller group of students who showed potential success for aural–oral education.

Oak School placed 3 Hispanic students in the self-contained DHH classroom full-time. Central School maintained the placement of 21 Hispanic students in the full-time DHH classroom. Twenty-eight Hispanic students stayed in the DHH classroom full-time at North School. Lassen School reported 23 Hispanics in the same placement arrangement. Oak and North Schools mainstreamed none of their Hispanic students. Central School mainstreamed 21 Hispanic students for art, physical education, and vocational training. Lassen School placed 10 Hispanic students in the regular classrooms for certain classes. Five students at Central School and one student at Lassen School were fully integrated with the hearing students.

With regard to the Deaf and Hard-of-Hearing ratio in the Hispanic group, Oak School had the most lopsided ratio: 147 Deaf and 5 Hard-of-Hearing students. By contrast, Central School classified 14 students to be Deaf and 12 to be Hard-of-Hearing. North School registered 20 Deaf and 11 Hard-of-Hearing. Similarly, Lassen School had 22 Deaf and 11 Hard-of-Hearing.

An interesting thing about the use of conventional amplification was that Oak and Central Schools, which served older students, reported few students that used hearing aids. Conversely, North and Lassen Schools, elementary schools, reported that most of their students wore hearing aids. It has been the experience of the investigator that middle school and high school students decide on their own to stop wearing hearing aids if they provide limited or no benefit.

Educators have long recognized the significance of good communication between parents and their Deaf children. It facilitates the children's language growth and helps with their socioemotional progress and their attainment of other developmental milestones. In view of these benefits, all schools polled in the study provided sign language classes after school for families of Deaf children. However, the classes were taught in American Sign Language and/or English. Only Lassen School was able to provide a separate sign language class for Spanish-speaking families. Furthermore, the school also provided free child care. Oak School provided a Spanish-speaking interpreter for a sign language class and charged one dollar an hour for child care. As noted earlier, a number of Spanish-speaking families cited the use of English as the reason for not signing up for sign language classes. It is anticipated that the percentage of Hispanic student enrollment will continue to rise in southern California. Therefore, it is hoped that schools and school programs will soon follow the initiative of Lassen School by offering sign language classes taught in the dominant language of linguistically diverse families.

All of the four schools provide interpreters for Spanish-speaking parents and families for individualized education program (IEP) meetings. Oak School was the only school that also provided Spanish interpreters upon request for other school activities such as open houses, graduation ceremonies, and plays, to name a few. Oak School holds an annual Latino Families Day open to Hispanic families and friends from southern California. The day includes a parent education program presented in Spanish. The attendees receive information on the growth and development of Deaf children. They also learn about special telephone devices, discipline for children, sign language, gangs, and other issues. The school also has a cross-cultural committee which sponsors cultural awareness months in recognition of the many cultures on campus. North and Lassen Schools would be willing to provide such service for some school activities. Despite the high percentage (65%) of Hispanic students in its program, Central School did not extend such services to Spanish-speaking visitors. Generally, schools make an effort to maintain communication with the families of their students about school affairs through periodic newsletters. Unfortunately, Schools A and C published newsletters only in English. Central School sometimes published newsletters in Spanish. Lassen School published newsletters in both English and Spanish. Oak, Central, and North Schools printed some school documents in Spanish. The survey from Lassen School did not mention its use of Spanish for documents. Cohen *et al.* (1990) stated that 30% of school programs for the Deaf provide documents in the native language(s) of the parents of Deaf children as well as in English.

The surveys indicated that all schools extend the same opportunities to Hispanic Deaf students for services and activities that are available to hearing Hispanic students. They, with the exception of Central School, also made sure that their Deaf Hispanic students enjoy extracurricular activities as part of the school experience. Lassen School applied for and received a grant to pay for sign language interpreters for after-school activities. As a result, the Hispanic Deaf students signed up for the activities such as recreational karate, creative drawing, and jazz. Only Oak School had an organization exclusively geared for Hispanic students. The organization is known as MEChA (Movimiento Estudiantil Chicano de Aztlán). MEChA is a school organization geared to Hispanic students and friends with the purpose of enhancing cultural awareness and promoting pride in Hispanic history and language. Central, North, and Lassen Schools did not have such an organization, although the organization is commonly found in middle schools and high schools for hearing students.

Nationwide, most bilingual education programs are offered to hearing children in elementary schools. Such programs are designed to allow Spanish-speaking students to keep up with their core study taught in Spanish while acquiring English skills as a second language (Weston, 1992). This study found that while North and Lassen Schools had a bilingual program for hearing students, they did not offer such a program to Hispanic Deaf students. Schools Oak and Central did not offer bilingual education. Oak, Central, and North Schools provided remedial services for all their students, including Hispanic students, but not in Spanish. Lassen School did not extend remedial services. Instead, students at Lassen School could stay after school for assistance with their homework at the Homework Center.

As expected of high schools, Oak and Central Schools provided vocational training. The middle school department at Oak School also provided such training. Consistent with elementary schools elsewhere, North and Lassen Schools did not include vocational training in their school curriculum. However, Cohen *et al.* strongly recommended that vocational education be offered in the early grades and continued throughout the school years in view of the persistent problems of unemployment and underemployment among multicultural Deaf people in the job market (1990). Once again, Apodaca, himself Hispanic and Deaf, shared his concern about the frequent assessment of Hispanic Deaf students as low-functioning for placement purposes in vocational training classes (1994). Cohen *et al.* and Apodaca have divergent proposals on vocational education. Hispanic Deaf students should or may have a combination of vocational education and academic coursework throughout the middle school and high school years.

The last and 34th question on the survey pertained to school support services such as special tutoring, resource teachers, classroom aides, volunteers, parent support groups, counseling, and materials printed in Spanish. All four of the schools provided a variety of school support services conducted in American Sign Language and/or English. Spanish was used only for interpreting and translation services. Oak School provided all services except resource teachers. The school had a center with several full-time signing counselors. Central School also provided all of the services listed. Further, they used itinerant teachers as resource teachers for mainstreamed students within the school district. The itinerant teachers also went to 12 other school districts to provide assistance with their mainstreamed students. In Central School, classroom aides and interpreters served as tutors for students at lunch break. In addition, Central School translated letters into Spanish and provided sign language books with a Spanish translation for home study. At North School, they provided counseling, classroom aides, volunteers, and a parent support group.

Lassen School provided special tutoring, classroom aides, volunteers, parent support groups, and counseling. In order to work closely with the community, the school had a family resource center on its campus. The school believed that the children would perform better in school if their families had a community resource center for their needs. The center assisted families with social security, employment, medical, and legal matters. A bilingual social worker worked with the parents who had children in the Deaf and Hard-of-Hearing program. Surprisingly, the center coordinator was trilingual (ASL, English, and Spanish). The coordinator had a Deaf son who signs. In addition, the school was fortunate that they had two interpreters who could use ASL, English, and Spanish. One of the interpreters was also proficient in Mexican Sign Language.

Although some east coast schools have Spanish-speaking resource specialists dedicated to the service of Hispanic Deaf students and their families, none of the four schools in the study had this special service. It is recommended that the schools in California seriously consider creating new positions for Hispanic resource assistants in response to the continued growth of the Hispanic Deaf student population.

NEED FOR SCHOOL PROGRAMMING REFORM

A major problem existing in educational programs for the Deaf is the predominant focus on Anglo-Saxon culture at the expense of all other cultural experiences (Mac Neil, 1990). Moreover, educators of the

Deaf have been unaware, hesitant, or slow to respond to this problem, often insisting that deafness precludes ethnic and/or racial "minority" group membership or status (Cohen *et al.*, 1990; Grace, 1993). Even Deaf professionals, some of whom are multicultural, have made the same argument that being Deaf takes precedence over any other background the child may have.

Erickson (1984) concluded that solutions to educational problems were complicated by the dearth of research, personnel, and appropriate evaluation and therapeutic procedures designed to serve the population of Hispanic Deaf students. Cohen (1993) claimed that there have been relatively few attempts to address the needs of Deaf children from diverse racial, ethnic, and linguistic backgrounds. It is now time for educators dealing with Deaf children to be aware of the special challenges of the multicultural groups. Educators have the responsibility to conduct research, develop materials, and implement more effective programs in this area (Delgado, 1984). This study involved only four schools across a broad geographical area. Therefore, it is recommended that this type of study be replicated with a much bigger corpus of participating schools in southern California and beyond. A more extensive study can provide further information on the extent to which special services are currently available to Hispanic students and families, as well as other ethnic groups.

Similarly, the National Association of the Deaf recommended that demographic data be developed, research undertaken, and educational programming developed to address the needs of these children. Programming for these children must be designed to meet established state and local standards for all students, and the accountability of programs must be emphasized (Innes, 1994, p. 8).

One of the 52 recommendations proposed by the Commission on Education of the Deaf (COED) states that "The Department of Education should monitor states to ensure that the evaluation and assessment of children who are deaf be conducted by professionals knowledgeable about their unique needs and able to communicate effectively in the child's primary mode of communication." As former chair of the COED, Bowe (1991) confirmed that COED Recommendation 12 has been partly accomplished as anticipated. The commission was keenly aware of the difficulty inherent in the proper assessment of Deaf children with many variables considered. Especially in small programs for the Deaf, it is difficult to find a psychoeducational specialist who is able to communicate effectively in the preferred method or language used by Deaf students and who knows the many variables involved when assessing Deaf children (Bowe, 1991; Mac Neil, 1990).

We can speculate that it is even more difficult to hire an examiner who can sign American Sign Language fluently and speak or sign Spanish. The population of Deaf students with diverse backgrounds continues to increase, particularly in California. This compounds the problem of having test administrators who are trained specifically to assess Deaf students with dual cultural status. This issue of concern relates to the increased risk for misdiagnosis of multicultural students.

To ensure better academic success, research needs to be focused on the nature of learning in multicultural Deaf children and adolescents in order to develop appropriate teaching strategies (Cohen, 1993).

RECOMMENDATIONS FOR MULTICULTURAL EDUCATION

Cohen *et al.* (1990) proposed that schools and programs for the Deaf also solicit consultants and resources from organized groups encompassing people of diverse backgrounds such as Hispanics, African Americans, Asians/Pacific Islanders, Jews, Native Americans, and so forth. Such organizations could include the National Hispanic Council of the Deaf and Hard of Hearing, the Black Deaf Advocates with chapters scattered across the nation, and the World Congress of the Jewish Deaf. The National Hispanic Council of the Deaf and Hard of Hearing (NHC) is a new national organization dedicated to the advancement of Deaf Hispanics. Its members work to ensure equal access in the areas of employment, social, recreational, cultural, educational, and vocational welfare.

Anecdotal evidence indicates that there has been a gradual increase in sensitivity training toward multicultural individuals on the preservice level. The national Council on Education of the Deaf (CED) standards now require teacher preparation programs to provide multicultural information in their curricula. For instance, in the linguistic or practicum classes, professors increasingly emphasize the consideration of linguistic and cultural needs when working with students from diverse backgrounds. Likewise, there has been a gradual increase in the number of teacher preparation programs of the Deaf in the United States offering American Sign Language as well as Deaf culture courses. However, much remains to be accomplished (Christensen, 1993, personal interview).

In response, San Diego State University and California State University at Northridge, for example, have incorporated multicultural coursework in their teacher preparation programs for the Deaf. The national Conference of Educational Administrators Serving the Deaf (CEASD) has sponsored symposia on multicultural issues in deafness and has an active committee on ethnic and multicultural concerns. The Convention of American Instructors of the Deaf (CAID) has a special interest group on multicultural issues in education of the Deaf (Christensen, 1993, pp. 24–25).

In order for a school program to show its commitment to serve each and every student, the school program needs to promulgate a mission statement that embraces developing the academic and vocational achievement and personal growth and esteem of multicultural children, incorporating respect for their culture and heritage (Cohen, 1993).

RECOMMENDATIONS FOR BETTER FAMILY–SCHOOL RESULTS

For better participation of parents in school affairs, educational programs with a sizeable population of students from Spanish-speaking families should strive to set up parent groups and run meetings in Spanish (Gerner de Garcia, 1993; Cohen, 1993). Further, in response to a common excuse for not coming to the parent meetings, school programs could arrange transportation and child care at reduced rates or no charge (Cohen, 1993).

Education experts have proposed the establishment of American Sign Language classes taught in Spanish. This plan would empower parents and increase familial interaction between family members and the Hispanic Deaf children (Delgado, 1984; Christensen, 1986; Gerner de Garcia, 1993). An experimental trilingual education project that presented televised signed language instruction for Spanish-speaking parents of Deaf children found that these parents were successful in the acquisition and use of a rudimentary signed language when instruction was provided in Spanish. In addition, their attitudes toward their children's deafness were improved (Christensen, 1986).

Spanish-speaking parents may benefit from a bilingual advocate to help navigate the educational bureaucratic channels. This resource could serve as an intermediary between the parents and the interdisciplinary team of specialists in the IEP or parent conference. Ferullo summarized succinctly that the parents' greatest sense of security is in the language of their culture, while the weakest sense of security is in the language of the "other culture" (1983).

Parents and their Deaf children need opportunities to meet Deaf role models for inspiration. The survey data from Hispanic families indicated that many of them either never met a Deaf adult or met a Deaf adult only once. They need to see successful Deaf adults as positive role models on a frequent basis. Unlike Oak and Central Schools, North and Lassen Schools did not have a single culturally Deaf credentialed teacher on staff. North School, however, had a few Deaf classroom aides and an ASL-using Deaf volunteer.

In order to bring the academic performance of multicultural Deaf students closer to that of their European American Deaf counterparts, the whole school community, including parents, must make a commitment to every student regardless of his or her ethnic/linguistic background.

CONCLUSION

The Hispanic population will continue to increase for the foreseeable future in California as well as across the United States. The persistent academic and subsequent employment difficulties besetting Hispanic Deaf individuals will continue unless schools and programs for the Deaf institute educational reform. On the basis of the survey responses, this reform should include publication of school newsletters in Spanish, increased recruitment efforts for teachers/administrators who are Deaf and/or from underrepresented ethnically and linguistically diverse groups, creation of positions for resource specialists, expansion of the battery of test instruments in Spanish and normed on Hispanic Deaf children, greater effort in dissemination of information on school services to parents, and modified services for Spanish-speaking parents.

> This problem can no longer be overlooked. It will not go away. Each of us, as dedicated educators, and each professional organization concerned with educating deaf children should marshal its resources, to influence national, state, and local authorities to give high priority to conducting research, developing materials, and implementing effective programs in this area. To do less would demonstrate a lack of sensitivity and professionalism. (Delgado, 1982, p. 94)

This challenge continues to exist.

REFERENCES

Abrams, M. (1993, Spring). A voice for positive change: Venita Gragg. *Pre-College Programs—Gallaudet University Preview*, 4–9.
Andrews, J., & Jordan, D. (1993). Minority and minority-deaf professionals. *American Annals of the Deaf*, 138(5) 388–396.

Apodaca, M. (1994, Summer). Is there hope for the Hispanic Deaf? *The National Hispanic Council of Deaf and Hard of Hearing Newsletter,* 1(1), 1–4.

Bowe, F. (1991). *Approaching equality—Education of the Deaf.* Maryland: TJ Publishers.

Christensen, K. (1986). Conceptual sign language acquisition by Spanish-speaking parents of hearing-impaired children. *American Annals of the Deaf,* 131, 285–287.

Christensen, K., & Delgado, G. (1993). A multicultural approach to education. In K. Christensen & G. Delgado (Eds.), *Multicultural issues in deafness* (pp. 17–27). New York: Longman.

Christiansen, J. (1987). Minorities. In *Gallaudet encyclopedia of Deaf people and deafness* (Vol. 1, pp. 270–276). New York: McGraw-Hill.

Cohen, O. (1993). Educational needs of African and Hispanic deaf children and youth. In K. Christensen & G. Delgado (Eds.), *Multicultural issues in deafness* (pp. 45–67). New York: Longman.

Cohen, O., Fischgrund, J., & Redding, R. (1990). Deaf children from ethnic, linguistic and racial minority backgrounds: An overview. *American Annals of the Deaf,* 135(2), 67–73.

Delgado, G. (1984). Hearing-impaired children from non-native-language homes. In G. Delgado (Ed.), *The Hispanic Deaf* (pp. 28–37). Washington, DC: Gallaudet University Press.

Delgado, G. (1982). International baseline data on hearing-impaired children with non-native home languages. *International Congress on Education of the Deaf* (Vol. 1, pp. 84–94). Herstellung, Germany: Julius Groos Verlag.

Erickson, J. (1984). Hispanic deaf children: A bilingual and special education challenge. In G. Delgado (Ed.), *The Hispanic Deaf* (pp. 4–11). Washington, DC: Gallaudet University Press.

Gerner de Garcia, B. (1993). Addressing the needs of Hispanic deaf children. In K. Christensen & G. Delgado (Eds.), *Multicultural issues in deafness* (pp. 69–90). New York: Longman.

Grace, C. (1993). A model program for home-school communication and staff development. In K. Christensen & G. Delgado (Eds.), *Multicultural issues in deafness* (pp. 29–41). New York: Longman.

Grant, J. (1984). Teachers of Hispanic hearing-impaired children: Competencies and preparation. In G. Delgado (Ed.), *The Hispanic Deaf* (pp. 182–194). Washington, DC: Gallaudet University Press.

Innes, J. (1994, December). NAD comments on IDEA in *The NAD Broadcaster* (Vol. 16, No. 2, pp. 5–8). National Association of the Deaf.

King, C., & Quigley, S. (1985). *Reading and deafness.* San Diego, CA: College Hill.

Lerman, A. (1984). Survey of Hispanic hearing impaired students and their families in New York City. In G. Delgado (Ed.), *The Hispanic Deaf* (pp. 38–56). Washington, DC: Gallaudet University Press.

Mac Neil, B. (1990). Educational needs for multicultural hearing-impaired students in the public school system. *American Annals of the Deaf,* **135**(2), 75–82.

Ogden, P., & Lipsett, S. (1982). *The silent garden.* New York: St. Martin's Press.

Weston, N. (1992). *The home–school library: Improving the educational success of students through family involvement.* Master's thesis, University of California, San Diego.

Chapter

9

Exploring Students' Personal Cultures

Ruth Fletcher-Carter and Doris Paez

Each individual is like all other people, like some other people, and like no other person.

Elsie J. Smith

Because culture influences how we think and behave in our daily lives, it has been suggested that an understanding of culture can serve as a "silent partner" to human services professionals (Wehrly, 1995). That is, knowledge of a student's culture can assist a professional in more effectively working with that student. For teachers of deaf or hard-of-hearing students, knowledge of their students' culture can serve as an important supplement to their teaching. A student, particularly one who is deaf or hard-of-hearing, attending school in the United States belongs to or is influenced by at least four cultural groups: (1) family, (2) neighborhood, (3) surrounding community, and (4) school. However, because family is the primary venue of a child's life experiences, professionals tend to identify the child's culture as simply reflecting that of the family, and educators neglect to analyze the contribution of the other three cultural influences. To understand the world of each student requires that we, as educators, explore the child's uniqueness or personal culture.

There is a growing appreciation among scholars and school personnel that awareness of the characteristics which distinguish cultural groups can increase effectiveness in working with children and adolescents served by special education (Baca & Cervantes, 1989; Bailey, 1989; Chamberlain & Medinos-Landurand, 1991; Correa, 1989; Turnbull & Turnbull, 1990). It has been suggested that without such awareness, misperceptions and miscommunications between the teacher and the student may occur, resulting in poorer classroom performance and impaired parent–school relationships (Chamberlain & Medinos-Landurand, 1991). This is particularly true for deaf students who may be members of more than one cultural group (e.g., Hispanic and Deaf; Native American and Deaf) (Christensen, 1993).

Indeed, students who are Deaf and Black, or Deaf and Asian, or Deaf and Native American, or Deaf and Hispanic seldom encounter teachers who are Deaf, let alone Deaf and representative of their ethnic/racial group. It significant to note that while culturally diverse groups make up 32% (i.e., Black, 16%; Hispanic, 12%; Other, 4%) of America's special education school population, only 14% of the special education teaching professionals represent those cultural diverse groups (Cook & Boe, 1995). Added to the dilemma of an imbalanced teacher–student cultural ratio is the reality for deaf students that more than 90% of their parents are hearing (Center for Demographic Studies, 1994). Thus, the primary responsibility falls upon the teachers, most of whom are European American and hearing, to expose deaf, culturally diverse children to their ethnic roots and their Deaf Culture.

Some teachers of deaf students are themselves deaf. However, they are faced with the same challenge of working with cultural diversity as are hearing teachers of hearing students. Teachers who are deaf share a common experience with their deaf students—deafness. Likewise, hearing teachers share a similar common experience with their hearing students—the ability to hear. The challenge is when cultural backgrounds alter that shared experience. Western European descendants have had cultural experiences different from the refugee family from South America or Vietnam or the African American family from Alabama or Georgia. These differences need to be acknowledge and incorporated into the classroom (Center for Education for the Deaf, 1996).

More often, teachers of the deaf are themselves hearing and, therefore, face two cultural challenges: that of the Deaf Culture, and that of the ethnic diversity of the students and their families. Such bi- or multiculturality among students who are deaf requires that teachers gain an understanding of the different or shared knowledge and belief systems, ways of living in the world, and acquired knowledge that people use to interpret experience and to generate social behavior (Bennett, 1995).

So significant is the issue of cultural diversity that national organizations have set standards for all beginning and continuing special educators that include a core set of knowledge and skills in this area. Specifically, the standards call for "special education professionals to continue to broaden their perspectives and to insure vigilant attention to the issues of diversity such as culture, language, gender, religion, sexuality and disability (CEC, 1996, p. 1; CED, 1996, p. 10)."

TEACHER'S ROLES IN THE IDENTIFICATION AND USE OF CULTURAL DIVERSITY

How do teachers of the deaf identify and attend to the variations in beliefs, traditions, and values across cultures and within society that may impact their students' worldview or personal cultures?

First, educators need a common definition for the term "multicultural" that incorporates the idea that all students, regardless of their gender, social class, ethnicity, race, or disability, have the right to equal opportunities to learn in school.

Second, educators need to understand the personal cultures of their students so that they can adapt curricula to ensure that they (a) increase students' personal (and their students' families') awareness and knowledge of the history, culture, and perspectives of all ethnic, racial, and cultural groups; (b) enhance students' identity within the curriculum; (c) promote valuing cultural differences so that they are viewed in an egalitarian mode by educators and learners; (d) identify and build on the commonalties and differences among groups; and (e) enhance academic performance of all students.

For teachers of the deaf, cultural and linguistic differences frequently mean the culture of deafness versus the culture of hearing individuals (Christensen, 1993). However, the culture of deafness may not be the only culture impacting students' and their families' life views. The case can be made that a student who is deaf attending school in the United States belongs to or is influenced by the four places in which he/she resides: (1) family, (2) neighborhood, (3) surrounding community, and (4) school. It can further be asserted that each of these places constitutes a cultural group (e.g., family culture, school culture). However, because family is the primary venue of a child's life experiences, professionals tend to identify the child's culture as simply reflecting that of the family. Educators frequently neglect to analyze the contribution of the other three cultural influences. Therefore educators of children who are deaf must explore and understand each child's cultural affiliations as a means to understanding the child's uniqueness or *personal culture.*

Exploring cultural groups, according to Phinney (1996), requires that three dimensions of ethnicity be addressed, including: (a) the cultural values, attitudes, and behaviors that characterize ethnic groups; (b) ethnic identity or the subjective sense of ethnic group membership; and (c) the experiences associated with underrepresented status, including powerlessness and discrimination. She also suggests that political, economic, and historical factors are relevant components of ethnicity (i.e., sociopolitical context). Moreover, Phinney acknowledges that these components are overlapping and confounding, but they can be separated conceptually for purposes of discussion, examination, and intervention.

Thus, exploring the *personal culture* of a deaf student requires that characteristics of the student as well as those of each of the influencing cultural groups (family, neighborhood, surrounding community, and school) be analyzed across the dimensions of ethnicity described. This suggests that variables must be identified which represent: (a) cultural values, attitudes, and behaviors; (b) subjective sense of group membership; (c) experiences associated with minority status; and (d) transforming life events. While not an exhaustive list, the cultural variables described in the next section have been identified in the anthropological, psychological, and educational literature as significant features which distinguish cultural groups. The examples provided within the discussions of each cultural variable and throughout this chapter reflect the core characteristics that are frequently cited in empirical studies. Cultures and individuals within cultures vary considerably.

PERSONAL CULTURE DIMENSIONS AND VARIABLES OF CULTURAL VALUES, ATTITUDES, AND BEHAVIORS

Cultural values, attitudes, and behaviors stem from a common culture of origin, which is transmitted across generations (Phinney, 1996). When discussions of culture occur within the special education arena these variables typically influence Individualized Educational Program goals, curriculum (e.g., choice of instructional materials), and family–school collaborations (e.g., extension of school activities to home settings). Considerations include the place or region of residence (demographics), verbal behaviors, nonverbal behaviors, achievement orientation and range of educational levels, temporal orientation, unique thinking/cognitive processes, religious/spiritual affiliations, and leisure activities.

Demographic Influences

It has long been recognized that differences exist among individuals who reside in different areas of the United States. Consequently, demographics influence the treatment of deaf students. Discussions on this cultural variable are related more to differences in rural, suburban, and urban areas than to Western versus non-Western culture. There tends to be a distinct difference among groups who reside in different regions according to human and technological resources, values, lifestyles, and economic factors (Alper & Retish, 1994). In special education, the distinction is often made that services for rural students are more limited than those for suburban or urban students because of a lack of human and technological resources (Helge, 1983). Moreover, values, lifestyles, and economic factors such as those related to farming communities as opposed to those related to industrialized communities permeate the choices made in the life of an individual and in his/her community and schools.

Linguistic Behaviors

Beyond discussing where a person/group resides, cultural groups are often described in terms of how, when, where, and why language is used (Chamberlain & Medinos-Landurand, 1991; Wehrly, 1995). Here we include both oral English and American Sign Language (ASL) because they reflect symbol systems which are organized and used systematically to convey information (i.e., communication) (Valli & Lucas, 1992). In the United States, we often describe cultures in terms of perceived overt uses and sound quality of languages. For example, the Irish are associated with verbal eloquence, although not for speaking out for negative feelings or to communicate a point (Wehrly, 1995). African Americans are described as having strong oral traditions and speaking in a forthright manner, while Asian Americans tend to be passive in discussions (Wehrly, 1995; Misra, 1994). Other cultures are known for the melodic aspects of their verbal behavior. For example, we speak of French as a beautiful or romantic sounding language. Similarities in verbal behaviors include language patterns which affect not only the way a word is pronounced but also the when and how one speaks; this includes dialects and sound omissions/transformations (Misra, 1994). For example, Hispanic Americans are described as varying in dialects with a tendency to omit final sounds. Similarly, there are the dialects found among Black Deaf signers and White Deaf signers of ASL. Specifically, differences in lexical characteristics are noted. In some instances, forms are not used with a person who is not a part of the Black Deaf Culture (Andersson, 1992; Valli & Lucas, 1992).

Nonverbal Behaviors

Nonverbal behaviors include facial expression, gestures and the use of space in communication (Chamberlain & Medinos-Landurand, 1991; Wehrly, 1995). The sending of effective messages through nonverbal behaviors and the use of space varies across cultures. Specifically, there are differences related to proximity, acceptable touching, and eye contact for communication (Chamberlain & Medinos-Landurand, 1991). For example, while Hispanic Americans often accept closer contact between people and physical touch during conversations, it is often unacceptable for Asian Americans (Misra, 1994). Moreover, in some contexts, cultural groups such as Asian Americans and Native Americans may avoid eye contact. Similarly, use of appropriate nonverbal behaviors is critical in working with deaf individuals (Padden, 1989).

Achievement Orientation/Education Level

The degree to which achievement is valued and educational levels obtained by individuals within a cultural group is an important variable in schools. It is necessary to understand the motivation for or the "meaning of school" for culturally diverse students. Ogbu (1991) suggested that the understanding of people's motives for and response to schooling requires knowledge of that individual's cultural group concept of status mobility; that is, the folk theory and methods the group adheres to for getting ahead in a society or a given population. From this perspective there is a corelationship between the socioeconomic characteristics of the group and educational expectations. For example, Asian parents in the United States tend to have high expectations for their children and are dissatisfied with average or below average school performance. This can be traced to the need for economic security (Lee, 1991). Given the typical academic challenges of deaf students, it follows that the issues of expectations would have to be addressed (Paul & Quigley, 1990).

Temporal Orientation

Temporal orientation refers to the concept of time. First, cultures vary with regard to their emphasis on the past, present, and the future (Wehrly, 1995). White middle-class culture is oriented toward the future. Other cultures are present and past oriented. Second, cultures vary in their concept of time and rules regarding time. While most North Americans emphasize using time efficiently and being on time, other cultures are more relaxed in their use of time and are more concerned with personal relationships than punctuality (Chamberlain & Medinos-Landurand, 1991). The concept of time is evident even in the phrases that cultures use for describing time. For example, in the United States time "runs" while in some Latin American countries time "walks" (Chamberlain & Medinos-Landurand, 1991, p. 118).

Thinking/Cognitive Process

Culture has an impact not only on what we think but also on the way we think (Sue, 1992). For example, English-speaking people who have been influenced by Western values tend to have linear thinking (Wehrly, 1995). Other cultures encourage looking at a topic from a variety of views or discussing a topic in terms of what it is not but never addressing the topic directly. Other cultures (e.g., Hispanic) use associative information processing in which all clues plus the context are necessary to understand and interpret the messages (Correa, 1989; Chamberlain & Medinos-Landurand, 1991; Sue, 1992). This is different from thinking styles which rely almost entirely on the spoken word and focus on verbalizations directly related to the topic under discussion (Sue, 1992).

Culture and cognitive process have also been discussed as an issue of perceptual style. It has been suggested that perceptual style varies along the dimension of field dependence/independence (Chamberlain & Medinos-Landurand, 1991). Individuals who are field independent perceive specific details apart from a whole, while field dependent individuals tend to see details in relation to the whole. For example, several researchers have reported that Mexican American students are more field dependent or field sensitive and, therefore, prefer to interact socially in physically close environments where they can be attentive to feelings and expectations of the people around them (Chamberlain & Medinos-Landurand, 1991; Misra, 1994).

Religious/Spiritual Affiliation

The cultural impact of the beliefs that the individual holds includes the following: the supernatural, the existence or nonexistence of a supreme being (or beings), the importance of religious or spiritual practices such as worshiping a supreme being (or beings), beliefs about life after death, and the number and ways in which life's rituals are accomplished (Misra, 1994; Turnbull & Turnbull, 1990; Wehrly, 1995). The healing powers of curanderos, witches, santeros, worlds of ghosts, and nature as a guiding force may be central to the lives of some cultural groups (e.g., Hispanic Americans) (Baca & Cervantes, 1989).

Leisure Activities

Turnbull and Turnbull (1990) suggested that leisure activity objectives for students in special education often have been given low priority.

However, leisure activities may represent an important function of the family and other cultural groups. They can provide an outlet for stress as well as a means of building communication and teamwork.

SENSE OF GROUP MEMBERSHIP

Individuals differ in the strength of their sense of belonging to or association with a cultural group. The perception of group membership relates to variability in ethnic identity, socioeconomic status, decision-making/action-taking attitudes, family practices, and length of legal citizenship status.

Dominant Ethnic Identity

The concept of ethnic identity is complex, multidimensional, and significantly related to the other cultural variables. However, within the Personal Culture Framework, the dominant ethnic identity of an individual or group is defined as the self-identification which occurs when a group label is consistently used. In the United States, self-identification is influenced by national origin/affiliation and ethnic density (Wehrly, 1995). Ethnic density influences the degree to which individuals maintain parts of their culture in their daily lives and in certain contexts.

Socioeconomic Status

Bailey (1989) and Correa (1989) discuss the need for gathering family information regarding socioeconomic status (SES) with regard to that of the surrounding community. While there are different types of SES indexes, for the purposes of this chapter the general categories of high, middle, and low will be used. Gathering SES information is important because it facilitates an understanding of stressors and strains placed on an individual, family, or cultural group.

U.S. Generational Context

Wehrly (1995) indicated that there are differences within cultural groups because of years of residence in the United States. Groups of first-, second-, or third-generation Americans differ in the amount of exposure to the dominant culture's values, beliefs, and behaviors. For example, the reluctance of a first-generation Hispanic mother to allow her deaf child to attend a state school for the deaf may be related to her lack of exposure due to shortness in residency and reluctancy to let go of a traditional parenting role, as well as other factors (P. Villa, 1995, personal communication).

Decision-Making/Action-Taking Attitudes

There are several cultural influences on how an individual will make a decision or take action, including: (a) the emphasis or value place on decision-making and action-taking, (b) the role of the individual versus nature in life activities, and (c) the role of the group in the decision-making process. With regard to the value and emphasis on decisions and actions, Western individualistic middle-class culture tends to place emphasis on "doing" and "planning" as opposed to some non-Western cultures which emphasize "being." Indeed, Western cultures are inclined to always be "doing something" (Wehrly, 1995). Moreover, Westerners tend to credit the individual's effort, as opposed to external factors, for successes and failures (Chamberlain & Medinos-Landurand, 1991).

Cultures which credit external factors view the person as part of nature, suggesting that life is to be accepted and not controlled. Moreover, it is because one is subjugated by nature that one just lives as part of the universe. The theme of collective and consensual group decision-making processes, as opposed to individualism in decision-making processes, is highlighted (Chamberlain & Medinos-Landurand, 1991; Phinney, 1996; Triandis, 1985). Specifically, it is suggested that

Western countries tend to emphasize the importance of the individual over the group and to view and value the independence of the individual. This is in contrast to some non-Western countries which stress the importance of the group and the interdependence of its members.

Observances

One of the features in discussions of cultures is differences in observation of or commemoration of a person or life event (Correa, 1989; Wehrly, 1995). This includes the celebrations, holidays, and ceremonies observed by groups.

Family Definition

The definition of "family," the group of people who are considered kin, varies across cultural groups from small nuclear families to an extended unit which includes many people (Wehrly, 1995). The definition reflects the influence the family has on the life activities of an individual and community. While Western societies are likely to be influenced by the small nuclear family and place a high value on individualism, non-Western cultures may see family or kin as an extended unit that does not necessarily limit itself to "blood" relatives (Correa, 1989; Sue, 1992; Wehrly, 1995). It is important to know which family members are involved with making critical decisions regarding a child's educational program.

EXPERIENCES ASSOCIATED WITH SOCIOPOLITICAL STATUS

The experiences and status of individuals, groups, and communities within society are strongly related to the sense of group membership (Phinney, 1996). Ogbu (1991) suggests that a person's behavior may be influenced by the current and historical sociopolitical context of a cultural group in the United States.

Sociopolitical Context

The sociopolitical context includes issues of residency status (e.g., refugee, naturalized citizen, legal resident, generation of U.S. citizenship) and an understanding of the historical forces which led their immigration to the United States (Ogbu, 1991; Wehrly, 1995). For example, there are cultural groups associated with immigrant societies who came because of opportunities for greater political freedom. This is in contrast to nonimmigrant groups whose ancestors came to the United States via slavery, conquest, or colonization. These individuals may perceive the majority community and institutions as oppressive. The sociopolitical context is directly related to the power and status of a group. The context, therefore, may explain fears related to trust and the degree to which their environment can be predicted (Correa, 1989; Ogbu, 1991; Sue, 1992).

Transforming Life Events

A family, like an individual, grows and changes over the course of time (Alper & Retish, 1994; Turnbull & Turnbull, 1990). Turnbull and Turnbull (1990) have described these changes by identifying five basic life cycle stages: (a) the couple, (b) childbearing and preschool years, (c) school age, (d) adolescence, and (e) adulthood. Evidenced in the titles of these stages is a relationship to the changes parents experience as their children develop. This is particularly significant for parents of deaf children because of the life events which are and are not experienced due to a child's deafness (Leutke-Stahlman & Luckner, 1993).

Critical and Normal Life Events

Bailey (1988) suggested that special education services personnel need to examine the *critical life events* (diagnosis of disability, attainment of developmental milestones, obtaining and participating in special education services, transitions, and medical crises) and the *normal life events* (common financial, family/home, social, and work changes) of the individuals and families with whom they work. Given that neighborhood, communities, and schools also change over time, it seems appropriate to look at their development as occurring due to critical and normal "life" events.

APPLICATION OF THE PERSONAL CULTURE FRAMEWORK

The Personal Culture Framework includes a strategy for exploring a student's personal culture and provides school personnel, particularly teachers, with a list of cultural features which can be incorporated into curriculum and/or approaches to the child and his/her family. The framework includes forms for identifying personal culture variables and generating curricular adaptation strategies.

The *Student's Personal Culture Form* (see Fig. 9.1) is to be utilized by teachers to identify the cultural variables within four dimensions and across five loci which influence the child. A second form, the *Strategy Form* (see Fig. 9.2), is used to summarize findings from the *Student's Personal Culture Form* and generate strategies for approaching cultural variables not shared across the five loci. Educators are cautioned not to overgeneralize nor rely solely on stereotypical information found in the literature. For example, the values of one American Indian Nation may or may not be shared exactly the same way by another Nation. There are over 500 Native American Nations in existence in the United States (Hopkins, 1996). Moreover, there are some 34 countries designated as "Asian," and "Black Americans" may come from Jamaica or Puerto Rico and not Africa (Andersson, 1992; Nishimura, 1996).

Having accepted the paradigm of personal cultures influenced by family, neighborhood, vicinity/community, and school and having gathered information on the personal cultures of their students, how can teachers put the information to work in the classroom?

The exploration of students' personal cultures requires the use of "cultural brokers" (Correa, 1989). These brokers are individuals who

Fig. 9.1
Student's Personal Culture Form

Student's Name:

Dimensions	Cultural Variables	L Family	O Neighbor-hood	C Vicinity/ Community	U School	S Child
Cultural Values, Attitudes and Behaviors	Demographic Influences (urban, suburban, rural)					
	Verbal Behaviors (the what, how, when, where and why of language)					
	Nonverbal Behaviors (show of affection, meaning of common facial expression/ gestures, use of space)					
	Achievement Orienta-tion/ Education Level					
	Temporal Orientation/ (past-, present-, future-oriented)					
	Thinking/Cognitive Processes					
	Religious/Spiritual Af-filiations					
	Leisure Activities (recreation,sports, hob-bies, stress relievers)					
Sense of Group Membership	Dominant Ethnic Identity (country of origin, national affiliations, ethnic density)					
	U.S. Generational Con-text (first-, second-, third- generation, etc.)					
	Socio-economic Status (low, middle, high)					
	Decision-making/Ac-tion-taking Attitudes					
	Observances (holidays, celebrations, cere-monies)					
	Family Definition (influ-ence of family/kin)					
Experiences Associated with Minority Status	Sociopolitical Context (immigration pattern, resident status, experiences with racism)					
Transforming Life Events	Normal Events (developmental transitions)					
	Critical Events (traumatic events, illness, surgeries)					

Fig. 9.2
Strategy Form

Cultural Variables	Locus	Strategies
	F = Family N = Neighborhood V = Vicinity/Community S = School C = Child	
	F N V S C	
	F N V S C	
	F N V S C	
	F N V S C	
	F N V S C	
	F N V S C	
	F N V S C	
	F N V S C	
	F N V S C	
	F N V S C	
	F N V S C	
	F N V S C	
	F N V S C	
	F N V S C	
	F N V S C	
	F N V S C	
	F N V S C	

© Doris Paez & R. Fletcher-Carter, 1996.

provide a bridge between cultures and school sites. They can be used as informants, mediators, and/or advocates. As cultural brokers, they can share information regarding cultural values, attitudes, and behaviors; issues related to group membership; experiences associated with minority status; and transforming life events. Depending on the situation, parents and other family members or members of the community may act as cultural brokers (Correa, 1989). Bilingual educators, English as Second Language specialists, migrant educators, Chapter 1 teachers, and staff may serve as resources in this area. Functionally, the use of a cultural broker requires that the teacher discuss all of the variables in the *Student's Personal Culture Form* with as many brokers as possible.

Following are the six steps used in applying the Personal Culture Framework, which includes the use of the Student's Personal Culture and Strategy Forms with the cultural broker(s).

Step 1: Based on information gathered from cultural broker(s)/informant(s) and research, the teacher writes down key words/phrases to complete each cell in the Student's Personal Culture Form.

Step 2: The teacher circles the variables on the Student's Personal Culture Form which are NOT SHARED across the five locus columns: (a) family, (b) neighborhood, (c) vicinity/community, (d) school, and (e) child.

Step 3: The teacher then lists the variables not shared in the first column of the Strategy Form.

Step 4: The teacher then circles the loci which do not share the variable in column 2 of the Strategy Form.

Step 5: Teacher and cultural broker(s) generate strategies for addressing these NOT SHARED variables within the four dimensions. These curricular strategies are written in column 3 of the Strategy Form.

Step 6: Strategies are then included in curricular methods and
content.

Garcia and Malkin (1993) advocate that the goals and objectives
on a child's Individualized Education Program (IEP) or Individualized
Family Service Plan (IFSP) should specify responsiveness to cultural
and linguistic variables. Instruction then should respond at the student's instructional level to expectations of the family; be sensitive to
culturally based responses to the disability; include a language use
plan; and address language development and ESL needs.

CASE STUDIES

Imagine that all of the subjects you are about to meet were in the same
classroom together and you were the teacher. What would you need
to know about your students and their families to make learning relevant and to ensure that information from their personal cultures is incorporated into your curriculum to enhance parent/family
involvement with the schools?

Case Study 1: Deaf Child of Hearing Parents—European American Heritage

The student in question is deaf (bilateral profound loss), the
parents are hearing. There are no other known family members
who are deaf. The parents have had no experience with Deaf
adults. The child is enrolled in a special day class for deaf students with mainstreaming services (e.g., interpreters) for selected courses. The community is rural; the special class is
located in a larger nearby urban community. The child is bused
daily. The family, neighborhood, community, and school are
predominantly European American and middle to upper class
socioeconomic status. The parents are professional musicians.

Completing the Student's Personal Culture Form (Fig. 1), the teacher and broker found that variables *not shared* among the child and her school, family, immediate neighborhood, and vicinity/community are (a) *verbal and nonverbal behaviors*—spoken English by all but the child, her special class, and selected members of the urban community; (b) *leisure activities*—the parents are musicians; and (c) *transforming life events*—for the parents, giving birth to a profoundly deaf child.

The teacher and cultural broker (adult European American Deaf member of the local school parent group) suggested strategies for the parents' *critical life event,* their child's deafness. There was a perceived need to increase the awareness of the parents, family members, and child with Deaf Culture (history, culture, perspectives, language). The parents were invited by other parents and the teacher to attend school and Deaf Community activities (e.g., school and class sponsored events). The parents met successful deaf adults, heard their stories (barriers to and supports of success), became familiar with communication technologies (e.g., decoders, alarms, toys), and became aware of Deaf Community resources and advocacy organizations.

To address the *verbal and nonverbal behaviors,* the parents were invited to participate in Deaf Community and school sponsored classes to learn American Sign Language and study Deaf History and applicable laws effecting deaf and hard-of-hearing persons in the United States. To assist in knowing what signs their child was learning, a weekly video tape was sent from school to the family in order to share the week's current vocabulary (Teller, 1996). The parents were invited to classroom sponsored parent training sessions which focused on reading to a deaf child and other activities that generally supported the acquisition of language and literacy skills (Luetke-Stahlman & Luckner, 1991). These parents were also directed to parent groups which support and advocate for school and support services (e.g., Gallaudet Regional Centers).

In the area of *leisure activities,* the teacher and parents agreed to an information exchange. Parents would be informed of their child's progress both in academics and in extracurricular and leisure activities. Teachers would be advised of upcoming family events for which the teacher could help the parents prepare their child. The parents also agreed to assist the class with access to community arts including children's concerts.

Case Study 2: Deaf Child of Deaf Parents—Recent Immigrants from Mexico

The second student is a recent immigrant from Mexico. He and his Deaf parents reside in a small *colonia* less than 40 miles from the border of Mexico. The majority of the neighbors speak Spanish and have strong family ties to Mexico. Homes are without water, gas, or sewers. The parents of the student read survival Spanish and use Mexican Sign Language that they learned from other deaf adults in Mexico. The father has two years of oral school attendance in Ciudad Juarez (a major city in northern Mexico). The mother attended one year in public schools and six months in special education (oral tradition) in Mexico City. Both hold menial jobs. The parents are the only deaf members of their families. Many visits are made to Mexico by the family to visit extended family members in Juarez and surrounding towns. The parents are very proud of their son and take him to all social events. The parents choose to live where they do so that their child can attend American schools with special classes for children who are deaf and hard-of-hearing. They prefer the use of American Sign Language for instruction.

Completing the *Student's Personal Culture Form* (Fig. 1), the variables *not shared* among the child and his family and the school, neighborhood, and vicinity/community were: (a) *verbal and nonverbal behaviors*—the family used Mexican Sign Language, and the school used American Sign Language and Signed English; the neighborhood was Spanish speaking, and the vicinity/community was English and

Spanish, the parents were limited in Spanish literacy; and (b) *sense of group membership*—the parents were first generation immigrants coming to the U.S. for better jobs and for a public education for their child. They were connected to the Deaf Community in Cd. Juarez, Mexico, but not to the small Deaf Community in the town where their child attended school. The active Deaf Community in the town was middle class with professional jobs. The parents of Subject 2 were low socioeconomic status. The established Deaf Community was predominantly of European American heritage, although younger-aged deaf adults attending the local college were more representative of the area's demographics (60% Hispanic and 40% European American).

The child's aunt knew both Mexican Sign Language and English, so the mother of the child and aunt served as the cultural brokers/informants. *Verbal and nonverbal behaviors* were addressed from the need for second language learning. The school worked with increasing the child's as well as members of the family's ASL skills. The mother frequently stayed at the school on special days (e.g., visit from the fire fighters, visits from emergency medical technicians, a visit to the zoo) and learned ASL. In addition, the family was provided with an ASL text to study. The text had both English and Spanish translations.

Experiences associated with status and sense of group membership were addressed through the community. The college held ASL classes and also sponsored an ASL Club for students and the Deaf Community which the mother, aunt, and student attended on a regular basis. At the ASL club, the mother and student met other deaf adults and children using ASL, as well as hearing persons trying to improve their ASL. Hearing persons were more representative of the cultural demographics of the area than the Deaf Community. The parents were encouraged to attend the local chapter of the National Association for the Deaf (more ASL, more networking with the American Deaf Community, and more exposure to assistive technology). The school invited the mother to teach Mexican Sign Language to a district parent advisor/interpreter. The college invited the mother to special multicultural presentations to share Mexican Sign Language (MSL).

Connections were made with the nearby interpreting program to share MSL with area interpreters.

At school, children's literature from Mexico was incorporated into story time. American and Southwestern history was already supplemented with stories of "Deaf heroes" in the preschool. The parents were encouraged to join the newly formed parent advocacy group. Because of proximity to the Mexican/United States border, the neighborhood, community, and school, in this instance, were heavily Hispanic. However, in the larger world, this family needed assistance in integrating successfully into the area's Deaf Community and the larger hearing world. An Individualized Family Service Plan (IFSP) was planned which allowed much assistance to go directly to the family.

Case Study 3: African American Deaf—Rural South

The third student is the only deaf member of an African American family from the rural South. The hearing parents have never met anyone who is deaf. The daughter is profoundly deaf. The parents are professionals who are themselves in a period of self-discovery regarding their African American heritage. The student attends the state school for the deaf, which has a larger representation of African American children than the neighborhood school and is two hours from home. Teachers are predominantly White European American and hearing. A number of African American women serve as teaching assistants. Several deaf adults serve as dormitory counselors.

The African American teaching assistant and parents served as cultural brokers for the teacher while completing the Student's Personal Culture Form. Results placed on the Cultural Strategies Form identified several cultural variables *not shared* among the child, family, and their neighborhood, community, and school including: (a) *verbal and nonverbal behaviors,* (b) *ethnic identity,* (c) *observances,* and (d) *critical life events.* Common for most hearing parents, the birth of their deaf child was a *critical life event.* The parents needed to be exposed to language and modality options, communication technology available for their child, and their legal rights and educational options. Early on the parents needed to be introduced to African American Deaf adults who were in a variety of positions of responsibility. Introductions were accomplished through either personal visits, published sources, or, today, the Internet.

To address *ethnic identity and social/cultural observances,* the parents needed to be given information on National Black Deaf Advocates (NBDA) and the National Alliance of Black Interpreters (NAOBI). The parents of the African American Deaf student and the student herself needed to be schooled in Deaf History (including recent achievements of Deaf African American persons, for example, Glenn Anderson, first African American Deaf person to serve as chairman of Gallaudet University Board of Trustees; Andrew Jackson Foster, first Black student to graduate from Gallaudet and founder of Christian Mission for Deaf Africans; Earnest E. Hairston, chief of Caption Films Branch of U.S. Department of Education). This family wanted to be able to share their (a) cultural knowledge through the oral tradition embedded in the African American experience; (b) communication styles which are different from standard English and ASL; (c) informal unspoken mores; and (d) cultural attire and behaviors for social and cultural events.

Nonverbal and verbal variances were addressed at school for the student through formal instruction in ASL, as well as signed English systems. Her parents were able to take signed language courses through the local chapter of the National Black Deaf Advocates in cooperation with the State School Parent Association. This afforded them the opportunity to learn standard ASL and the cultural dialects of Black ASL.

To involve the child directly in *ethnic identity and social/cultural observances,* the school invited the parents to participate with the school in introducing African American cultural events to the students, such as preparing the students for Kwanzaa and Martin Luther King Day. Because of their interest in their African roots, they helped in developing African American studies—including art, music, dance, and the celebration of Kwanzaa. In this case, instructional modifications for the cultural diversity of the student were accommodated within curricular content which incorporated the Black Deaf experience, Black Deaf History, ASL linguistic variables, Black social/cultural events, and Black literature.

Case Study 4: Native American Indian Deaf Child of Hearing Parents

The fourth student is a Native American Indian child—one of two siblings, both of whom are deaf. The child has two paternal uncles who are also deaf. The uncles did not attend formal schooling for deaf children. To date, these uncles do not hold jobs within or outside of the tribe. The uncles do participate in cultural dances and traditions historically not participated in by Native American Indian Deaf students who attend state residential schools. These parents elected to have their son attend a distant public school district where they offered day classes for deaf and hard-of-hearing students.

The child attends a day preschool for deaf and hard-of-hearing children in a metropolitan area that is composed primarily of White non-Hispanic and Hispanic groups. Native American Indians represent less than 1.0% of that school district's student population. The parents speak the tribal language and English, and they understand the home signs of the uncles. The parents choose to live on the reservation although the father works off the reservation. The mother drives the son to school daily and spends the day in town waiting for him. The family is actively involved in cultural ceremonies and events on the reservation. The deaf son may attend ceremonies, but ceremonies that are considered sacred are not accessible to the child, since all children are covered with blankets during sacred dances. The student is unable to hear the chanting and drumming. The mother has tried unsuccessfully to have the tribal policy on children not viewing scared dances waived for her son. The teachers at the preschool are European American and hearing except for one Deaf (also European American) teacher. Several classroom assistants are Hispanic and one is a Native American Indian. Mentors who are deaf are invited to the school to share Deaf Culture.

The teacher completed the *Student's Personal Culture Form* with the child's mother and bilingual specialist serving as cultural brokers. The findings revealed that the child, family, and neighborhood share a number of cultural variables. The child differs from the neighborhood and community due to *verbal and nonverbal* communication (e.g., need for formal ASL, expressive faces, eye contact, and pointing for ASL). High affect, eye contact, and pointing are in conflict with tribal communication styles and mores. The tribal language is tonal and the uncles' sign language is primarily home sign.

Regarding *dominant ethnic identity,* there was strong family identity with the tribal heritage. The parents asked for help in taking their sons request to "watch sacred dancing" before the tribal council. They also offered to bring tribal customs to school. The student was the only Native American Indian in the school. Teachers needed to work with the family to have them serve as cultural brokers to share religious/spiritual affiliation, observances, ceremonies, leisure activities, attire, and foods. The family needed to advise the school of any taboos such as not permitting the touching of snakes or story telling during certain times of the year. Information not sacred was incorporated into class thematic teaching. For example, when teaching about houses, structures included were hogans, and pueblos, and tepees. Similarly, when teaching about dance, ceremonial dances were included with tap and ballet. Class trips were made on feast days to the reservation. Foods and traditions were brought to the classroom for sharing information about the student's Native American culture.

For *verbal and nonverbal* communication, ASL clearly requires pointing for pronominalization. The school provided parents information on alternative communication modes. The mother and father chose to set aside tribal taboos against pointing in order to use ASL, stating that their son needed to have the information. The parents, student, and uncle were put in contact with the Intertribal Deaf Council (IDC). Interpreters for Native American Indians were located. *Experiences associated with status* were addressed also. For example, American holidays which presented the European view were also viewed from the Native American Indian perspective (e.g., Columbus Day, Feast Days). Vocabulary for explaining tribal events and items were given to the parents so that they might share information spontaneously with their son during true "teachable moments." Literature and children's stories from the Native American Indian tradition were incorporated into story telling time. Deaf adult mentors were taught Native American Indian folklore in order to be able to tell the story in ASL. In this case study, the mother was an integral part of her child's schooling. Cultural experiences were openly shared by the family with the school. Cultural variables were addressed through curricular modifications provided by the family to the teacher.

Case Study 5: Asian American Deaf Child of First Generation Immigrant Hearing Parents

The fifth case study involves an Asian American child who became deaf following an illness. His mother speaks Mandarin and no English. His father speaks both but uses Mandarin in the home. The child understood Mandarin before becoming deaf at age 4. His brothers speak Mandarin only at home and English outside of the home. Without understanding why, the Asian Deaf child was taken to the residential school for the deaf and left there by his father. When at school he uses American Sign Language and written English. There are no other Asian Deaf students at the school. At home, he cannot communicate with his mother at all. He writes notes to communicate with his brothers and father during his short visits at home. His sister is learning ASL from community classes. She is the only one in the family with whom he can sign. He does not participate in family religious practices although he is aware that it is different at home (Taoism) than at school (Judeo-Christian). The parents expect high educational achievement from their children. Work is everything. No leisure activities are encouraged. Parents are separated from the school in distance and language, although the son is an excellent student and highly literate in English.

Unlike the other cases, the parents could not and did not serve as the cultural brokers for this student's education. This individual, in essence, grew up without knowledge of his biological race/culture. As an adult, he has recommendations for the schools. He identified cultural variables *not shared* between the school and his family and gave suggestions: *Verbal and nonverbal*—He wanted knowledge of his family/home language as well as family knowledge about ASL. (At least, he says, he could have written to his mother in her language.) *Sense of group membership*—He needed explanations about the home religion. He could have studied about the home beliefs through a cultural broker so that when at home, he might have been more aware of what was happening. *Experiences associated with status*—He should have been introduced to other Asian Deaf persons. Again, this could have been in person, over the Internet, or through correspondence. In American Deaf History, the role of Asian Americans in American Deaf Culture needed to be incorporated (e.g., playwright Shanny Mow). In history, the role of Asians in American and World History should be included.

This Asian Deaf adult wanted as much of his family's culture included in the curricular experiences as possible so that misperceptions and miscommunications between the student, the school, the family, the neighborhood, and the community could be reduced.

SUGGESTIONS FOR TEACHERS

Beyond the application of the Student's Personal Culture Form, it is suggested that teachers of the deaf become familiar with the cultures included in their school and community. This allows one to identify materials, strategies, and resources that are inclusive of the students taught on a regular basis. Teachers are then asked to update the information annually to avoid stereotypes. Sources used should acknowledge within-group differences. Educators are asked to obtain information that is beyond *holiday/tourist* curriculum. Historical experiences, migration patterns, accomplishments of members of the group, values and belief systems, and communication styles are to be included (Garcia & Malkin, 1993). To incorporate racial and ethnic cultures with the Deaf Culture, teachers should contact ethnic Deaf organizations (e.g., Intertribal Council of the Deaf, Asian Deaf Conference, Hispanic Deaf Conference, Black Deaf Advocacy). Computer literacy skills with the Internet and Worldwide Web afford teachers access to information that is contemporary and up-to-date from online libraries, bulletin boards, or chat rooms.

In conclusion, the Personal Culture Framework has helped us to understand that:

Each student was like all other students, like some other students, and like no other student.

REFERENCES

Alper, S., & Retish, P. (1994). Nontraditional families of children with disabilities. In S. Alper, P. J. Schloss, & C. N. Schloss, (Eds.), *Families of students with disabilities: Consultation and advocacy* (pp. 123–142). Needham Heights, MA: Allyn & Bacon.

Andersson, Y. (1992). Sociological reflections on diversity within the deaf population. In Mervin D. Garetson (Ed.), *A Deaf American monograph.* (Vol. 42). Silver Spring, MD: National Association of the Deaf.

Baca, L. M., & Cervantes, H.T. (1989). *The bilingual special education interface.* Upper Saddle River, NJ: Prentice-Hall.

Bailey, D. (1989). Assessing critical events. In D. Bailey & R. Simeonsson (Eds.), *Family assessment in early intervention* (pp. 119–138). Columbus, OH: Merrill.

Bennett, C. I. (1995). *Comprehensive multicultural education: Theory and practice* (3rd ed.). Boston: Allyn & Bacon.

Center for Demographic Studies (1994). *Annual survey of deaf and hard of hearing children and youth: 1993–1994 School year state by state summaries.* Washington, DC: Gallaudet University Press.

Chamberlain, P., & Medinos-Landurand, P. (1991). Practical considerations in the assessment of LEP students with special needs. In E. Hamayan & J. Damico (Eds.), *Limiting bias in the assessment of bilingual students* (pp. 111–154). Austin, TX: PRO-ED.

Christensen, K.M. (1993). A multicultural approach to education of children who are deaf. In K. M. Christensen & G. L. Delgado (Eds.), *Multicultural issues in deafness* (pp. 17–27). White Plains, NY: Longman.

Cook, L., & Boe, E. (1995). Who is teaching students with disabilities? *Teaching Exceptional Children,* **28**(1), 70–72.

Correa, V. (1989). Involving culturally diverse families in the educational process. In S. Fradd & J. Weismantel (Eds.), *Meeting the needs of culturally and linguistically different students: A handbook for educators* (pp. 130–144). Boston: College Hill.

Council for Exceptional Children (CEC) (1996). *Common core knowledge and skills essential for all beginning special education teachers.* Reston, VA: author.

Council of Educators of the Deaf (CED) (1996). *Draft standards knowledge & skills beyond the core.* Paper presented at the 22nd Annual Conference of the Association of College Educators-Deaf/Hard of Hearing (ACE-DHH), Williamsburg, VA.

Garcia, B., & Malkin, D. H. (1993). Toward defining programs and services for culturally and linguistically diverse learners in special education. *Teaching Exceptional Children,* **26**(1), 52–58.

Hall, S. (1989). Train-gone-sorry: The etiquette of social conversations in American Sign Language. In Sherman Wolcon (Ed.), *American deaf culture: An anthology.* Burtonsville, MD: Linstok Press.

Helge, D. (1993). The state of the art of rural special education. *National Rural Project.* Murray State Univ., Murray KY: ERIC ED 241202.

Hopkins, J. (1996, September). *Enhancing racial and ethnic diversity in the interpreting profession.* Symposium conducted at a telecast in interpreter training, Waubonsee Community College, Sugar Grove, IL.

Lee, Y. (1991). Koreans in Japan and the United States. In M. Gibson & J. Ogbu (Eds.), *Minority status and schooling* (pp. 3–36). New York, NY: Garland.

Luetke-Stahlman, B., & Luckner, J. (1991). *Effectively education students with hearing impairments.* New York: Longman.

Misra, A. (1994). Partnership with multicultural families. In S. Alper, P.J. Schloss, & C.N. Schloss (Eds.), *Families of students with disabilities: Consultation and advocacy* (pp. 143–158). Needham Heights, MA: Allyn & Bacon.

Nishimura, J. (1996, September). *Enhancing racial and ethnic diversity in the interpreting profession.* Symposium conducted at a telecast in interpreter training, Waubonsee Community College, Sugar Grove, IL.

Ogbu, J. (1991). Immigrant and involuntary minorities in comparative perspective. In M. Gibson & J. Ogbu (Eds.), *Minority status and schooling* (pp. 3–36). New York, NY: Garland.

Padden, C. (1989). *The Deaf Community and the culture of deaf people.* In Sherman Wilcon (Ed.), American Deaf Culture (pp. 1–16).

Paul, P.V., & Quigley, S. P. (1990). *Education and deafness.* New York: Longman.

Phinney, J. S. (1996). When we talk about American ethnic groups, what do we mean? *American Psychologist, 51*(9), 918–927.

Schirmer, B. R. (1994). *Language and literacy development in children who are deaf.* New York: Macmillan.

Simpson, R. L. (1990). *Conferencing parents of exceptional children.* Austin, TX: PRO-ED.

Smith, G. P. (1996, March). *The teacher education knowledge base for cultural diversity.* Handout in Barbara Gerner de Garcia Multicultural/Diversity Workshop: Preparing Teachers of Deaf/Hard-of-Hearing Children for Diversity, 22nd Annual Conference Association of College Educators-Deaf and Hard of Hearing, Williamsburg, VA.

Smith, M. A. (1994, Summer). Enhancing educational opportunities for Hispanic students who are deaf. *New York State Association for Bilingual Education, 9,* 7–13.

Sue, D. W. (1992). Culture-specific strategies in counseling: A conceptual framework. *Professional Psychology, 21,* 424–433.

Teller, H. (1996, March). *The video camera in the classroom: A great tool for parent support and involvement.* Paper presented at the 22nd Annual Conference of the Association of College Educators-Deaf/Hard of Hearing (ACE-DHH), Williamsburg, VA.

Triandis, H. (1985). Some major dimensions in cultural variation in client populations. In P. Pedersen (Ed.), *Handbook of cross-cultural counseling and therapy* (pp. 21–28). Wesport, CT: Greenwood.

Turnbull, A.P., & Turbull, H.R. III (1990). *Families, professionals, and exceptionality: A special partnership* (2nd. Ed.). Columbus: Merril Publishing.

Wehrly, B. (1995). *Pathways to multicultural counseling competence: A developmental journey.* Pacific Grove, CA: Brooks/Cole.

Valli, C., & Lucas, C. (1992). *Linguistics of American Sign Language.* Washington, DC: Gallaudet University Press.

Chapter

10

Teacher Expectations and Their Implications for Ethnically Diverse Deaf Students

Reginald Lee Redding

Teacher expectations may very well be the key to educational success for the increasing population of deaf students of color in schools and programs for the deaf (p.5).

Students of color are over-represented in lower academic skills classes and continue to underachieve. Changing demographic trends indicate a movement toward increased numbers of minority students among the school-aged population, while the majority of teachers of the hard-of-hearing continue to be predominantly White, hearing, females. Therefore, the characteristic differences between students and teachers are becoming more pronounced. This chapter discusses how the impact of teacher expectations may be an important factor in addressing the current dilemma facing students of color in the educational system.

The impact of teacher expectations for ethnically diverse deaf students in schools and programs for the deaf across this nation has not been discussed at any length by researchers or professional organizations, nor has it been sufficiently covered in the literature. However, the importance of teacher expectations and their implications for students in the general school-age population has been well documented (Wigfield *et al.*, 1998).

At no other time has there been so much attention given to the field of special education at both federal and state levels than in the past three decades (Banks & Banks, 1989). Various educational initiatives have been developed and implemented, giving more attention than ever before to children with special needs. These efforts have been extended to children with culturally diverse backgrounds. Head Start and Chapter 1 programs are both examples of such initiatives (Janesick & Moores, 1992). Unfortunately, the same has not been true for children who are deaf/hard-of-hearing and from culturally diverse backgrounds. There has not been a widespread concentrated effort to attend specifically to the needs of ethnically diverse deaf students, who present their own unique educational needs (Anderson & Grace, 1991). Three commissioned reports, (a) Education of the Deaf: A Report to the Secretary of Health, Education, and Welfare (Babbidge, 1965), (b) Toward Equality: Education of the Deaf (Commission on the Education of the Deaf, 1988), and (c) the State of Education of the Deaf in the United States (National Association of State Directors of Special Education, 1991), revealed that the educational attainment for deaf students from underrepresented ethnic groups was an alarming disgrace. However appalling, very little attention was given in these federally commissioned reports toward addressing the dilemmas faced by deaf students of color by way of recommendations or mandates to the field. Even professional organizations specializing in deafness have not made significant strides to remedy the academic achievement problems of this population.

Most recently, however, some attention has been given to the status of deaf children who are members of both the Deaf Culture and racial, ethnic, and/or linguistic groups such as African American, Hispanic American, Native American Indian, and Asian American populations by those educators on the front lines of this battle for equity. One reason for this new concern is the growing number of these students in school systems, coupled with the alarmingly low level of educational attainment among these students. By the year 2000, deaf students of color will comprised at least 40% of school-age children (Cohen *et al.,* 1990; Andrews & Jordan, 1993; Shildroth & Hotto, 1993). In spite of this new awareness on the part of some educators, a general sense of apathy exists in the field.

CURRENT EDUCATIONAL ATTAINMENT

As one examines the current educational attainment among deaf students, it is noteworthy that White deaf students tend to fare much better than their non-White peers. There were an estimated 57,555 deaf and hard-of-hearing students in the United States in 1990 (MacLeod-Gallinger, 1993). A significant number of them did not achieve reading levels adequate for successful completion of high school (MacLeod-Gallinger, 1993; Nash, 1992). Additionally, Allen (1992), reported that 80% of the deaf and hard-of-hearing students were leaving high school with reading levels below the 4th-grade level, with a mean score of 3rd grade. The Center for Assessment and Demographic studies at Gallaudet University in 1989 reported an even greater crisis for deaf and hard-of-hearing children from ethnically diverse, other than Anglo, backgrounds. Allen (1990) found that of the deaf and hard-of-hearing youths of color tested between the ages of 17 and 20 years, only 3% Black, 5% Hispanic, and 18%

White were reading at or above, the 7th-grade level. The enormity of the problem is overwhelming. Likewise, Nash (1992) reported that at best, not more than 200 African American or Hispanic deaf students nationwide will enter postsecondary educational institutions in any given year for the remainder of this decade. Of this number, less than 45% of those students who do enter college will make it to graduation at either the associate or bachelor's degree level.

DEMOGRAPHICS

The literature documents the rapid growth of deaf students of color in the educational system. Ethnically diverse deaf students are defined as those individuals coming from linguistic, cultural and/or ethnic backgrounds other than White American (e.g., African American, Hispanic American, Native American, and Asian American students). According to a 1990 study, deaf children of color comprise 36% of the school-age deaf and hard-of-hearing population (Center for Assessment and Demographic Studies, 1990). As previously stated, as of the year 2000, deaf students of color comprise at least 40% of the deaf student population.

TEACHER EXPECTATIONS

Research has demonstrated time and time again how teacher expectations play an instrumental role in promoting educational success among students in the general population. A review of the literature indicates that the underachievement of students of color is well documented (Redding, 1995). Hearing students of color who fare less well than their White peers is a recurring theme (Anderson & Grace, 1991; Andrews & Jordan, 1993; Cohen *et al.,* 1990; Hale-Benson, 1982). In general, the literature supports the notion that public schools have not been successful in educating students of color, as evident in the higher dropout rates among Black and Hispanic students than among White students (Hillard, 1989). There is a substantial gap between achievement scores for students of color and the national average (Gault & Murphy, 1987).

The achievement gap between deaf students of color and their White peers has also been proven to exist. It is a dilemma that beckons us to ask why. We must begin to address the culprit and reverse the low educational attainment among ethnically diverse deaf students. Repeatedly, studies of the general population have pointed to one prominent factor that may affect academic success: *teacher expectations.* Multiple studies among the general population have examined the possible factors influencing the formulation of teacher expectations and behaviors. One study reported that, "when teachers are in tune culturally with minority students...communication is enhanced, instruction is effective, and the positive teacher effect is maximized" (Irvine, 1980, p. 2). Teacher attitudes and perceptions of their students, more specifically students of color, are important in the level of expectations set for their students and in the kind of treatment these students receive in their classrooms (Larke *et al.,* 1990). Rosenfield (1973) reported that teachers expected greater achievement from European American students than was warranted by previous measures of their performance and, significantly, that teachers underestimated achievement gains for Mexican American and African American students. Hillard (1989) calls these underestimations "killer assumptions," which must be rejected when setting expectations for African American, Hispanic American, Asian American, and Native American youth.

Interactions between teachers and students of color is to be an important consideration. Cohen (1982) and Dean (1988) reported that positive interactions increased cultural awareness and that sensitivity training has been shown to change teacher attitudes and expectations of students of color.

IMPLICATIONS

Teacher expectations may very well be the key to educational success for the increasing population of deaf students of color. While there is a dearth of literature on the impact of low expectations on racially diverse underrepresented deaf students, it is speculated that the potential negative impact found for the general population holds true for the overall deaf student population as well. A study conducted in 1995 examined the influence of racial and ethnic backgrounds of deaf and hard-of-hearing students in one northeast region of the United States on the level of expectations teachers set for both academic performance and behavioral areas (Redding, 1995). Additionally, the study examined the kind of classroom behavior interventions teachers were likely to use. Although this study did not find evidence of stereotypical behaviors on the part of the teacher sample, it did bring forth some areas of concern. There was strong resistance to the study due to the potential for identifying the racial biases of the teachers. One reason the study did not find statistically significant results was due to the neutral scores teachers chose in their responses. These neutral responses were characterized as "safe" and did not reveal teachers' personal perspective on the issues. This demonstrated that teacher participants were unwilling to make strong statements about their feelings one way or the other.

The majority of the teaching force in education of the deaf is White. This represents at least 90% of all teachers in both schools and programs for students who are deaf and hard-of-hearing. This statistic is evidence that the trend in enrollment in teacher preparation programs is not reflective of the rapid shift in demographics among the deaf student population (Cohen *et al.,* 1990; Andrews & Jordan, 1993; Mobley, 1991; Corbett & Jensema, 1980). This presents an interesting challenge for teachers who may not have the skills, understanding, knowledge, and/or attitudes to work with diverse populations of deaf students. Deaf students of color may have difficulty making a cultural connection with their White teachers (Redding, 1995; Anderson & Grace, 1991).

PRESERVICE TRAINING PROGRAM

In the education of the deaf one is required to acquire specialized skills and knowledge to teach deaf students through preservice training programs that meet rigorous standards for certification by the Council on Education of the Deaf and/or local state licenses. In light of current demographic trends and research into the achievement of students of color, preservice training programs must be examined to ensure that future teachers are prepared to deal with the multicultural issues facing the diverse students that they will educate. In the early 1990s, teacher preparation programs were expected to include in their course offerings some concentration on the issues facing all ethnic and racial groups of deaf students. We have yet to see the impact that this has had on future teachers just now entering classrooms. However, in the opinion of this writer, more needs to be done to address this dilemma. The achievement of deaf children of color is at a crisis level and urgent care is needed to remedy the problems they face.

RECOMMENDATIONS

Central to the implementation of multicultural education is the integration of race and ethnicity, class, and gender issues throughout the curricula and activities of schools (Gollnick and Chinn, 1994). Teacher preparation programs must assume the responsibility of preparing all teachers, regardless of race, to teach in culturally diverse classrooms. The framework must be comprehensive and holistic and include much more than a single course on multicultural education or human relations (Garibaldi, 1992). Teacher education programs can help teacher candidates begin the process of critical examination of the practices of educators. Teacher preparation must include understanding the difference between culture and class and the implications for

1. Planning and organizing instruction

2. Educational assessment

3. Classroom management

4. Motivational techniques

5. Textbook selection.

Home, Community, and School Collaborations

The elimination of racism, classism, sexism, and discrimination against children and the elderly within society is the goal for all instruction. The recognition and elimination of these behaviors within schools is the beginning. This requires a critical analysis of current practices and the courage to change them.

In addition, the presence of faculty members of color is attractive to students. When students of color see faculty of color, they conclude that school administrators are interested and committed to equity issues and to diversity. Students' feelings of isolation and exclusion can be lessened, especially if the faculty of color are tenured and visible as power brokers in the system. Therefore, greater efforts must be made on the part of teacher preparation programs to recruit diverse scholars and nontraditional students. In turn, these professionals will provide the accepting atmosphere and positive expectations needed so that African American, Hispanic American, Asian American, and Native American Indian Deaf students can succeed.

REFERENCES

Allen, T. E. (1992). Subgroup differences in educational placement for deaf and hard of hearing students. *American Annals of the Deaf,* 137(5), 381–388.

Anderson, G. B., & Grace, C. A. (1991). Black deaf adolescents: Adverse and underserved population. *The Volta Review,* 93(5), 73–86.

Andrews, J.F., & Jordan, D.L. (1993). Minority and minority deaf professionals. *American Annals of the Deaf,* **138**(5), 388–396.

Babbidge, H. (1965). *Education of the deaf: A report of the advisory committee on education of the deaf.* Washington, DC: U.S. Department of Health, Education, and Welfare.

Banks, A., & Banks, M. (Eds.) (1989). *Multicultural education: Issues and perspectives.* Boston: Allyn & Bacon.

Center for Assessment and Demographic Studies (1990). *Annual survey of hearing impaired children and youth, 1988–1989 school year.* Washington, DC: Gallaudet University Press.

Cohen, E.G. (1982). Expectation states and interracial interactions in school settings. *Annual Review of Sociology,* **8,** 209–235.

Cohen, O.P., Fischgrund, J.E., & Redding, R., (1990). Deaf children from ethnic, linguistic and racial minorities: An overview. *American Annals of the Deaf,* **135**(2), 67–73.

Commission on the Education of the Deaf (1988). *Toward equality: Education of the deaf.* Washington, DC: U.S. Government Printing Office.

Corbett, E., & Jensema, C. (1981). *Teachers of the deaf: Descriptive profiles.* Washington, DC: Gallaudet University Press.

Dean, T. (1988). Multicultural classrooms, monocultural teachers. *College Composition and Communication,* **40**(1), 23–27.

Garibaldi, A.M. (1989). *Teacher recruitment and retention: With a special focus on minority teachers.* Washington, DC: NEA.

Gault, A., & Murphy, J. (1987). The implications of high expectations for bilingual students. *Journal of Education Equity and Leadership,* **7**(4), 301–317.

Gollnick, D.M., & Chinn, P.C. (1994). *Multicultural education in a pluralistic society* (4th ed.). New York: Maxwell Macmillian International.

Hale-Benson, J. (1982). *Black children, their roots, culture, and learning styles.* Provo, UT: Brigham Young University Press.

Hillard, A.G. (1989, December/January). Teachers and cultural styles in a pluralistic society. *Rethinking Schools,* 3.

Irvine, J.J. (1980). *Black students and school achievement: A process model of relationship among significant variables.* Paper presented at 1989 American Educational Research Association Conference, March 1993.

Janesick, V.J., & Moores, D.F. (1992). Ethnic and cultural considerations. In T.N. Kluwin, D.F. Moores, & M.G. Faustad (Eds.), *Toward effective public school programs for deaf students: Context, process and outcomes* (pp. 49–65). New York: Teachers College Press.

Larke, P.J., Wiseman, D., & Bradley, C. (1990). The minority mentorship project: Changing attitudes of preservice teachers for diverse classrooms. *Action in Teacher Education, 3,* 5–11.

MacLeod-Gallinger, J. (1993, April). *Deaf ethnic minorities: Have they a double liability?* Presented at the Annual Meeting of the American Educational Research Association, Atlanta, GA.

Mobley, R. (1991, February). *Deaf teachers of the deaf.* Paper presented at the Conference of Association of College Educators in Hearing Impaired, Jekyll Island, GA.

Nash, K. (1992). The changing population: A challenge for postsecondary education. In S.B. Foster & G.G. Walter (Eds.), *Deaf students in postsecondary education.* New York: Routledge.

National Association of State Directors of Special Education (1991, February). *State of education of the deaf in the United States.* Paper presented at the NASDSE Action Seminar, Las Vegas, NV.

Redding, R. (1995). *Factors influencing academic and behavioral expectations of teachers in classes for deaf and hard of hearing students with diverse racial, ethnic, and linguistic backgrounds.* Doctoral dissertation, Gallaudet University, Washington, DC.

Rosenfield, L.R. (1973). *An investigation of teachers stereotyping behavior: The influence of mode of presentation, ethnicity, and social class on teacher's evaluation of students* (ERIC Document Reproduction Service No. ED 090 172).

Schildroth A., & Hotto, S. (1993). Annual survey of hearing impaired children and youth: 1991–1992 School year. *American Annals of the Deaf,* **138,** 163–168.

Wigfield, A., Eccles, J., & Rodriguez, D. (1998). The development of children's motivation in school contexts. In P. Pearson & A. Iran-Nejad (Eds.), *Review of research in education* (pp. 73–118). Washington DC: AERA.

11

Shifting the Margins

Kathee M. Christensen

There is an intimate relationship between language and culture. Without language, culture cannot be acquired effectively nor can it be expressed and transmitted. Without culture, language cannot exist. The linkage between language and culture in the process of knowledge acquisition, as well as in the context of the whole development of young humans, cannot be stressed enough. While there is no contention about this linkage, its nature and consequences need to be addressed.

H. Trueba

This chapter links the ideas of this book to the opportunities of the future. A new educational paradigm is suggested which emphasizes school reform and restructuring from a multilingual and multicultural perspective. The need for collaboration among new sets of partners is described. As we enter the new millennium, teachers, parents, administrators, and members of the deaf community are called upon to make connections with the larger world of bilingual–multicultural research and practice. Such linkages will place the field of ASL/English bilingual–multicultural education of learners who are deaf firmly within the broadly defined field of bilingual–multicultural education.

Shifting Cultural Boundaries

As we move into the 21st century, our cultural definitions are becoming more complex. In the 20th century, middle class, Anglo, hearing, heterosexual English speakers were considered to be the "norm"...at least in the United States. Other groups were marginalized, more or less, according to their standard practices with regard to the norm. Majority leadership defined and set standards for marginalized groups. For the most part, the less challenging a group was perceived to be, the less marginalized it was. White, hearing women, for example, were able to work their way into middle management positions long before people of color or people with disabilities were considered even at the interview level.

Throughout the 20th century, however, voices of disenfranchised groups became stronger and louder. The Civil Rights Act of 1964 made it illegal for public institutions to discriminate against persons on the basis of race. Further legislation expanded the rights of persons to equal treatment regardless of religion, national origin, sexual orientation, gender, marital status, age, or disability. Immigration increased substantially. Cultural trends emerged. In many parts of the United States, particularly Miami and Los Angeles, neighborhoods evolved where Spanish was the dominant language. African Americans entered the political arena in greater numbers. Asian Americans excelled in business ventures. Native American Indian nations stepped forward to claim their birthright—equal and just treatment under the law. Women excelled in higher education and pursued a variety of careers formerly held exclusively by men. The educational and vocational expectations for people with disabilities were expanded by law. American Sign Language entered the ranks of the top five most studied languages in some regions of the United States. Cross-racial and cross-cultural intermarriages, and the children born to these families, tended to make cultural boundaries less clearly defined. The word "minority" no longer held the same meaning with regard to women, people of color, biracial/bicultural people, and people with disabilities. These groups, when perceived collectively, were becoming the majority.

A visit to a typical urban elementary school will confirm the fact that our society is becoming multilingual and multicultural at a rapid and consistent rate. In major urban areas in southern California, for example, more than half of the children enrolled in public school programs come from families that regularly use a language other than English. This rich linguistic resource is further enhanced by the cultural experiences of the children and their families, many of whom have survived great odds to attain their current residential status.

When major shifts occur, it is logical to assume that a state of chaos will exist, at least temporarily, while individuals and groups struggle to define their roles in the evolving social structure. Personal identity, within the complex social structure, presents an additional challenge. Ultimately, the way in which an individual decides to identify himself or herself is a matter of personal choice. For example, a Deaf man, born and raised in the Navajo nation, might choose to identify himself as Deaf Navajo, Navajo Deaf, Deaf Native American Indian, American Indian Deaf, or one of another set of descriptors which he feels best communicate the way in which he chooses to identify himself. The guidelines for self-identification are flexible and adaptable according to each individual's personal rights and self-image. Members of particular ethnic groups may promote the use of one label over another for sociopolitical reasons and attempt to marginalize individuals who fail to conform. In so doing, a new definition of discrimination emerges. The division which results has the potential to diminish the progress of the group at large.

A way of guarding against self-destructive practices within a community is to maintain respect for a diverse, bilingual, multicultural identity and, at the same time, present a strong, collaborative presence. The multifaceted Deaf Community can benefit from allegiances with diverse national organizations. Well-established national organizations which promote linguistic and cultural diversity can and should welcome Deaf constituencies. In a recent article, Cohen (1997) outlined the need for educators of children who are Deaf to move toward structural and social change in the profession. He suggested that anti-racist, multicultural education is beneficial for all children, regardless of ethnicity or hearing status. In addition, he promoted the creation of national affiliations among organizations in education of the Deaf and organizations responsive to the needs of children of color.

The National Association of the Deaf (NAD) has demonstrated a positive model with regard to collaboration by promoting dialogue among their leaders and the leaders of national educational organizations. Deaf leadership and a strong Deaf presence at the national level can influence decision-making beyond the tiny field of education of the Deaf and enhance the practice of American Sign Language and ASL–English bilingualism. The joint affiliation of NAD and the American Sign Language Teachers Association (ASLTA) with the American Council on the Teaching of Foreign Languages (ACTFL) is an example of a collaborative strategy at the national level. As NAD and ASLTA work to develop a strong, positive presence within ACTFL, the cause of bilingual–multicultural education of children who are Deaf will be promoted nationally and internationally.

Much can be accomplished through the development of strong collaborations with established national organizations. Connections at the national level between the Deaf Community and TESOL (Teaching English to Speakers of Other Languages) have lost ground in recent years. The rejuvenation of TEDS (Teaching English to Deaf Students) Special Interest Group of TESOL would be a logical goal for the 21st century. Recently, the National Council of Teachers of English (NCTE) recognized the use of a learner's native language as a resource for learning both academic content and English. The National Association of Bilingual Education (NABE) has long promoted academic use of native/natural languages in public schools. Linkages with these and other national educational organizations could enhance two-way understanding of ASL–English bilingualism. The academic option of visual learning is grounded in multiple intelligence theory (Gardner, 1983) and could take root and flourish in ASL-English bilingual classrooms.

SHIFTING THE RESEARCH FOCUS

There is much to explore and accomplish in order to enhance education of Deaf learners in the 21st century. As a profession, we have some idea of how bilingual–bicultural ASL–English education has been successful with Deaf children of Deaf parents (Brasel, 1975). A primary question to address in the next century is that of bilingual–multicultural education of Deaf children from hearing families, especially those hearing families who, for the most part, speak languages other than English at home and in their communities. What will work best to promote academic and social success in Deaf Culture, ASL, English, and the heritage, language, and culture for this large and needy population?

Recent research in bilingual education of hearing children has concluded that:

1. Substantial use of the native language did not impede children's acquisition of English (Ramirez *et al.,* 1991; Ramirez, 1992).

2. The most effective programs in terms of academic achievement are two-way developmental bilingual programs (Collier & Thomas, 1989; Thomas & Collier, 1995; Olsen & Leone, 1994). Typically these programs follow either the 50/50 model where learners receive instruction for equal amounts of time in

each language, or the 90/10 model, where 90% of the instruction, initially, is in the native/natural language and the target language instruction gradually is increased to equal time by about the fourth year. In both approaches, all languages are given equal status.

3. Successful bilingual teachers actively resist the hegemony of English and actively promote the status of the other languages in the classroom (Faltis & Hudelson, 1998).

If these conclusions are valid for bilingual education of hearing children, to what extent are they valid also for Deaf learners? Researchers in the field of education of children who are Deaf must design studies which replicate these findings in schools with two-way developmental bilingual ASL–English programs.

CONCLUSION

The contributors to this text have underscored the importance of at least two basic concepts. First, bilingualism and multilingualism, including ASL, enhance the communication potential of all individuals, whether Deaf or hearing. Second, biculturalism and multiculturalism, including Deaf Culture, enrich the quality of life for all individuals, whether Deaf or hearing. As we face the increasing diversity and complexity of the 21st century, we, as educators, must be committed to the development of quality educational programs for all learners. Teachers and administrators must have an in-depth understanding of the diverse cultural and linguistic challenges which confront our profession. Universities must take leadership in areas of research. Universities and schools must collaborate effectively to put research principles into effective practice. All of these shifts in attitude and practice will take time, energy, positive leadership, and personal commitment to quality and progress. Rigorous leadership training is necessary, and persons must be willing to dedicate themselves to leadership activities in order to move multilingual and multicultural programs forward in the 21st century.

There is an old Spanish dicho, or saying, which sums up the situation. "Poco a poco, se va lejos"...Little by little, we will make progress. We will shift the paradigm away from a hegemonic English-centered approach, away from a medical disability perspective, and toward a multicultural focus with Deaf-Plus cultural and linguistic resources at the center. How will you fit into the new paradigm?

REFERENCES

Brasel, K. (1975). *The influence of early language and communication environments on the development of language in deaf children.* Ph.D. dissertation, University of Illinois.

Cohen, O. (1997). Giving all children a chance: Advantages of an anti-racist approach to education for deaf children. *American Annals of the Deaf,* **142,** 80–82.

Collier, V., & Thomas, W. (1989). How quickly can immigrants become proficient in English? *Journal of Educational Issues of Language Minority Students, 5,* 26–38.

Faltis, C. & Hudelson, S. (1998). *Bilingual education in elementary and secondary school communities: Toward understanding and caring.* Boston: Allyn & Bacon.

Gardner, H. (1983). *Frames of mind.* New York: Basic Books.

Olsen, R., & Leone, B. (1994). Sociocultural processes in academic, cognitive, and language development. *TESOL Matters, 4,* 1–18.

Ramirez, J. (1992). Executive summary. *Bilingual Research Journal,* **16,** 1–61.

Ramirez, D., Yuen, S., Ramsay, D., & Pasta, D. (1991). *Final report: Longitudinal study of structured English immersion strategy, early-exit, and late-exit bilingual educational programs for language-minority children,* (Vol. 1). San Mateo, CA: Aguirre International.

Thomas, W., & Collier, V. (1995). *Language minority student achievement and program effectiveness.* Washington, DC: National Clearinghouse for Bilingual Education.

Trueba, H. (1989). *Raising silent voices: Educating the linguistic minorities for the 21st century.* New York: Newbury House.

Index